KT-167-928

Contents at a Glance

Table of Contents

About the Author

Michael Miller is a top eBay seller and a successful and prolific author. He has a reputation for practical, real-world advice and an unerring empathy for the needs of his readers.

Mr. Miller has written more than 50 how-to and reference books in the past 15 years for Que and other major publishers. His books for Que include *Absolute Beginner's Guide to eBay, Absolute Beginner's Guide to Computer Basics,* and *Absolute Beginner's Guide to Upgrading and Fixing Your PC.* He is known for his casual, easy-to-read writing style and his ability to explain a wide variety of complex topics to an everyday audience.

Mr. Miller is also president of The Molehill Group, a strategic consulting and authoring firm based in Carmel, Indiana. You can email Mr. Miller directly at ebay-business@molehillgroup.com. His Web site is located at www.molehillgroup.com.

Dedication

This book is dedicated to successful eBay sellers everywhere—keep up the good work!

Acknowledgments

Thanks to the usual suspects at Que, including but not limited to Greg Wiegand, Angelina Ward, Christy Miller Kuziensky, Cari Skaggs, Benjamin Berg, Charlotte Clapp, Sheila Schroeder, and Sharry Lee Gregory.

We Want to Hear from You!

As the reader of this book, you are our most important critic and commentator. We value your opinion and want to know what we're doing right, what we could do better, what areas you'd like to see us publish in, and any other words of wisdom you're willing to pass our way.

As an associate publisher for Que Publishing, I welcome your comments. You can email or write me directly to let me know what you did or didn't like about this book—as well as what we can do to make our books better.

Please note that I cannot help you with technical problems related to the topic of this book. We do have a User Services group, however, where I will forward specific technical questions related to the book.

When you write, please be sure to include this book's title and author as well as your name, email address, and phone number. I will carefully review your comments and share them with the author and editors who worked on the book.

Email: feedback@quepublishing.com

Mail: Greg Wiegand
         Associate Publisher
         Que Publishing
         800 East 96th Street
         Indianapolis, IN 46240 USA

For more information about this book or another Que Publishing title, visit our Web site at www.quepublishing.com. Type the ISBN (excluding hyphens) or the title of a book in the Search field to find the page you're looking for.

Introduction

On any given day there are more than 12 million items listed for auction at eBay, the world's largest online trading community. In the year 2002, almost $15 billion worth of merchandise, in more than 638 million individual auctions, was traded over eBay. That's $50 million a day—or *$579 every second.*

So who's making all that money?

While most eBay users are simple hobbyists, a surprisingly large number of users sell enough items to actually make a living from their eBay auctions. Officially or not, these users are running eBay businesses. They purchase inventory, market their products, collect payments, and ship merchandise, just like an Amazon.com or L.L. Bean does. They're businesses, pure and simple, that operate on and through the eBay auction service.

Does the prospect of running your own business, from the comfort of your own home, appeal to you? Do you think you can sell with the best of them and make enough from your eBay auctions to support yourself, either part-time or full-time? If so, then you should consider launching your own eBay business.

What do you need to know to make it on eBay? More than you think. You need to determine what kind of business you want to run, write an instructive business plan, establish an effective accounting system, set up a home office, obtain starting inventory, arrange initial funding, and establish an eBay presence.

And that's before you sell a single item.

Once you start selling, you have the entire auction management process to deal with. You have to list items for sale, manage your inventory, correspond with winning bidders, handle customer payments, deal with deadbeat customers, and pack and ship all those items you sell. To be truly successful, you need to do all this as efficiently as possible; you'll need to automate those repetitive tasks, manage your costs, and find a way to increase the success rates of the auctions you run.

As you can see, there's a lot of work involved in managing the day-to-day operation of a high-volume business. After all, running a successful online business isn't quite as simple as listing a few items for sale on eBay. Fortunately, you don't have to reinvent the wheel. You're not the first person to dream about running their own eBay business, so you might as well learn from others who've already done it.

Which is where this book comes in.

Absolute Beginner's Guide to Launching an eBay Business shows you everything you need to know to launch and run your own business, using eBay auctions to sell your merchandise. I don't profess to know everything there is to know about managing a successful eBay business, but I can definitely help you get your business off the ground. All you have to do is follow the instructions and advice between these two covers, and before you know it, you'll be selling—profitably—on eBay. Just be prepared for a lot of work; the more you sell, the more work is involved—and, of course, the more money you'll make!

How This Book Is Organized

This book is organized into four main parts, as follows:

- **Part 1, "Learning the Ropes,"** serves as a primer on eBay basics. Start here if you've never used eBay before—or if you need a quick refresher course!

- **Part 2, "Setting Up an eBay Business—Step by Step,"** walks you through the "homework" you need to do before you start selling on eBay. You'll learn how to create a business plan, evaluate your funding needs, deal with legal and tax issues, set up a record-keeping system and back office, find and manage your inventory, and establish your initial eBay presence.

- **Part 3, "Managing Your Day-to-Day Business,"** shows you how to list and manage your ongoing eBay auctions. You'll learn how to create item listings, handle post-auction correspondence, manage customer payments, pack and ship your merchandise, and deal with customers—and any problems that might come up.

- **Part 4, "Moving from Seller to PowerSeller,"** helps you make your auctions more successful—and your business more profitable. You'll learn all about eBay's PowerSeller and eBay Stores programs, as well how to work with photographs, utilize professional auction tools, set up your own Web site for online sales, and promote your eBay auctions. You'll also discover tons of tips for creating more successful auctions—sure-fire ideas you use to become an eBay PowerSeller!

Taken together, the 24 chapters in this book will help you launch and run a successful eBay business. By the time you get to the end of the final chapter, you'll know just about everything you need to know to make money on eBay. Now all you have to do is do the work!

Conventions Used in This Book

I hope that this book is easy enough to figure out on its own, without requiring its own instruction manual. As you read through the pages, however, it helps to know precisely how I've presented specific types of information.

Web Page Addresses

There are a lot of Web page addresses in this book—including addresses for specific pages on the eBay site. They're noted as such:

www.ebay.com

Technically, a Web page address is supposed to start with `http://` (as in `http://www.ebay.com`). Because Internet Explorer and other Web browsers automatically insert this piece of the address, however, you don't have to type it—and I haven't included it in any of the addresses in this book.

Special Elements

This book also includes a few special elements that provide additional information not included in the basic text. These elements are designed to supplement the text to make your learning faster, easier, and more efficient.

Finally, in various parts of this book you'll find big *checklists*. Use these checklists to prepare for the upcoming task—just check off the items on the list, and you'll be ready to go.

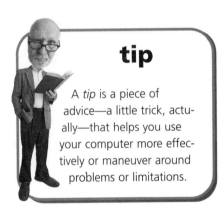

tip

A *tip* is a piece of advice—a little trick, actually—that helps you use your computer more effectively or maneuver around problems or limitations.

note

A *note* is designed to provide information that is generally useful but not specifically necessary for what you're doing at the moment. Some are like extended tips—interesting, but not essential.

caution

A *caution* will tell you to beware of a potentially dangerous act or situation. In some cases, ignoring a caution could cause you significant problems—so pay attention to them!

"Mike Sez"

This element is my personal opinion or recommendation regarding the topic at hand. Remember—I might not always be right, but I'll always have an opinion!

Let Me Know What You Think

I always love to hear from readers. If you want to contact me, feel free to email me at ebay-business@molehillgroup.com. I can't promise that I'll answer every message, but I will promise that I'll read each one!

If you want to learn more about me and any new books I have cooking, check out my Molehill Group Web site at www.molehillgroup.com. Who knows—you might find some other books there that you'd like to read.

PART

i

LEARNING THE ROPES

1

REVIEWING EBAY BASICS

What is eBay? I think the site's official mission statement does a good job of summing up what eBay is all about:

"eBay's mission is to help practically anyone trade practically anything on earth."

eBay fulfils its mission by creating millions of online auctions, in which sellers offer merchandise to potential buyers. While eBay is billed as a person-to-person auction site, there are also a good number of businesses that use eBay to sell their merchandise to customers across the country and around the world.

If you haven't used eBay yet, you're missing out on something. eBay is a terrific place to find just about anything you might want to buy—and to sell anything you have to sell. Since this book is about the selling part of the equation, we won't focus much on bidding and buying on eBay; still, you owe it to yourself to check out everything that the eBay site has to offer.

This chapter provides a brief refresher course on what eBay does and how to use the site. If you've already mastered these eBay basics, feel free to skim this chapter and then move ahead to more advanced material elsewhere in the book.

How an eBay Auction Works

In essence, an online auction on eBay works pretty much like an old-fashioned real-world auction—you know, the type where a fast-talking auctioneer stands in the front of the room, trying to coax potential buyers into bidding *just a little bit more* for the piece of merchandise up for bid. The only difference is that there's no fast-talking auctioneer online (the bidding process is executed by special auction software on the auction site), and all the bidders aren't in the same room—in fact, they might be located anywhere in the world, as long as they have Internet access.

Sellers like you post a listing for each item they want to sell; they select the merchandise category, length of the auction, and the starting bid price. From there the auction process takes over, with interested buyers making increasing bids on each item. At the end of the auction, the user with the highest bid wins, and pays for the item. When payment is received, the seller ships the item to the buyer.

It's not much more complicated than that—so let's go ahead and look at the entire process in more detail, from the seller's perspective.

This chapter isn't meant to replace a full-featured tutorial for beginning users. For that, read my companion book, *Absolute Beginner's Guide to eBay* (Que, 2003), available wherever books are sold.

eBay is kind of like a newspaper that runs classified ads—eBay isn't the actual seller, and isn't even really a "middleman." All eBay does is facilitate the transaction, and therefore can't be held responsible for anything that goes wrong with any particular auction or sale. When someone buys an item on eBay, they buy it directly from the seller—they don't pay any money to eBay.

Step 1: Register

Before you can list an item for sale, you first have to register with eBay. There's no fee to register, although eBay does charge the seller a small *listing fee* to list an item for sale, and another small *transaction fee* when the item is sold. eBay doesn't charge any fees to buyers, however.

For more information on creating your eBay account, see Chapter 10, "Step Eight: Establish Your eBay Presence."

Step 2: Create an Item Listing

Once you know what you want to sell, you have to create an "advertisement" for your auction. This item listing, like the one shown in Figure 1.1, consists of a headline, descriptive text about your item, one or more pictures (optional), payment and shipping information, and the starting bid price.

FIGURE 1.1

A typical eBay item listing.

You create item listings from eBay's Sell Your Item page. You specify both the length of the auction (3, 5, 7, or 10 days) and the minimum bid you will accept for that item. eBay will charge you anywhere from $0.30 to $3.30 to list your item.

For more information on creating item listings, see Chapter 11, "Creating Item Listings."

Step 3: Let the Bids Come In

Once the auction starts, your work is done—for the moment. What happens next, hopefully, is that a potential buyer searching for a particular type of item (or just browsing through all the merchandise listed in a specific category) reads your item listing and decides to make a bid. The bidder specifies the *maximum* amount he or she will pay; this amount has to be above the *minimum* bid you previously set.

eBay's built-in bidding software automatically places a bid for the bidder that bests the current bid by a specified amount—but doesn't reveal the bidder's maximum bid. For example, the current bid on an item might be $25. A bidder is willing to pay up to $40 for the item, and enters a maximum bid of $40. eBay's "proxy" software places a bid for the new bidder in the amount of $26—higher than the current bid, but less than the specified maximum bid. If there are no other bids, this bidder will win the auction with a $26 bid. Other potential buyers, however, can place additional bids; unless their maximum bids are more than the current bidder's $40 maximum, they are informed (via email) that they have been outbid—and the first bidder's current bid is automatically raised to match the new bids (up to the specified maximum bid price) .

Step 4: The Auction Ends

At the conclusion of the auction, eBay informs the highest bidder of his or her winning bid; as the seller you also receive an email informing you of the auction results. You're responsible for contacting the high bidder and requesting payment, although buyers also have the option (at your request) of using eBay's online checkout to provide shipping information and, if offered, to use the PayPal service to pay via credit card.

For more information on managing end-of-auction activities, see Chapter 12, "Managing Your Auctions."

Step 5: Receive Payment and Ship the Item

When you receive the buyer's payment, you then ship the merchandise directly to the buyer. In most cases the buyer pays all shipping and handling costs.

For more information on shipping merchandise, see Chapter 14, "Managing Packing and Shipping."

Step 6: Housecleaning

Concurrent with the close of the auction, eBay bills you, the seller, a small percentage (starting at 5.25%) of the final bid price. This selling fee is directly billed to your credit card or automatically debited from your checking account.

You should also, at this point, leave feedback about the buyer. If it was a smooth transaction, you leave positive feedback; if the buyer stiffed you, you leave negative feedback. When he or she receives the item, the buyer should also leave feedback about you. (Learn more about feedback in Chapter 2, "Using eBay's Advanced Features.")

Other Types of Auctions

eBay offers four basic variations on the main online auction theme—reserve price auctions, Dutch auctions, private auctions, and auctions with the Buy It Now option. We'll look at each in turn.

Reserve Price Auctions

A reserve price auction is one in which your starting bid price really isn't the minimum price you'll accept. Even though bids might exceed the initial bid price, if they don't hit your reserve price, you don't have to sell.

Many buyers—especially those just getting started—don't like reserve price auctions, and shy away from them. That's probably because they appear more complicated than regular auctions (and they are, just a little), and also because the reserve price is never disclosed to bidders. In this case, lack of familiarity definitely breeds contempt, at least from a certain class of bidders.

But there's something to the confusion factor. Let's say you set a minimum price of $5 for an item (really low, to get a buzz going and attract some early bidders) but a reserve price of $50 (because that's what you believe the item is really worth). If the high bidder bids $25, that bid doesn't win—because it's less than the $50 reserve. Unfortunately, bidders have no idea how much more to bid to hit the undisclosed reserve price. Messy and confusing, eh?

Why, then, would you opt for a reserve price auction? There are two possible scenarios:

- When you're unsure of the real value of an item—and don't want to appear to be asking too much for an item—you can reserve the right to refuse to sell the item if the market value is below a certain price.

- When you want to use a low initial bid price to get the bidding going more quickly than if the true desired minimum price (now the reserve price) was listed, the reserve price still guarantees that you won't have to sell below a minimum acceptable price.

Remember, if no one bids the reserve price or higher, no one wins.

Dutch Auctions

Dutch auctions are those in which you have more than one quantity of an identical item to sell. It's great if you have a dozen Scooby Doo Pez dispensers, 10 copies of *Lord of the Rings* on DVD, or a hundred units of white extra-large boxer shorts to sell.

In a Dutch auction, you specify both the minimum bid and the number of items available in the auction. As in a normal auction, bidders bid at or above that minimum bid for the item—although, in a Dutch auction, bidders can also specify a specific *quantity* that they're interested in purchasing.

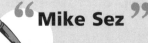

"Mike Sez"

I personally don't like reserve price auctions, and only run them on the rarest of occasions. My experience is that you turn a lot of potential bidders off by using a reserve price; it's better to create a regular auction with a higher minimum bid price, and be up front about everything.

Determining who "wins" a Dutch auction is a little different from determining who wins a normal auction. In a Dutch auction, the highest bidders purchase the items, but all buyers pay only the amount that matches the lowest successful bid.

Let's work through an example. Say you're selling 10 identical copies of a particular *Lord of the Rings* t-shirt. You indicate the number of items available (10), and the minimum bid (let's say $5). Potential buyers enter their bids, which must be equal to or higher than the minimum bid of $5; each buyer also indicates the quantity (from 1 to 10) that he or she is interested in purchasing.

If 11 people bid $5 each (for one shirt apiece), the first 10 bidders will win the auction, each paying $5 for their items, and the last bidder will be out of luck. But if the 11th person had placed a higher bid—$6, let's say—then that 11th bidder would be listed as the #1 bidder, and the last $5 bidder (chronologically) would be knocked from the list. All 10 winning bidders, however—including the person who bid $6— would only have to pay $5 for the item. (Highest bidders, lowest bids—get it?)

In a Dutch auction, the minimum price ends up being raised only if enough bidders place bids above the minimum bid. In our example, if 9 bidders bid over the minimum, but the 10th bidder bid $5, all bidders would still pay $5. But if the lowest bid was $6 (and the other bidders bid from $6 to $10), all 10 bidders would pay $6 (the lowest current bid). So posting a higher bid increases a buyer's chances of

caution

You can't make a Dutch auction private.

winning an item at a Dutch auction, but it also increases the risk of raising the price for everybody.

In any case, eBay handles all the details automatically, as long as you specify multiple quantities when listing your item.

Private Auctions

The next oddball auction type is relatively simple, compared to the others. If you're auctioning off something that is a little delicate, sensitive, or downright embarrassing, choose a Private auction and none of the bidders' names will ever be revealed publicly. It's great for items in the Adult category, although some bidders on ultra-high-priced items—such as rare collectibles—might also want to remain anonymous.

Buy It Now

eBay's Buy It Now (BIN) option lets you add a fixed-price option to your auction listings. The way BIN works is that you name a fixed price for your item; if a user bids that price, the auction is automatically closed and that user is named the high bidder. Note, however, that the BIN price is active only until the first bid is placed. (Or, in a reserve price auction, until the reserve price is met.) If the first bidder places a bid lower than the BIN price, the BIN price is removed and the auction proceeds normally.

The BIN option is popular among professional eBay sellers with a lot of similar inventory. That is, they're likely to place the same item up for auction week after week; in this scenario, the BIN price becomes the de facto retail price of the item, and you can ship items as soon as you find a willing buyer—you don't have to wait the standard seven days for a normal auction to end.

You might also want to consider BIN around the Christmas holiday, when buyers don't always want to wait around seven whole days to see if they've won an item; desperate Christmas shoppers will sometimes pay a premium to get something *now*, which is where BIN comes in.

Navigating the eBay Site

On any given day, eBay has more than 12 million items listed for auction. These items are organized into categories, some of them quite specific. Potential buyers can find merchandise by browsing through these categories, or by using eBay's search feature.

As you might suspect, all those millions of item listings make the eBay Web site (www.ebay.com) rather large and often cumbersome to navigate. The truth is that eBay has a ton of content and community on its site—if you know where to find it. (And the home page isn't always the best place to find what you're looking for!)

eBay's Home Page

When you're getting to know eBay, the place to start is the home page, shown in Figure 1.2. From here, you can access eBay's most important features and services.

The big chunk of space in the middle of the page is probably best ignored; it's nothing more than a big advertisement for the category or items du jour. Better to focus on the links along the top and left side of the page.

Across the top of the home page—across virtually every eBay page, as a matter of fact—is the Navigation Bar. This bar includes buttons that link to the major sections of the eBay site: Browse, Search, Sell, My eBay, and Community. When you click one of these links, you not only go to the main page for that section, you also display a list of subsections underneath the Navigation Bar.

FIGURE 1.2

Access the most important parts of eBay from the home page (www.ebay.com).

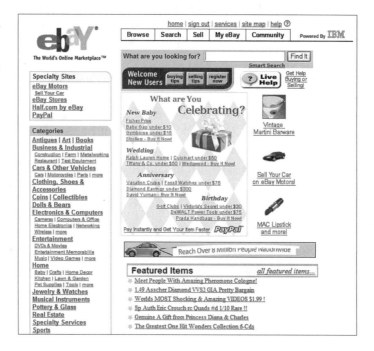

Along the left side of the home page is a collection of links to specific eBay item categories and specialty sites. When you want to find a particular type of item, it's easy to click through the categories listed on the left of the home page—or to search for items using the Search box (labeled "What are you looking for?"), located underneath the Navigation Bar.

Where to Find Everything Else: eBay's Site Map

Unfortunately, there's just so much stuff on the eBay site—and it's so haphazardly organized—that most users never find some of eBay's most interesting and useful features. In fact, you simply can't access many features from the home page. To really dig down into the eBay site, you need a little help—which you can get from eBay's Site Map page.

note

There are also six links *above* the Navigation Bar—Home, Register, Sign In/Sign Out/Register, Services, Site Map, and Help. Like the Navigation Bar, these links also appear at the top of most eBay pages.

You can access the Site Map page by clicking the Site Map link above the Navigation Bar. This page serves as the true access point to eBay's numerous and diverse features.

How People Make Money on eBay

Chances are you're just starting out on your online auction adventures—learning how to buy and sell and take advantage of everything eBay has to offer. As you gain more experience, however, you may decide that you want to try to make a living from selling goods online. (That's why you bought this book, after all.)

For tens of thousands of eBay users, making a living from online auctions isn't a dream—it's reality. It's definitely possible to sell enough items to generate a livable income from eBay auctions. It takes a lot of hard work and it's as complex as running any other business, but it can be done.

While most eBay users are simple hobbyists, a surprisingly large number of users sell enough items to actually make a living from their eBay auctions. Officially or not, these users are running eBay businesses—and many of them make really good money from it.

There are two keys to making money on eBay. First, you have to sell a large volume of merchandise. (Alternately, you can sell a small number of high-priced items—

which isn't as easy as it sounds.) Second, you have to control your costs. Sell enough items while keeping your costs under control, and you'll have a profitable business on your hands.

That sounds simple, but there's a lot that goes into the process. Still, the big difference between the occasional eBay seller and the person running a successful eBay business is nothing more than volume. Whether you're selling one item a month or a hundred, the process is basically the same. It's just that the professional seller has to manage a lot more activity—and do so with the lowest possible expenditure of time and money. Manage this process well, and you'll have a successful eBay business on your hands.

Which, of course, is what the rest of this book is all about. So now that you have the basics down, read on to discover how to become a true eBay power seller.

THE ABSOLUTE MINIMUM

eBay is the largest online auction site in the world. Whether you're a relatively new or totally experienced user, keep these facts in mind:

- An online auction is similar to a traditional auction, except that automated bidding software replaces the role of the human auctioneer.

- Other types of auctions available on eBay include reserve price auctions, Dutch auctions, private auctions, and auctions with the Buy It Now fixed-price option.

- eBay's home page (www.ebay.com) lets you access the most important operations—although the Site Map page is better for finding all of eBay's features and services.

2

USING EBAY'S ADVANCED FEATURES

In the last chapter we revisited how an online auction works and how to get around the eBay site. In this chapter we'll go beyond those basics into some of eBay's more advanced features—features that you, as a budding eBay businessperson, might find particularly interesting.

The Ins and Outs of User Feedback

Next to every buyer and seller's name on eBay is a number and (more often than not) a colored star. (Figure 2.1 shows my personal star and feedback number.) These numbers and stars represent that user's feedback rating. You can use this feedback information to determine the trustworthiness of your fellow eBay users; in general, the larger the number, the better the feedback—and the more trustworthy the user.

FIGURE 2.1

Check the feedback rating next to a member's name.

How Feedback Ratings Are Calculated

eBay automatically calculates total feedback ratings based on feedback from individual users. Every new user starts with 0 points. (A clean slate!) For every positive feedback received, eBay adds 1 point to your feedback rating. For every negative feedback received, eBay subtracts 1 point. Neutral comments add 0 points to your rating.

Let's say you're a new user, starting with a 0 rating. On the first two items you sell, the buyers like the fact that you shipped quickly and they give you positive feedback. On the third transaction, however, you forgot to ship the item for a few weeks, and the buyer (rightly so) left you negative feedback. After these three transactions, your feedback rating would be 1. (That's $0 + 1 + 1 - 1 = 1$.)

If you build up a lot of positive feedback, you qualify for a star next to your name. Different colored stars (from yellow to green—and on into "shooting stars") represent different levels of positive feedback.

Obviously, heavy users can build up positive feedback faster than occasional users. If you're dealing with a shooting-star user (of any color), you know you're dealing with a trustworthy eBay pro.

Reading Feedback Comments

You can also read the individual comments left by other users by going to the user's Feedback Profile page. To access this page, just click the number next to a user's name. (Figure 2.2 shows a typical Feedback Profile.)

FIGURE 2.2

A typical feedback profile; hey, people like this guy!

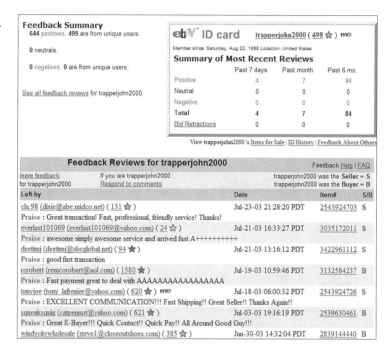

The Feedback Profile page includes the ID Card box (at the top) that summarizes feedback left in the past seven days, month, and six months. The individual feedback comments are shown below, and you can jump back to the auctions in question if you want by clicking on the item # links.

View Feedback About You

There are at least three ways to view all feedback left about you.

- Go to your My eBay page and select the Feedback tab (page).
- Click the feedback rating next to your name in any auction.
- Go to the Feedback Forum (discussed next) and click the Review and Respond to Feedback Comments Left to You link.

Using the Feedback Forum

eBay's Feedback Forum is the central clearinghouse for all things feedback related. You access the Feedback Forum by clicking the Services link in the Navigation Bar and then clicking the Feedback Forum link—or by going directly to pages.ebay.com/services/forum/feedback.html.

From the Feedback Forum you can

- Learn more about feedback
- Review and respond to feedback comments about you
- View feedback about other eBay users
- Leave feedback about other users—and see all the auctions where you *need* to leave feedback
- Review and follow up on feedback you've left for other users
- View feedback a member left about other users
- Access eBay's Star Recognition program, where you can earn prizes based on your feedback rating

How to Leave Feedback

You can leave feedback from the Feedback Forum or from any item listing page. (Click either the Leave Feedback to Seller or Leave Feedback to Bidder link.) You can then choose to leave Positive, Negative, or Neutral feedback, along with a brief comment (80 characters maximum).

Make sure your feedback is accurate before you click the Leave Comment button; you can't change your comments after they've been registered.

Dealing with Negative Feedback

Many eBay users are zealous about their feedback ratings. Although it's a good thing to want to build up a high rating, some users get quite obsessive about it.

For that reason, you want to be very sure of yourself before you leave negative feedback about a user. Some overly zealous users might retaliate by leaving negative feedback about you—even if it wasn't warranted.

> **"Mike Sez"**
>
> I recommend that, whether a transaction went swell or went south, you leave feedback about your partner in every transaction. It really is a good way to judge the quality of the other party in your eBay transactions.

Unfortunately, there's not much you can do if you receive negative feedback; feedback comments cannot be retracted. (That's one of eBay's faults, if you ask me.) What you can do is offer a response to the feedback, which you do by going to the Feedback Forum and clicking the Review and Respond to Feedback Comments Left to You link. When the feedback comments list appears, click the Respond link next to a particular comment and then enter your response. Your new comment is listed below the original feedback comment on the Feedback Profile page.

Using My eBay to Track Your eBay Activity

If you're running a lot of auctions simultaneously (and maybe even bidding in a few), how do you keep track of all your eBay activity?

eBay's My eBay feature is not only a way to track your auction activity, but also a way to personalize your eBay experience. It's a page—actually, a set of pages—that you customize to your own personal preferences to track your own bidding and selling activity in your own way. I highly recommend you avail yourself of this useful feature.

You access My eBay, shown in Figure 2.3, by clicking the My eBay button on the Navigation Bar.

There are actually seven pages (or tabs) in your My eBay, accessed from links at the top of the page, including:

- Bidding/Watching
- Selling
- Favorites
- Accounts
- Feedback
- Preferences
- All

note

The person who posted the negative feedback also gets a chance to respond to your response—so they get the last word!

note

If you're using eBay's Selling Manager feature (discussed in Chapter 12, "Managing Your Auctions"), the Selling tab in My eBay is replaced by a Selling Manager tab.

FIGURE 2.3

The My eBay
Bidding/Watchin
g page.

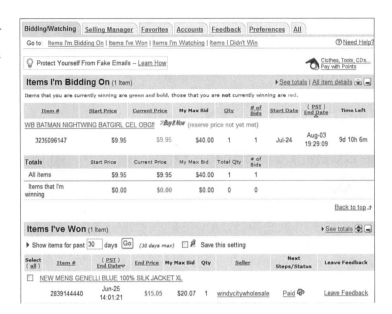

Showing Off Your Business with About Me

The My eBay page is a personalized Web page just for you—nobody else can view it. If you want a page to show to other users—to tell potential bidders a little bit about yourself—eBay lets you create your very own About Me page.

eBay's About Me page is a personal Web page just for you. It's easy to create (no HTML coding necessary), and lets you tell other eBay users a little bit about yourself. It also lets you show other users your current auctions, most recent feedback, and interesting items you've found online.

Although eBay uses a trio of templates to construct users' About Me pages, there is sufficient personalization available to make your About Me page different from your neighbors'. Figure 2.4 shows *my* About Me page, which you can access directly at members.ebay.com/aboutme/trapperjohn2000/.

You can view any user's About Me page by clicking the Me icon next to their user name on any item listing page. (If there's no icon displayed, that user doesn't have an About Me page.) You can search for other users' About Me pages by clicking the Search link on the Navigation Bar and then clicking Find Members to display the Find Members page; scroll down to the bottom of the page to search for About Me pages by user ID.

FIGURE 2.4

About *Me*, your author!

This page is maintained by trapperjohn2000 (498) ☆

Michael Miller: Best-Selling Author and eBay Professional

Listings

Current Items for Sale

Item	Start	End	Price	Title	High Bidder/Status
2547785148	Jul-25-03	Aug-04-03 09:29:31	$0.99	CD: The Rembrandts L.P.	No Bids Yet

About Michael Miller

Michael Miller is an author, consultant, musician, and the President of The Molehill Group, an Indianapolis-based writing and consulting firm. He has been an eBay member since Saturday, Aug 22, 1998.

Among the more than fifty books he has authored over the past fifteen years are the award-winning **The Complete Idiot's Guide to Online Auctions**, as well as numerous books about computer, business, and music topics. His most recent book, **Absolute Beginner's Guide to eBay**, was released in February, 2003. It's already hitting the best-seller lists at bookstores across the nation.

Feedback

User: cla.98 (131) ☆ **Date:** Jul-23-03 21:28:20 PDT

Praise: Great transaction! Fast, professional, friendly service! Thanks!

User: everlast101069 (24) ☆ **Date:** Jul-21-03 16:33:27 PDT

Praise: awesome simply awesome service and arrived fast A+++++++++++

User: deetimj (94) ★ **Date:** Jul-21-03 13:16:12 PDT

Praise: good fast transaction

Creating Your About Me Page

You don't have to be a Web programmer to create your own About Me page. All you have to do is click a few options and fill in some blanks, and you're ready to go.

Follow these steps:

1. From the Navigation Bar, click Services and then click Create My About Me Page.

2. When the About Me Login page appears, click the Create and Edit Your Page button.

3. When the About Me Styles page appears, select either a two-column, newspaper (three-column), or centered (single-column) layout.

4. When the Select Template Elements page appears, it's time to fill in the blanks. In particular, you need to enter a title for your page;

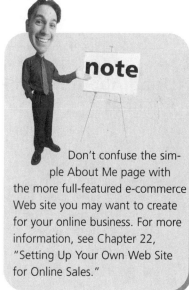

note

Don't confuse the simple About Me page with the more full-featured e-commerce Web site you may want to create for your online business. For more information, see Chapter 22, "Setting Up Your Own Web Site for Online Sales."

a short welcome message; one or more other paragraphs; and a link to a picture. You can also opt to display your most recent feedback comments; the items you currently have for sale; links for up to three of your favorite Web pages; and up to three items currently listed on eBay. Click the Preview Your Page button when you're done.

5. You now see a preview of your About Me page. If you like what you see, click the Save My Page button. If you want to change a few items, click the Edit Some More button to return to the previous page. If you'd rather fine-tune the page with your own HTML, click the Edit Using HTML button.

6. If you clicked the Save My Page button, you now see the Confirm Your Selection page, otherwise known as the Ready to Save Your Page? page. If you want to edit some more, click the Keep Editing for Now button. If you're sure you're done, click the Save My Page button.

You'll now be taken directly to your brand new About Me page.

Using About Me to Publicize Your Auctions

The great thing about the About Me page is that it's a page with a non-changing URL that always lists your current auctions. When you want to direct other users to your eBay auctions, it's easier to direct them to your About Me page than it is to enter the individual URLs for all your item listing pages.

The address for your About Me page is shown in the address box of your Web browser. The address is typically in the form of

`members.ebay.com/aboutme/`*userid*`/`; just replace *userid*

> **" Mike Sez "**
>
> If you have a separate personal Web page outside of eBay, list it in the favorite links section. That's a better use of space than the favorite eBay items section, which is almost immediately out of date when the auctions end and is better ignored. Also, you can include multiple descriptive paragraphs by entering a <p> paragraph break tag in either the Welcome Message or Another Paragraph text.

> **tip**
>
> You can edit your About Me page at any time by repeating steps 1 and 2, which will take you to your preview page. Click the Edit Some More button to make changes to your page.

with your own user ID and you should have the URL. (My eBay ID is trapperjohn2000, so my About Me address is `members.ebay.com/aboutme/ trapperjohn2000/`.)

You can then insert this URL into your personal Web page, your email signature, or any other item you can think of. It's a great way to publicize your ongoing eBay activity for free!

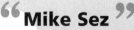

" Mike Sez "

The About Me page is also a good way for other eBay users to get to know you—especially those who are bidding in your auctions. Make sure you include text and photos that position you as a reputable eBay seller—and not some goofball flake who's likely to cause trouble.

THE ABSOLUTE MINIMUM

When it comes to eBay's advanced features, keep these key points in mind:

- You can use feedback ratings and comments to judge the trustworthiness of other eBay users; view other users' feedback by clicking on the feedback rating number next to their user name.

- The My eBay page lets you track all your eBay activities and information in one place; it includes separate tabs/pages for tracking items you're bidding on or watching, items you're selling, your favorite searches and categories, your eBay account, your feedback, and your preferences.

- The About Me page is your personal page on the eBay site—which you can create in less than five minutes, no HTML coding necessary.

PART

SETTING UP AN EBAY BUSINESS

3

STEP ONE: CREATE A BUSINESS PLAN

Before you can start your eBay business, you have to determine just what type of business you want to start. Yes, you know that's it's going to involve selling (lots of) stuff on eBay, but what kind of stuff are you going to sell? And where are you going to get that stuff? And just how are you going to manage the selling and shipping of all that stuff? And, if everything goes well, how much money do you expect to make—versus how much money you have to spend?

When—and only when—you can answer all these questions, then you're ready to start building your new business. Until then, you're just fooling around. Not that there's anything wrong with fooling around, of course—that describes millions of typical eBay sellers, most of whom do just enough work to make a little money. But if you want to make a *lot* of money—if you want to run a true business on eBay—then you have to do your homework and figure out where you want to go and how you're going to get there.

This act of figuring out what kind of business you'll be running is best done by preparing a *business plan*. If that sounds terribly formal and complicated, don't stress out—it doesn't have to be. The plan for your business can be as simple as some bullet points written out in longhand, or as sophisticated as a professional-looking desktop-published document. The key thing is to set down on paper the details about the business you want to create, and then follow the steps in your plan to build that business.

Thinking It Through—Before You Start

The key to planning your eBay business is to sit down and give it some serious thought. You don't want to rush into this new endeavor without thinking through all the details. While it is possible to stumble into eBay profitability, the most successful sellers know what they want to do and how they want to do it. In other words, they have a plan for success.

The easiest way to begin this planning process is to ask yourself a series of questions. When you can comfortably answer these questions, you'll have the framework of your business plan.

What Type of Business Do You Want to Run?

The first question to ask is the most important: What type of business do you want to run? Or, put more pointedly, what types of merchandise do you intend to sell on eBay?

For some sellers, the answer to this question is easy—especially if you already have a product. For example, if you're an artist, your product is your artwork. If you make hand-sewn quilts, your product is your quilts. Your business is based on your product; your plan is to use eBay to sell your artwork or your quilts. Everything you do from this point forward is designed to accomplish that goal.

If you don't already have a product to sell, answering this question will take some serious thought—and not a little work. You can't just sell "stuff" on eBay; that's not a real business, that's an online garage sale. No, you have to determine what *kind* of "stuff" you want to sell. And you probably want to specialize.

Maybe you're a comic book collector; you probably have a large collection of your own, as well as continuing access to new items from other collectors. Your plan, then, will be to create an eBay business based on the selling of collectible comic books. Or perhaps you have a source for handmade gift baskets. That's your business, right there—selling gift baskets on eBay.

Or maybe you base your business on the way you acquire merchandise, rather than a specific category of merchandise. Perhaps you specialize in acquiring items at estate sales. Your eBay business would be the selling of items acquired at estate sales. Or maybe you acquire large lots of liquidated merchandise from distressed wholesalers. Your eBay business, then, would be the selling of liquidated merchandise.

If you don't yet have a source of merchandise—if you could, in fact, sell *anything* on eBay—then you have to decide what type of merchandise you want to sell. That involves determining the type of item you want to work with (smaller and lighter is good, for shipping purposes; cheap to acquire but commands a high price from bidders is also good) and then finding a source for those items. This probably means doing some research as to what sells well on eBay and where that merchandise can be obtained.

The point is that you have to know what you're going to sell before you can figure out how to sell it. That's why this step is so crucial to putting together your business plan.

How Much Money Do You Want to Make?

Knowing what you want to sell is one thing. Knowing how much money you want to make is another. And, unfortunately, sometimes they don't match up. (This is why planning is important—so you'll know what works before you're hip-deep in things.)

Start from the top down. For your business to be successful, you have to generate an income on which you can comfortably live—unless, of course, you're looking for your eBay business to supplement an existing income. In any case, you need to set a monetary goal that you want to achieve. This number will determine how many items you need to sell.

Let's work through an example. You've talked it over with your family, and decided that you would be extremely happy if you could quit your current job and generate the same income from your eBay business. You currently earn $30,000 a year, so this becomes the financial goal of your eBay business.

That $30,000 a year translates into $600 a week, on average. (Figure on fifty working weeks a year, giving yourself two weeks of vacation; also keep in mind that certain weeks—around the Christmas holiday, especially—will generate more sales than others.) Now you have to determine how you're going to hit that $600/week target.

We'll also assume that you've already decided what types of items you want to sell. For the purposes of this example, let's say that you're selling gift baskets. Based on your research (primarily by looking at sales of similar items on eBay), you've established that you can sell these gift baskets for $20 each, on average. So you do some quick math and determine that you need to sell 30 of these $20 gift baskets every week to reach your $600/week goal. (That's $600 divided by $20.)

Stop right there! There's something wrong with this calculation. Can you figure out what it is?

Here's the problem: This simple calculation fails to take into account any of your expenses! That $20 per item represents your gross revenue, *not* your net profit. So we have to go back and figure out the costs involved with the sale of each item.

The first cost you have to take into account is the actual cost of the merchandise. Let's say that you pay $5 for each gift basket. Subtract that $5 product cost from your $20 selling price, and you have a $15 profit for every item you sell.

But that's not your only expense. You have to pay eBay for every item you list, and for every item you sell. If you accept credit card payments, you'll pay a percentage for all purchases made with plastic. And if you avail yourself of an auction management service, you'll pay for that, too.

Altogether, these non-product costs can add up to 5–10% of your total revenues. Let's use the top figure—10%—and subtract $2 for each $20 sale.

Now let's do the math. Take your $20 selling price, subtract your $5 product cost and $2 for other expenses, and you have a net profit of $13. To generate $600 a week in profit, you have to sell about 46 gift baskets. (That's $600 divided by $13.)

That's not the end of the math, however. Based on additional research, you determine that about only about half of the eBay auctions in this category end in a sale. So to sell those 46 items, you have to launch 92 auctions every week, half of which will end with no bidders.

That's a lot of work.

Now is when you start thinking about the options available to you. What if you could find a better-quality gift basket that you could sell for $40 instead of $20? Assuming you could keep the rest of your costs in line, that would cut in half the number of auctions you have to run every week. Or what if you decided you could live on $20,000 a year instead of $30,000? That would reduce your financial nut by a third.

You see where we're going with this. By working through these types of details ahead of time, you can fine-tune the amount of money you expect to make and the amount of effort you have to expend. Want to make more money? Then find a higher-priced (or lower-cost) item to sell, or plan on listing a larger quantity of items every week. It's all related; plan where you want to go, then you can figure out how to get there.

How Much Time Can You—and Do You Want to—Devote to Your Business?

Now you're at a point to ask if all this work seems reasonable. Taking our previous example, can you physically manage close to a 100 auctions a week? Can you pack and ship almost 50 items a week? And, more importantly, can you realistically *sell* almost 50 items a week? Are there enough potential customers to support that sort of sales volume?

If you plan on making eBay a full-time activity, you'll have eight hours a day, five (or six) days a week, to devote to managing your auctions. If, on the other hand, your eBay business is only a part-time job, you'll have less time to spend. Think it through carefully; can you reasonably expect to do what you need to do to reach your desired level of sales?

The point is that you have to realistically estimate the amount of work involved to run your eBay business, and then determine if you have that kind of time—and if it's worth it to you. If you only have a few hours per week to spend, then you might not be cut out to be a high-volume seller. (Unless, of course, you're selling very high-priced items.) If you're willing to put in the hours, however, higher income can result.

Why You Need a Business Plan

Okay. You've thought through what you want to sell and the amount of work involved, and you're convinced that it's doable. Why not just get started now?

There are several good reasons to put your planning down on paper. First, by formally writing down your plan, you're guaranteeing that you'll actually think through what you're going to do—you won't slide by without doing the critical thinking. Second, by committing your plan to paper, you have a real plan—something you can follow in the future, and use as a benchmark when evaluating your success. And third, if you need to obtain any funding for your business—to purchase inventory, for example—potential lenders or investors will want to see the plan you've put together.

This last point can't be ignored. Most potential lenders and investors require that you present a detailed business plan before they will even consider giving you money. Since your business plan contains information about your potential market, your business, your strategy, and your planned operation, any investor or lender can read the plan to get a quick snapshot of you and your business.

For that reason, a business plan should not only reflect how you plan to run your eBay business, it should also contain everything a potential lender or investor needs to make an informed decision about whether or not to give you money. Without a business plan, you won't even get in the door.

How to Create a Business Plan

You may think that a business plan has to be a complex document, full of long sentences, overly technical terms, convoluted legalese, and detailed financial data. Nothing could be further from the truth. If you can talk about your business—and you no doubt can, at length—then you can create an effective business plan.

The best business plans are conversational in tone, are easy to read and understand, avoid as much legalese as possible, and only include enough financial data that is necessary to paint an accurate picture of your business's potential. In fact, you could probably dictate the bulk of your business plan in a single sitting, based on your inherent knowledge of what it is that you're trying to accomplish and why.

Imagine you're sitting in a restaurant or a coffeehouse, and someone you know comes up and asks you what you're up to these days. You answer that you're in the process of starting up a new eBay business, and then you start to tell a little story. You tell this person what your business is all about, why you've decided to get into this eBay thing, what kind of opportunity you see, and how you intend to exploit that opportunity. If you're on good terms with the person you're talking to, you might even share the revenues and profits you hope to generate.

Here's the type of story you tell:

> "Let me tell you about what I plan to do. You see, there's a big market out there for gift baskets. They're very popular with women, especially older women, who buy them for gifts. They're so popular, eBay has created a dedicated gift basket category on their site.

> "I did a search on eBay and found that the average gift basket sells for about $20, and in a typical week there were more than 500 auctions for these items. I've found a source for gift baskets that are better than what you typically find online, and think I can provide eBay's buyers with a better product than they're currently getting, but for a similar price.

> "My source will sell me these gift baskets for $5 apiece. If I sell them for $20, on average, I think I can take 10% of the sales in the category. That means I'll be selling close to 50 gift baskets a week. Taking all my costs into account, that should generate about $30,000 in profit a year.

"To handle this volume of sales, I plan to set up kind of an assembly line in my spare bedroom. I'll buy the gift baskets in bulk and store them in my garage. I can purchase shipping boxes from my local box store, and ship the baskets via Priority Mail. The buyers will pay all shipping costs, which I'll inflate a little to cover the cost of the box and packing material.

"In addition, I'm going to subscribe to one of those auction management services, which will make it easier to manage all my customer communication and keep track of who's paid and what needs to be shipped. And I'll sign up for PayPal, so I can accept credit card payments.

"At the start, I think I can manage the entire business myself—which is what I'm quitting my job to do. If things really take off, I can hire my cousin Helen to help me out with the packing and shipping. But that's probably down the road; for now, it'll be just me, which is all I'm planning for. If I can hit my numbers, I'll be very happy to take home $30,000 a year for my efforts."

As you can see, this short story (a little more than 300 words) tells your audience everything they need to know about your planned eBay business. They know why you're starting the business, they see the opportunity presented, they understand how you expect to profit from that opportunity, they sense the unique things that you intend to do, and they learn how much money you expect to make. It's all there, presented in a logical order; everything important is included, with nothing extraneous added.

In short, you've just created your business plan—orally. Now all you have to do is put it down on paper.

The Components of a Winning Business Plan

Now that you have the outline of your business plan in your head, let's look at how to translate your story into a written document.

In essence, you take your oral story and write it down, in a logical order. The typical business plan is divided into several distinct sections—each of which maps to a part of your business story. What you have to do is take the story you just told and sort it out into short sections that help the reader understand just what it is your business is about.

Of course, your particular business plan can contain more or fewer or different sections than presented here, but it should contain the same information—because this information will describe and drive your new business. If you were writing a business plan for a big corporation, each section might be several pages long. For the purposes of your eBay business, though, think along the lines of a few sentences or paragraphs, instead.

You see, the length of your business plan document depends entirely on your particular circumstances. If your business plan is solely for your own personal use, there's no need to make it any longer or fancier than it needs to be; it's even okay to write in bullets rather than complete sentences. If you expect to present your business plan to others, then by all means go a little fancier and use proper grammar and punctuation. The key thing is to include all the information necessary to get your points across.

Next, we'll look at the individual sections of your business plan separately.

Mission

This part of the plan, typically just a sentence or so long, describes your dream for your business—why you're doing what you're doing. Although this is the shortest section of your plan, it is sometimes the most difficult section to write. That's because many people find it difficult to articulate the reasons why they do what they do.

Sometimes called a *mission statement*, this section describes the *what*—what your business does and what you're trying to achieve. Someone reading your Mission section should know immediately what your business does—and what you *don't* do.

Using our ongoing example, a relevant mission statement might be something like: "I intend to sell high-quality gift baskets to targeted buyers on the eBay online auction site." It should *not* be "I plan to make a lot of money on eBay;" that isn't a very specific mission, and it certainly isn't market-driven.

Opportunity

This section, sometimes called the *market dynamics* or *market analysis* section, describes the compelling reason for your business to exist—in other words, it

note

This chapter presents the type of bare-bones business plan you need for a small eBay business. If you want to create a really serious business plan—or a plan for a larger business opportunity—check out my companion book, *Teach Yourself Business Plans in 24 Hours* (2001, Alpha Books).

note

A mission is different from a goal in that a mission defines a general direction, while a goal defines a specific target. A business will have but a single mission but can have many individual goals.

presents the market opportunity you've identified. Typically, this section starts out by identifying the target market, sizing it, and then presenting growth opportunities.

The goal of this section is to describe the market opportunity you seek to pursue, and to convince potential investors that it's a significant enough opportunity to be worth pursuing. As such, this section will include narrative text (you have to tell a story about the market) and some amount of numerical data. Which data you choose to present, how you choose to present it, and how you weave it into your narrative will determine the effectiveness of this section.

When the Opportunity section is complete, the reader should understand the basic nature of the market you choose to pursue, the size of that market, the market's growth potential, and the types of customers who comprise the market. You can obtain most if not all of this data by searching eBay for similar types of merchandise, or by browsing through relevant categories.

Why do you need to present market data in your business plan, anyway? The answer is simple—to help you sell prospective lenders and investors on your specific business strategy. You also need to realistically size the opportunity for your own needs; you don't want to pursue merchandise categories that aren't big or robust enough to achieve your financial goals.

In the case of our ongoing example, you might want to include data on the number of similar auctions during a particular period, the average selling price for these items, and the close rate (number of auctions that result in a sale) for this category.

Strategy

This section of your plan describes how you'll exploit that immense market opportunity described in the previous section, and puts forward your potential eBay activities. This section typically includes information about the products you'll be selling, as well as how you plan to obtain and market these products. In essence, you want to describe the business you're in, what you plan to sell, and how you'll make money. You'll probably want to include some sort of timeline that details the major milestones you will likely face in successfully implementing your new business.

For our ongoing example, you'd explain that you're selling gift baskets (and maybe describe what a gift basket is), present where and how you're obtaining your merchandise, describe how you'll be selling the items on eBay, and then detail the selling price, cost, and profits associated with your sales.

Organization and Operations

This section describes your company structure as well as the back-end operations you use to bring your products and services to market. If your employee base consists of you and no one else, that's okay; if you have plans to hire an assistant or two, throw that in. The key thing in this section is to describe your "back office," how you plan to get things done. That means describing how you'll create your item listings, how you'll warehouse your inventory, and how you'll pack and ship your merchandise.

In short, this section of your business plan is where you detail how your business is structured and how it will work.

Strengths and Weaknesses

This is the last text section of your plan. A lot of businesses don't include this section, but I think it's well worth writing. In essence, this section lays bare your core competencies and the challenges you face—which are good to know *before* you actually go into business.

I like including strengths and weaknesses in a business plan, for several reasons. First, summarizing your unique competitive advantages serves to highlight those unique aspects of your business strategy. In addition, ending the text part of your plan with a list of your strengths is a great way to wrap things up; you leave your readers with a summary of the key points you want them to remember. Finally, by detailing potential challenges you might face, you get the chance to reassess the reality of what you're about to attempt—and to proactively address these issues before they become real problems.

Remember, when you answer potential challenges with distinct strategies, you turn your weaknesses into strengths—and present yourself as being both realistic and proactive.

Financials

The final section of your business plan document is the Financials section. This is where you present the financial status of and projections for your business. Put simply, these are the numbers—at minimum, an income statement and a balance sheet. You'll want to include your current statements (if your business is already up and running), and projections for the next three years.

Whether you're borrowing money or trying to attract investors, your potential business partners will want to know what size of a business you're talking about, how profitable that business is likely to be, and how you expect to grow revenues and profits over the years. Your financial statements provide that critical information. In addition, this section helps you come to grips with the financial realities of what you plan to do.

In a way, the Financials section defines the goals you have for your eBay business. The revenues and profits you project for future years *are* your company's financial goals—they're the yardstick with which you'll measure the success of your business strategy over the next several years.

When you're making your projections, you should make sure that the numbers you forecast actually make sense. Is there a logic to the revenue buildup over the period? Do the projected expenses make sense in relation to the projected revenues? Are these numbers realistic? Are they achievable? Are they *comfortable*—to both you and to your investors? Bottom line, do the numbers feel right?

Remember, the numbers you put together quantify your financial goals; once you accept them, you're committing yourself to running a successful eBay business.

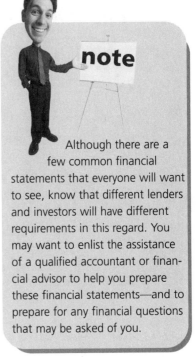

note

Although there are a few common financial statements that everyone will want to see, know that different lenders and investors will have different requirements in this regard. You may want to enlist the assistance of a qualified accountant or financial advisor to help you prepare these financial statements—and to prepare for any financial questions that may be asked of you.

Writing the Plan

Now that you know what goes into a successful business plan, all you have to do is write it. As daunting as that sounds, it isn't that difficult. The hardest part is just sitting down and getting started. Carve out a few hours of an evening or on the weekend, close the door, turn off the radio, and disconnect the telephone and the Internet. Concentrate on the task at hand, starting with a rough outline and filling in the details as if you were telling them to a friend. Take as much time as you need; a few hours, a few evenings, or a few weeks. Don't overthink it, just start writing and worry about editing later.

Once you have a rough draft down, re-read it as if you were a stranger to the story. Even better, give it to someone else to read and see if it tells them everything they need to know. See what questions they have, and incorporate these into any changes you need in your second draft.

After all the words are right, you can spend a few minutes making your document look pretty. Print it out, give it a final proofreading, and you're done. Then, and only then, you can start *using* the plan—to get your eBay business up and running.

THE ABSOLUTE MINIMUM

Before you start your eBay business, you need to determine what type of business you'll be running—and how you'll run it. Keep these points in mind:

- Successful sellers don't engage in random selling; they have a plan that describes and focuses their eBay activity.

- A written business plan is also necessary if you need to borrow money for your business—or if you want to attract investors.

- Good business plans are conversational—as if you're telling the story of your business to a friend.

- Your business plan doesn't have to be long or formal—a few pages is fine, as long as it achieves what it needs to.

- Every business plan should include the following sections: Mission, Opportunity, Strategy, Organization and Operations, Strengths and Weaknesses, and Financials.

IN THIS CHAPTER

- How much money do you need—and why?
- Where can you find the funding you need?
- Which is the right funding option for you?

4

STEP TWO: EVALUATE YOUR FUNDING NEEDS

It's quite possible that you can start your new eBay business with zero dollars in your pocket. It's more likely, however, that you'll have some startup costs involved—to purchase inventory and shipping boxes, if nothing else. How much money you need depends on the type of business you're setting up and how you plan to handle your day-to-day operations. And if you need more up-front money than you currently have in your pocket, you're going to have to find a source for these additional funds.

This chapter is all about this initial funding—and your ongoing financial needs. You'll need to determine how much money you need, how much money you have, and where (and how) to obtain the difference.

How Much Money Do You Need—and Why?

Before you go seeking funding for your new business, you first have to determine how much money you need. This isn't as easy as it may sound.

First you need to establish *why* you need this funding—because the why will sometimes determine the who (to ask for money). Assuming that you're starting your business from scratch, you'll need enough cash in the bank to pay for all your *operating expenses* until the time when you start generating real profits—which could be a period of months or even a year or more. You'll also need cash to purchase your opening inventory, as well as any capital expenses you need to make (for computers and similar items).

Use the following checklist to help figure out your funding needs.

Operating expenses are the ongoing, day-to-day costs of doing business—rent, utilities, office supplies, packing supplies, and the like.

Funding Calculation Checklist

- ☐ Estimate your startup and day-to-day costs for the first 12 months of operation
- ☐ Project your sales revenue for the first 12 months of operation
- ☐ Use your cost and revenue numbers to calculate your cash flow for the first 12 months of operation

Estimating Costs

Let's start on the costs side of things. Just what do you need to buy to get your business up-and-running?

Your business costs fall into a handful of major categories, which you should enter into a monthly planning sheet. These categories include:

- ■ **Capital expenses**. These are the big one-time purchases you need to make just to get started. Examples include personal computers, printers, digital cameras, scanners, office furniture, and similar expensive pieces of equipment. Lower-cost equipment, such as postal scales, typically don't fall into this category. You should enter the total expense for each item in the month you plan to purchase it.

- **Rent and utilities.** For most small eBay sellers, you operate out of your home, so you have no additional space expenses. However, if you need to rent a storage bin or warehouse space, or plan to lease office space, then you should include those expenses here. This is also where you track the fixed monthly costs of your Internet service, auction management tools, and the like. Do *not* include any rent or utility expenses (for your house) that are already being paid; only include new expenses directly related to your eBay business.

- **Sales expenses.** This is where you track your eBay and PayPal fees. These are variable expenses, typically figured as a percent of your projected sales. (You can do the figuring yourself, based on the various services you sign up for; in a pinch, I've found that these expenses average about 10% of total revenues.)

- **Packing supplies.** This is where you'd put that postal scale, as well as boxes, labels, sealing tape, and the like.

- **Office supplies.** This category is for all your consumable office items— paper, pens, paper clips, printer toner or ink cartridges, staples, and so on.

- **Inventory.** While not an operating expense per se, this is probably the biggest ongoing expenditure for most eBay sellers. If you have to purchase the items you intend to sell, you include those inventory costs here. This is also where you put your "manufacturing" costs if you're making the items you intend to sell.

You should plan out your costs in each category on a month-by-month basis, for at least twelve months. Adapt the following worksheet for your own individual circumstances, and for the particular items you intend to sell. (If you're spreadsheet savvy, you may even want to plug it into Excel.)

Cost Estimation Worksheet

Month	1	2	3	4	5	6	7	8	9	10	11	12	TOTAL
Capital Expenses													
Computer													
Printer													
Furniture													
Rent and Utilities													
Office rent													
Warehouse rent													
Utilities													
Internet													
Sales Expenses													
eBay fees													
PayPal fees													
Shipping													
Packing Supplies													
Boxes													
Labels													
Other													
Office Supplies													
Paper													
Toner													
Other													
Inventory													
Item 1													
Item 2													
Item 3													
TOTAL													

Now you know how much money you'll need every month for the next twelve months. This is not how much cash you actually need, however; after the first month or so, your ongoing revenues should help cover these costs—as you'll discover as we continue working through this process.

Projecting Revenues

It's hard to gaze into a crystal ball and say with absolute certainty how successful you're going to be with your eBay sales. All you can do is make a reasonable guess, based on all the planning you did back in Chapter 3, "Step One: Create a Business Plan."

Use the following worksheet to detail your projected sales over a twelve-month period.

> **caution**
>
> You shouldn't plan on hitting your stride right out of the gate. It's reasonable to expect it to take a few months for your sales to ramp up to their full potential, so it's best to plan for lower sales when you're first starting out. One of the most common business mistakes is to overestimate the time it takes a new business to start generating significant revenues.

Sales Projection Worksheet

Month	1	2	3	4	5	6	7	8	9	10	11	12	TOTAL
Sales													
Item 1	__	__	__	__	__	__	__	__	__	__	__	__	__
Item 2	__	__	__	__	__	__	__	__	__	__	__	__	__
Item 3	__	__	__	__	__	__	__	__	__	__	__	__	__
Item 4	__	__	__	__	__	__	__	__	__	__	__	__	__
Item 5	__	__	__	__	__	__	__	__	__	__	__	__	__
Item 6	__	__	__	__	__	__	__	__	__	__	__	__	__
TOTAL	__	__	__	__	__	__	__	__	__	__	__	__	__

Determining Cash Flow

Now that you know how much money you think you'll have going out (costs) and coming in (revenues) every month, you can calculate your monthly cash flow. This isn't your monthly profit, by the way, although it's probably close; all it is is a measure of your business's cash position.

You calculate your cash flow by starting with the amount of cash you have on hand (typically the ending cash from the previous month), adding your cash sales for the month, then subtracting your cash expenses for the month. The resulting number is your *cash position* at the end of the month—which becomes your starting *cash on hand* for the next month.

If your cash position at the end of the month is a negative number, your outflow exceeds your intake, and you'll need to come up with additional funds to meet the cash shortfall. If you get a positive number, you've generated extra cash that month—which you can use to pay next month's bills, put in your savings account, or go out and buy something nice for yourself.

note

The *breakeven point* is that point in time when your expenses and your revenues become equal. Any business conducted before that point was done at a loss; any business after the breakeven point is generating an operating profit.

Use the following worksheet to calculate your monthly cash flow. Remember that the Cash on Hand number is equal to the Cash Position number from the previous month. If you're profitable, the Cash Position number will keep growing—and the first month it goes positive is the month that your business breaks even.

Cash Flow Worksheet

Month	1	2	3	4	5	6	7	8	9	10	11	12
Cash on hand	—	—	—	—	—	—	—	—	—	—	—	—
plus Total sales	—	—	—	—	—	—	—	—	—	—	—	—
minus Total expenses	—	—	—	—	—	—	—	—	—	—	—	—
Cash Position	—	—	—	—	—	—	—	—	—	—	—	—

Now here's the thing with cash flow: It doesn't matter how much cash you end up with at the end of the year; if you don't have the cash when you need it, you're short. That's why you need to project your cash flow on a monthly basis. (Or, if you want to get really anal, you can calculate it weekly; after all, your expenses build up at least that frequently.)

Let's work through a quickie example, as shown in the following worksheet.

Cash Flow Worksheet: Mike's Gift Baskets

Month	1	2	3	4	5	6	7	8	9	10	11	12
Cash on Hand	$0	(2950)	(2600)	(1950)	(1000)	$275	$1550	$2825	$4100	$5375	$6650	$7925
Total Sales	$1000	$1500	$2000	$2500	$3000	$3000	$3000	$3000	$3000	$3000	$3000	$3000
Capital Expenses	$3000	$0	$0	$0	$0	$0	$0	$0	$0	$0	$0	$0
Rent & Utilities	$200	$200	$200	$200	$200	$200	$200	$200	$200	$200	$200	$200
Sales Expenses	$100	$150	$200	$250	$300	$300	$300	$300	$300	$300	$300	$300
Packing Supplies	$200	$225	$250	$275	$275	$275	$275	$275	$275	$275	$275	$275
Office Supplies	$200	$200	$200	$200	$200	$200	$200	$200	$200	$200	$200	$200
Inventory	$250	$375	$500	$625	$750	$750	$750	$750	$750	$750	$750	$750
Total Expenses	$3950	$1150	$1350	$1550	$1725	$1725	$1725	$1725	$1725	$1725	$1725	$1725
Cash Position	**(2950)**	**(2600)**	**(1950)**	**(1000)**	**$275**	**$1550**	**$2825**	**$4100**	**$5375**	**$6650**	**$7925**	**$9200**

If you look to the end of the twelfth month, you can see that you're in a very good cash position. You're generating $1,275 in cash each month, and should have a total of $9,200 cash on hand. However, if you look at your very first month, you see that you end that month $2,950 in the hole—and you stay in a negative cash position for the first four months of operation. It takes you until the fifth month to dig yourself out of the hole, when your cash position becomes positive.

caution

If you have to borrow money just to pay your rent or mortgage, then you're in no position to be launching a major eBay business. Make sure that all your basic needs are met *before* you invest more money to become a high-volume eBay seller.

All of which means that you need to come up with additional cash to get you through those first four months.

So how much additional cash do you need? All you have to do is look at the biggest monthly loss in the Cash Position line; this number represents the funding requirements for your new initiative. In essence, you want to obtain enough funding to pay for all your expenses until your business becomes self-funding through monthly operating profits. Anything above that figure is a safety net; anything less is a disaster waiting to happen.

In our example, the biggest negative cash position comes in the first month. That number—$2,950—is the amount of initial funding you need to get your business up and running.

Now for the tough question—where do you get the money?

Where to Find Funding

When you need to finance the start up of your business, where you go for funding depends a lot on how much money you need. The less money you need, the easier it will be to find it. If you need really big sums, your options become more limited—and the process more involved.

Let's look at all the places you can find funding for your new eBay business.

Personal Savings

The easiest place to look for money is in your own bank account. If you've been frugal with your money, you might have enough cash on hand to cover the startup costs of your eBay business. Just remember to work through your monthly cash flow to determine when you'll generate enough cash to pay yourself back.

The advantages of going the self-financed route are obvious. You don't have to spend time wooing a multitude of lenders and investors, and you don't have any obligations (legal or financial) to anyone else. The disadvantage, of course, is that it's all your money—and you could lose it all if your new business fails. You also lose whatever interest that your money could have been otherwise earning.

It's possible that you don't have enough money to completely fund your eBay business. So self-funding isn't always a viable option; if you have the money, however, it's the fastest and least-complex option available.

Credit Cards

Getting an advance on your credit card is another way of borrowing money from yourself. The big difference between this method and withdrawing funds from your savings account is that you have to pay interest on the funds advanced—which could be a percentage point or more every month. You may also be charged a fee for making a cash advance to yourself. So when you're calculating your payback schedule, make sure you factor in these additional costs.

Friends and Family

If you don't have the funds, maybe someone you know does. Depending on who you know (or who you're related to), you may want to consider borrowing your startup funds from a friend or family member.

The upside of dealing with friends and family is that you're dealing with friends and family. The downside is also that you're dealing with friends and family. Borrowing money from friends or family is always a little tricky; even the best of friendships can be tested when the issue of money is involved.

Loans

If you need more than a few thousand dollars, you may be forced to visit your friendly neighborhood bank or lending company and apply for a small-business loan.

> **" Mike Sez "**
>
> If you decide to hit up someone you know for a loan, my advice is to keep things as professional as possible. That means starting with a well-written business plan, and then writing up the entire transaction as a proper loan, complete with an agreed-upon payback schedule and a reasonable rate of interest. Treat your friend just as you would a banker, and make all your payments as scheduled. This way you'll avoid (as much as possible) having this business interfere with your personal relationships.

Lenders, of course, require you to give them back the money you borrowed—which means you have to include the loan payback in your financial plans. (This is also the case when you borrow money from friends and family.) You also have to factor in interest payments, which can be significant. This means, of course, that when you're putting together your financial plans, you have to make sure you generate enough profits to cover the loan and interest payments.

Still, if your funding needs are large enough, taking out a loan may be your only option. If this is the case, make sure you borrow no more (or no less) than you really need and that you can realistically pay back on a regular basis.

> **tip**
>
> If you have trouble getting a bank to lend you money, you can enlist the services of the Small Business Administration (SBA). The SBA offers a number of different types of loans as well as loan assistance. Learn more at the SBA's Web site at www.sba.gov.

When you're preparing to approach a banker or a loan official to ask for a loan, remember that lenders aren't expecting some huge payback on their investment; they merely want their principle back along with the designated amount of interest. What they're interested in, then, is your ability to repay the loan. So keep these points in mind when making a presentation to a lender:

- **Show stability.** Show your personal stability. Show the stability of your business model. Show anything you can that says "stable" and "low risk."

- **Concentrate on cash flow.** Lenders are less interested in your profitability (although they *are* interested in that, too) than in your ability to make loan payments. This means you want to stress your cash flow, which hopefully is positive and hopefully is large enough to cover your loan payments.

- **Look professional.** When you deal with professionals, you need to look professional. That means creating a solid business plan and printing it out in a professional fashion. It also means working through your financials so that they're as solid as possible.

- **Show a real use for the money.** Bankers won't want to lend you money without a good justification for it. (On the other hand, they also won't want to lend you money if you're so down on your luck that you really need it to survive; you'll have to strike a balance.) Show exactly how the money will be used, and be precise; bankers are nothing if not detail oriented.

Most lenders will want to see not only your business plan, but also your current balance sheet and projected P/L. (That's your profit and loss statement projected over the next year or two.) You may also be asked to put up collateral for the amount of the loan. For this reason, many small businesspeople get their startup funding by taking out a second mortgage or line of credit on their houses or other property.

Investors

When you need more funds than you can get with a simple loan—when you want to raise really large amounts of money, typically in the tens or hundreds of thousands of dollars—you need to consider equity funding. It's called equity funding because you sell equity in your business in return for the funding dollars. The people or companies that buy shares of equity are called investors; they're investing their money with the hope that their equity position will be worth more at a later date than it was when they purchased it.

When you take on investors—of any type—you're gaining partners. An investor buys a share of your business and thus has a lasting equity stake. Even though that equity stake can be small, it's still there—which means for every investor you add, the business adds a new co-owner.

The stake of the business that an investor purchases is called a share. Each share of your company's stock that you sell is assigned a specific price; this price can vary for different types of investors and will vary over time. As long as your company is private, you set the value of your shares. Once your company goes public (and it doesn't ever have to, of course), the value of the shares is set on the open market of a stock exchange.

There are many types of investors you can pursue for equity funding. In most cases, you'll be going after small investors—sometimes called "friend and family" or "angel" investors, people you know from other business dealings who are willing to invest in the future of your business. If your funding needs are *really* large, you'll be dealing with venture capital (VC) firms, who will demand a major stake in your business in return for their investment—and will expect high growth numbers to make their investment worthwhile.

The ins and outs of equity funding are beyond the scope of this book, and (fortunately) beyond the needs of most eBay sellers. If you think you want to form a business with equity partners, you'll need to bring in expert legal and financial help to put the deal together.

Which Is the Right Option for You?

Among these various funding options, which are the best for you and your company?

If you have relatively modest goals and funding needs, you're probably not large enough to show up on the radar of the big venture capital firms. This is probably for the best, as it's unlikely you'd want the hassle (and control issues) associated with venture capital funding.

Equity placement with small investors is also out of the question for most eBay businesses. Again, this is probably for the best, as you have all sorts of legal issues, not the least of which is developing a payout for your partners.

A more popular source of funding for eBay sellers is the bank. It's much easier to get a loan than to solicit investments. Borrow enough money to get up and running, make sure you pay it back in time, and then you're free of all obligations.

Even more popular is the self-funding option. If you start modestly (and you should), you probably have enough cash in the bank (or a high enough credit card limit) to handle your minimal start-up costs. Just make sure that the costs of launching your business don't keep you from paying your rent or mortgage!

THE ABSOLUTE MINIMUM

Figuring out how much money you need is essential for anyone setting up a high-volume eBay business. Keep these points in mind:

- Your eBay business will have a variety of expenses—capital expenses, ongoing rent and utilities, office and packing supplies, and cost of inventory.

- You calculate your monthly cash position by taking your starting cash on hand, adding your projected revenues, and then subtracting your estimated expenses for the month.

- The amount of funds you need to obtain is equal to your cumulative cash position for all the months before your business breaks even.

- Viable sources of funding include yourself, friends and family, your local bank or lending company, and large or small investors.

5

STEP THREE: DEAL WITH BUSINESS AND LEGAL ISSUES

Now that you have a plan for your business and know how to arrange funding to get things started, it's time to work on the nuts and bolts of setting up an official and legal business.

Wait a minute, some of you are probably thinking. There are millions of sellers on eBay who don't go through any of this legal stuff, who sell items out of their garage and do just fine, thank you.

That is true. But those sellers aren't trying to make a business of it; for them, selling on eBay is a hobby or an occasional pursuit. If you want to make serious money on eBay, you have to treat your activity as a serious business—which means setting yourself up as a legitimate business entity.

Choosing a Type of Business

When you're setting up your eBay business, you first need to decide what type of structure you want your business to have. The different types of businesses—sole proprietorship, partnership, and corporation—each have their pros and cons, and you should seriously evaluate which structure is best for your individual situation.

" Mike Sez "

I am not a lawyer, nor am I an accountant. For that reason, you should take the information in this chapter as general in nature, and consult a professional for more specific legal and tax-related advice.

Sole Proprietorship

Most eBay businesses are set up as sole proprietorships. In this type of structure, you are your business—and vice versa.

A sole proprietorship is the easiest type of business to form, and the easiest to manage on an ongoing basis. You don't have to file any papers of incorporation, nor do you need to pay payroll taxes and the like. You file income tax for the business under your own name, using your social security number as your tax identification number; you'll file and pay this tax as quarterly estimates (described in the "Dealing with Taxes" section, later in this chapter), but the paperwork burden is minimal, compared to other forms of businesses.

On the downside, the owner of a sole proprietorship is personally responsible for the debts and legal obligations of the business. That means if the business owes money, you're on the hook for it—and if your business gets sued, you end up in court.

Registering as a sole proprietorship is relatively easy and relatively cheap. You can probably handle all the paperwork yourself—although using an accountant or attorney isn't a bad idea. Your business can share your name, or you can do business under an assumed name or *dba* (doing business as). To do this legally, you'll need to file a *fictitious name affidavit* in the county in which you do business. If you choose to open a bank account under your business name, you'll need to present this fictitious name affidavit.

note

For more information about the legalities of starting a small business, check out the Small Business Association's BusinessLaw) Web site (www. businesslaw.gov), the Small Business section of the Nolo site (www.nolo.com), or the Entrepreneur's Help Page (www. tannedfeet.com). Another good source of information is your local secretary of state's office or Web site, which should have all the forms you need to get started.

Partnership

A partnership is like a sole proprietorship, but with more than one owner. The two or more partners have to contractually agree as to who is responsible for what, and how to share the business's profits or losses. You'll definitely want to draw up formal partnership papers, which means bringing in a lawyer. Legal registration is similar to that of a sole proprietorship.

" Mike Sez "

One of the most effective ways to ruin a good friendship is to go into partnership together. Even the best friendships are tested in the stressful environment of running a day-to-day business.

In a partnership, all partners are held personally liable for losses and other obligations. This also means that one partner is liable for the other's actions; if your partner runs up a huge debt or is sued, you can be held responsible.

In addition, breaking up or selling a partnership is often problematic. If one partner wants to quit, the other one(s) have to buy out his share—and valuing a business at the breaking point is seldom quick or easy.

A partnership has to file a tax return and must have a Federal Employer Identification Number (EIN), although the business itself pays no income tax. The individual partners report the company's income on their personal tax returns.

Corporation

Almost all large businesses are incorporated. Small businesses can also incorporate, although for many it's more trouble than it's worth.

One of the main advantages of incorporating your business is that it separates you personally from the business entity. That means that your personal liability is reduced if the business falls into debt or gets sued—in theory. In practice, however, lenders will often require the owners of small corporations to sign personal guarantees, which pretty much obviates that purported advantage.

Another advantage is that if you eventually have to hire one or more employees to help you run your eBay business, you can set up health insurance and retirement plans for your company's employees. In addition, if you ever decide to get out of the business, it's easier to sell a corporation than it is to sell other forms of businesses. Corporations can also sell stock, so if you have dreams of going big time, this is the way to start. There may also be tax advantages of incorporating; consult your accountant for details.

A corporation must have a Federal EIN, and must pay tax on all income. In addition, any dividends paid to stockholders (that includes you) are subject to personal income tax. You can minimize the corporate tax burden by taking all the profit out of your corporation, typically in the form of a big year-end bonus to yourself, so that the business has no net profit.

The most popular type of small corporation is the *subchapter S corporation*. This type of incorporated business is the simplest to set up, and the profits of such businesses aren't subject to corporate taxes. (You're still subject to personal income taxes, of course.) A subchapter S incorporation also enables you to offset any business losses against your personal income.

> **❝Mike Sez❞**
>
> I can only speak for myself here, but I've found that whatever slight advantages incorporation might offer to a small business are more than offset by the increased paperwork. For most small eBay businesses, sole proprietorship is probably the way to go.

If you have additional investors in your business, you might want to consider filing as a *limited liability corporation (LLC)*. In an LLC, the business's income and losses are shared by all investors, although investors are subject to limited liability (hence the name) for the corporations debts and obligations.

Whichever type of corporation you decide to set up, be prepared to deal with a lot of fees and paperwork. You'll probably need an attorney or accountant to handle the details for you.

Filing and Registering

While it's possible to just go online and start selling on eBay, if you're running a business you probably have to register with your local government. A good attorney or accountant can fill you in on what specifically you need to do where you live, as can the staff at your county clerk's office or chamber of commerce.

Many states, counties, and cities require that you register any new business with them. Some locales require you to obtain a permit or license for your activity; you should also check to see if your location is zoned for the type of business you plan to conduct.

As we'll discuss next, you'll also need to collect, report, and pay sales tax on all sales you make to residents of your state. That means obtaining a tax license and number from the state, and possibly a sales permit or reseller license from your local government. Your sales tax number

> **tip**
>
> For a state-by-state list of where to obtain business licenses, check out the Where to Obtain Business Licenses page on the SBA Web site (`www.sba.gov/hotlist/license.html`).

also functions as a *resale certificate*. You can present this number to any wholesalers you work with, which saves you from paying sales tax on the goods you purchase.

Dealing with Taxes

The only things sure in life are death and taxes. We'll skip the death conversation and focus on the tax side of things, as that's (hopefully!) more relevant to budding eBay sellers.

Collecting Sales Tax

If your state has a state sales tax (and all but Alaska, Delaware, Montana, New Hampshire, and Oregon do), you'll need to charge sales tax on all sales made to buyers who live in the same state you do. You do not have to, at this point in time, charge and collect sales tax on sales made to out-of-state or out-of-country buyers.

Of course, when you collect sales tax from a customer, you also have to report and forward that tax to your state government. This procedure varies from state to state, so you'll have to check with your local authorities (or your accountant) to get the proper details. You can also find this information online; check out the list compiled by the Multistate Tax Commission (www.mtc.gov/txpyrsvs/actualpage.htm).

Paying Taxes on Your eBay Income

While we're on the subject of taxes, here's another one you're not going to like. When you're running a legitimate eBay business, you're going to have to report the income you generate from your eBay sales. Failure to report your income is definitely actionable.

Again, if you're just selling a few items a month, the government probably isn't going to come

note

eBay makes it relatively easy to collect sales tax on your in-state sales. All you have to do is check the appropriate item on the Sell Your Item listing form; see Chapter 11, "Creating Item Listings," for more information."

caution

Not that I'm recommending it, but occasional eBay sellers can probably get by without collecting sales tax—just as most individuals running garage sales fly under the tax radar. When you're running a legitimate day-to-day business, however, there's no sliding by this requirement—you *must* collect sales tax, and you must report your collections to your state tax authorities. Failure to do so has legal implications.

after you for nickels and dimes. (Although they could if they wanted to.) But when you become a high-volume professional seller, your eBay activity is a real business—and real businesses have to pay taxes. That's all there is to it.

If you're running a sole proprietorship, the income you generate from your eBay sales, less any expenses related to those sales, is your business income, which you report on IRS form Schedule C. Your business income then becomes part of the calculation for your personal income tax, which you report on your normal form 1040.

caution

Let me repeat—if you're generating significant income from sales on eBay, you *must* report that income to the government!

Since you're working for yourself, there's no employer to withhold taxes from your paycheck (what paycheck?); instead, you'll need to estimate and pay these taxes quarterly, using IRS form 1040-ES. (You'll also need to pay state quarterly estimated taxes, using the appropriate state form.)

Of course, most everything you spend money on that's related to your business can be deducted as an expense. And I mean *everything*—Internet service, your computer, automobile trips to the bank or office supply store, even a fair share of your household utilities (for that portion of your house you use as a home office) may all be legitimate deductions—and the more deductions you have, the lower your reportable income for tax purposes. This is another reason to hire a professional to handle your business accounting and taxes; he or she will know just what you can and can't deduct. Chances are your accountant will find things to deduct that you never thought of—which will more than pay for his or her fee.

That said, when it comes to taxes, you should definitely seek the advice of a trained professional—a certified public accountant (CPA) or enrolled agent (EA). You can also get "official" tax information from the Internal Revenue Service; check out the IRS's Small Business One Stop Resource Web site (www.irs.ustreas.gov/businesses/small/), shown in Figure 5.1.

"Mike Sez"

It's important that you factor your quarterly tax payments in your budget. If you're used to having a regular job, with your taxes automatically deducted from each paycheck, this will be a new thing for you. When you run your own business, you're responsible for estimating your own taxes—and for making those payments every three months.

FIGURE 5.1

Get small business tax advice from the IRS.

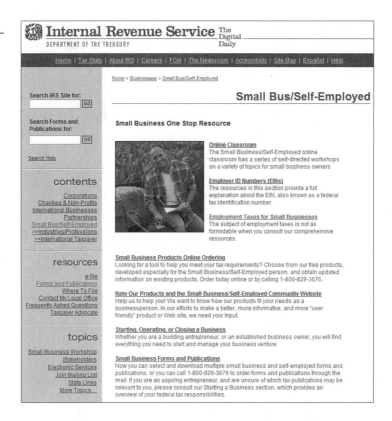

Withholding Employee Tax

If you have employees working for you in your eBay business, you'll need to withhold income tax from their paychecks, and then report and pay this tax to the state and Federal government. (This is yet another good reason to employ the services of a qualified accountant.) The Federal form you need to file is the SS-4. More information is available on the IRS Web site.

For state withholding information, check out the state-by-state list compiled by the Federation of Tax Administrators (www.taxadmin.org/fta/link/forms.html).

Setting Up Your Bank Accounts

When you're running a business, your banking needs are likely to be different from your previous personal needs. While you *can* make do by running your eBay payments through your personal savings and checking accounts, it's much cleaner to establish a separate banking identity for your business.

Merchant Checking Account

The best business practice is to set up a merchant or business checking account separate from your personal accounts. While you're not required to do this, if nothing else it will make your record keeping easier. Having a bank account in your business name should also minimize any potential confusion when it comes to depositing or cashing checks made out to your business name or dba.

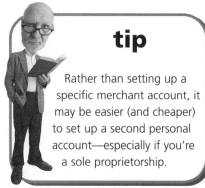

tip

Rather than setting up a specific merchant account, it may be easier (and cheaper) to set up a second personal account—especially if you're a sole proprietorship.

To set up a merchant account, you'll need that fictitious name affidavit we talked about earlier. If you're running a partnership, the partnership's bank account should be separate from all the partners, and should require more than one name on the checks. (That's to protect against any one partner running off with all the funds.)

Dealing with Credit Cards

While you're at the bank, you should ask about what's involved in establishing a merchant credit card account. You'll need to accept credit card payment for your eBay auctions, and if you can easily and affordably set up a merchant account with your bank, all the better. Know, however, that most banks make it difficult for small businesses to do this; you're probably better off going with PayPal for your credit card payments.

Obtaining Insurance

If you're going the self-employed route, you'll need to obtain health and disability insurance for yourself and your family (if you don't already have it)—and, if you're incorporated, for your employees. While eBay offers a health insurance plan to PowerSellers, all other sellers are on their own.

Fortunately, you're not in this alone; there are many health care providers that offer plans for small businesses and the self-employed. In addition, many business organizations and associations offer group insurance plans to their members. Here are some Web sites you can use to search for small business health insurance:

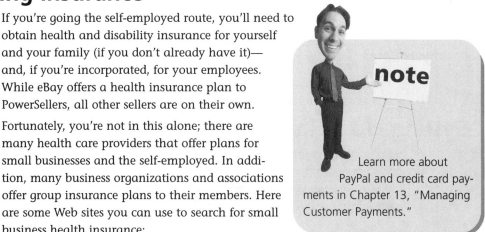

note

Learn more about PayPal and credit card payments in Chapter 13, "Managing Customer Payments."

- HealthInsurance.com (www.healthinsurance.com)
- Insure.com (www.insure.com)
- National Association of Socially Responsible Organizations (www.nasro-co-op.com)

You should also consider obtaining insurance on your business itself. This type of business insurance is designed to protect you from specific business liabilities, such as creditors and potential lawsuits. Check with your insurance agent to shape a policy that works for you.

Working Through the Checklist

Confused yet? Then use the following checklist to help you pull everything together for your new eBay business:

Business Startup Checklist

- [ ] Choose a legal structure for your business (sole proprietorship, partnership, or corporation)
- [ ] Register your business with local authorities
- [ ] Obtain any necessary business permits or licenses
- [ ] Obtain a tax license and number
- [ ] Arrange to collect sales tax on all in-state sales, if appropriate in your state
- [ ] Arrange for quarterly income tax payments
- [ ] Arrange to withhold and pay any necessary employee taxes
- [ ] Set up a business checking account
- [ ] Obtain health and disability insurance

Hiring Professional Help

Now that I've sent your head spinning with all the paperwork required to get your eBay business off the ground, let me tell you how to make most of these details go away:

Hire someone to do it for you.

That's right, when it comes to setting up and managing a small business, there is a definite advantage to hiring professionals to handle all the paperwork and record keeping. Yes, it's an additional cost you'll have to pay, but for most of us it's not only worth it—it's a necessity.

What kinds of professionals am I talking about? Just two: an accountant and an attorney. The attorney is necessary to help you get your business registered and legal, while the accountant is necessary to keep track of your taxes and finances on an ongoing basis. While you might be able to do all this work yourself (or not), a professional is more likely to know what's required, and thus keep you out of any potential hot water. Professionals also do this for a living, so they can do it better and faster than you can. Let the professionals handle all this busy work—so you can focus your attention on the important job of running your business!

And remember—all professional fees are tax deductible.

note

Learn more about hiring an accountant and setting up your business's accounting in Chapter 6, "Step Four: Set Up a Record-keeping System."

THE ABSOLUTE MINIMUM

When it's time to set up your eBay business, there are certain legal requirements you need to take care of. Keep these points in mind:

- You need to choose an appropriate legal structure for your business—sole proprietorship, partnership, or corporation.

- You'll need to check with your local government(s) to obtain all necessary permits and licenses.

- You'll also need to obtain a tax license and number, and then collect sales tax on all in-state sales.

- Since you're now self-employed, you'll need to file quarterly estimated taxes on your eBay auction income.

- Fortunately, almost all of these activities are best handled by employing the services of a qualified attorney and accountant.

6

Step Four: Set Up A Record-keeping System

When you're running a business, you need to keep track of what you're doing. That means keeping records about what you sell, who you sell it to, and how much money you make (or don't) from what you sell. These records not only help you manage your business on a day-to-day basis, they also help you prepare your yearly taxes.

This chapter walks you through the records you need to keep, and suggests how to set up your own recordkeeping system.

Why You Need to Keep Good Records

How profitable is your business? You'll never know if you're not keeping track—which is reason enough to set up some sort of recordkeeping system.

Keeping records can be both a defensive and an offensive (in a good way) activity. It's defensive in that you have key information about your business in case you ever need it in the future—to answer a query from the IRS, to investigate a customer complaint, or to notify customers in the case of a product recall. It's offensive in that you can use this information to generate more sales, by selling additional items to your existing customer base.

And then there's that matter of tracking the progress of your business.

You need to know how much things cost and how much you sell them for in order to gauge the success of your business. If nothing else, you have to report your business income to the Internal Revenue Service at the end of each year, and you can't do that if you don't know what you've sold, and for how much. The more detailed and accurate your record-keeping, the easier it is to put together your yearly tax returns—and to claim all the allowable deductions against your income.

In addition, setting up a simple accounting system lets you generate monthly financials, which tell you on a near-real-time basis just how well your business is (or isn't) doing. After all, you don't want to wait until the end of the year to find out that you're going broke—or getting rich!

Components of a Bare-Bones Record-keeping System

When we talk about setting up a record-keeping system for your eBay business, we're talking about assembling and tracking some very bare-bones data. We'll talk about each component of your record-keeping system in detail; you can use the following checklist to get a head start on what you'll need to track.

Record-keeping Checklist

- ☐ Inventory records (quantity, date in, date out, cost, sales price)
- ☐ Customer records (name, address, email, payment type, what was purchased, and when)
- ☐ Financial records (all business-related receipts and invoices)

Inventory Records

Setting up an inventory management system sounds like an extremely complex undertaking. It's really not. Just think of it in these simple terms:

You want to track when you got your stuff, how much it cost you, when you sold it, and how much you sold it for.

That's not rocket science.

In the old (pre-PC) days, many businesses tracked their inventory on 3"×5" index cards. (I know; I used to work with a system like this.) Each card included the information shown in the following checklist:

Inventory Management Checklist

- ☐ Item name
- ☐ Item description
- ☐ Item model number (if appropriate)
- ☐ Item serial number (if appropriate)
- ☐ Cost of the item
- ☐ Date the item was purchased
- ☐ Date the item was sold
- ☐ Final sales price of the item

The one bad thing about "the old days" was that we had to enter all this information by hand, and then manually add up the numbers on all the cards at the end of each month. Now that we all have personal computers, however, a lot of this manual work is automated.

The simplest way to track your inventory on a PC is to use a database program, such as Microsoft Works Database or Microsoft Access. You can also use a spreadsheet program, such as Microsoft Excel, as a kind of simple database; Excel's database functions are good enough for most small business inventory management.

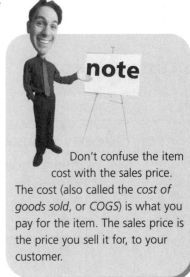

note

Don't confuse the item cost with the sales price. The cost (also called the *cost of goods sold*, or *COGS*) is what you pay for the item. The sales price is the price you sell it for, to your customer.

Just set up your database with fields for each of the items listed previously. Then create a new record for each item in inventory. Whenever you purchase new inventory, create new records. When you sell an item, mark the record for that item sold, and fill in the date sold and sales price fields.

At the end of each month, have your program run a report that lists the total cost of all the inventory you currently have in stock. You should also run a report showing all items sold, and calculating your total profit (sales price less cost of item) on these items. That should provide the basic inventory and sales information you need for your accounting system (discussed later in this chapter).

Once you get good at it, you can use your inventory management system to help you decide when to order more items for sale. Set a minimum quantity that you want to keep in stock, and program your database to alert you when the number of units on hand drops below this number. This is particularly useful when you're selling large quantities of each item, and when you have to purchase each item in quantity.

Another option for tracking the inventory of your eBay business is to use one of the advanced auction management tools offered by various third-party sites. These tools are discussed in more detail in Chapter 12, "Managing Your Auctions," and Chapter 20, "Using Professional Auction Tools." The best of these tools will track both your inventory and your customer activity, and include

- Auctionworks (www.auctionworks.com)
- ChannelAdvisor Pro (www.channeladvisor.com/solutions/pro.htm)
- eBay Selling Manager Pro (pages.ebay.com/selling_manager_pro/)
- Vendio's Sales Manager Pro (www.vendio.com)

Customer Records

Just as it's important to track what it is you sell, it's also important to track who it is that buys it. Establishing a customer management system not only lets you recall who you've sold to, it also lets you match up your customers with specific item purchases—and possibly leverage that information for future sales.

Just as you can use Access or Excel to track your inventory, you can also use these programs to store your customer information. In addition, you can use eBay Selling Manager or most other auction management tools to track your customers and their sales activity.

What customer records should you keep? Here's a short list:

Customer Management Checklist

- ☐ Customer name
- ☐ Customer address (street, city, state, ZIP code)
- ☐ Customer email address
- ☐ Item number purchased
- ☐ Item description
- ☐ Price of item purchased
- ☐ Date item listed for auction
- ☐ Date auction closed
- ☐ Date item paid for
- ☐ Payment method
- ☐ Date item shipped
- ☐ Shipping method

In addition, you might find it useful to track all the communications you send to each customer. This way you'll know who've you contacted about payment and who might need a reminder email.

Once you have all this customer information stored, what do you do with it? First, it's good to have, *just in case*—just in case a customer claims not to have received an item, or just in case a customer has a complaint and wants his or her money back. In addition, some sellers use their customer lists to solicit additional sales, mailing or emailing them when they have new merchandise available or a sale coming up. It's always good to know who your good customers are; it costs less to make additional sales to an existing customer than it does to acquire a completely new customer.

Financial Records

You can use the information stored in your inventory and customer management systems to help you prepare your ongoing financial records. In particular, you'll want to transfer the data relating to item cost, date sold, and sales price; this information will form the key lines on your monthly income statement.

You'll also need to track additional information relating to the costs of running your eBay business, and then use that information to perform your regular business accounting. In particular, there are certain items you'll need to hold onto for tax purposes—specifically those little pieces of paper that document items you've purchased or sold. Even if your "system" consists of throwing all your receipts in an old shoebox or file folder, you need to hold onto all these items—not only for your monthly accounting and end-of-year tax preparation, but also in case the IRS ever decides to audit you.

How long should you hold onto your original documentation? Some experts say to hold onto all your receipts and invoices for a minimum of three years, but that might not be long enough. For example, the IRS requires that you keep documentation on all your assets for the life of the asset. And if the IRS thinks you've filed a fraudulent return, there's no statute of limitations at all.

Which means you might want to hang onto this basic documentation *forever*. Just clear out a corner of your garage or attic where you can store all your shoeboxes, and be done with it.

What kind of hard-copy documentation should you be holding? Use the following checklist as a guideline:

Financial Records Checklist

- ☐ Bank statements
- ☐ Credit card statements
- ☐ Receipts for all business-related purchases and expenses (including shipping expenses)
- ☐ Invoices for all inventory purchases
- ☐ Invoices or sales receipts for all items sold
- ☐ Automobile mileage (keep a log for all business-related travel)

Setting Up an Accounting System

Throwing all your receipts in a shoebox is just a start. To truly track your business's finances, you need to incorporate all the data from those receipts and from your inventory and customer management systems into some sort of an accounting system.

This chapter isn't the place to go into all that's involved in setting up a detailed small business accounting system; there are lots of books and online resources that are more appropriate to the task. We can, however, take a look at what you need to track to make your accounting system work.

Tracking Your Business Activity

All accounting systems track basic types of activities: *revenues* and *expenses*. Revenues are the sales you make to your eBay customers. Expenses are the costs you incur in the running of your business—the inventory you have to purchase, as well as all those other things you need to buy to make your business run.

In accounting terms, the money you take in creates a *credit* on your books. The money you spend creates a *debit*. When your credits exceed your debits, you're making a profit (or at least generating positive cash flow). When your debits exceed your credits, your business is losing money. Obviously, the former position is preferable.

To make your accounting system work, you have to enter each and every financial activity of your business. Make a sale, enter it in the books. Buy some supplies, enter that in the books. At regular intervals—typically at the end of each month—you add up all the credits and debits (after putting them in the proper slots) and take a snapshot as to how your business is doing. These snapshots are the financial statements you use to measure the financial condition of your business.

Key Financial Statements

There are two key financial statements that you should prepare at the end of each month. These are the *income statement* (sometimes called a *profit and loss statement*, or *P/L*) and a *balance sheet*. These documents measure the condition of your business from two different angles.

Income Statement

The income statement reflects the revenue your business generates, the expenses you pay, and the profit (or loss) that filters down. This is done by showing your revenues, subtracting the cost of goods sold (which reveals the gross profit), and then subtracting all your operating expenses to show your net profit.

As you can see in Figure 6.1, the top of the statement lists all the money your business took in—your business's revenues. The bottom of the statement lists all the money you paid—your business's expenses. Subtract the bottom from the top and the number you get, expressed on the last line of the statement, is your business's profit or loss.

Your operating expenses are typically broken out into multiple line items. In addition, you'll see the gross profit and net profit described as percentages of net revenues. (When shown this way, they're called *gross margin* and *net margin*.)

Here's a brief explanation of the most important line items on the income statement:

FIGURE 6.1

A typical
income
statement.

Income Statement

Gross Sales (Gross Revenues)	**$53,697**
Returns	$767
Net Sales (Net Revenues)	**$52,930**
Cost of Goods Sold (COGS)	$12,642
Gross Profit	**$40,288**
Gross Profit Margin (Gross Margin)	76.1%
Operating Expenses	
Salaries (Wages)	$14,672
Marketing	$1,200
Selling	$5,463
General & Administrative	$1,767
Utilities	$650
Automobile	$1,165
Travel & Entertainment	$542
Dues/Subscriptions	$273
Loan Payments	$1,750
Total Operating Expenses	**$27,482**
Net Profit (Loss)	**$12,806**
Net Margin	24.2%

- **Gross Revenues**. This line (also called *Gross Sales*) reflects all of your dollar sales for the period, not counting any damaged or returned goods.

- **Returns**. Sometimes called *Returns and Allowances*, this line reflects the cost of any returned or damaged merchandise, as well as any allowances and markdowns.

- **Net Revenues**. Net Revenues (also called *Net Sales*) reflect your Gross Revenues less your Returns and Allowances.

- **Cost of Goods Sold**. This line (also called *COGS* or *Cost of Sales*) reflects the direct costs of the products you sold for the period.

- **Gross Profit**. This line reflects the direct profit you made from sales during this period. It is calculated by subtracting the Cost of Goods Sold from Net Revenues.

- **Gross Margin**. This line (also called *Gross Profit Margin*) describes your Gross Profit as a percent of your Net Revenues. You calculate this number by dividing Gross Profit by Net Revenues.

■ **Operating Expenses**. This line reflects all the indirect costs of your business. Typical line items within this overall category include Salaries, Advertising, Marketing, Selling, Office, Office Supplies, Rent, Leases, Utilities, Automobile, Travel and Entertainment (T&E), General and Administrative (G&A), Dues and Subscriptions, Licenses and Permits, and Training. *Not* included in this section are direct product costs (which should be reflected in the Cost of Goods Sold), loan payments, interest on loans, taxes, depreciation, and amortization.

■ **Net Profit (Loss)**. This line (also called *Net Earnings* or *Net Income*; the words "income," "earnings," and "profit" are synonymous) reflects your reported profit or loss. You calculate this number by subtracting Operating Expenses from Gross Profit; a loss is notated within parentheses.

note

In all financial statements, a loss is typically noted by inserting the number in parentheses. So if you see ($200), you note a loss of $200. An alternative, although less accepted, method is to put a negative sign in front of any losses. If you're printing in color, you would use red (in addition to the parentheses) to notate all losses.

■ **Net Margin**. This line describes your Net Profit as a percentage of your Net Sales. You calculate this number by dividing Net Profit by Net Sales.

Most businesses will create an income statement for each month in the year, and then a comprehensive income statement at the end of the year. Many businesses like to track their progress over the course of the year, and create a year-to-date income statement at the end of each month, as well.

Balance Sheet

The other essential financial statement is the balance sheet. The balance sheet looks at your business in a slightly different fashion from an income statement. Instead of looking at pure monetary profit (or loss), the balance sheet measures how much your business is worth. It does this by comparing your assets (the things you own—including your cash on hand) with your liabilities (the money you owe to others).

As you can see in Figure 6.2, the assets go on the left side of the balance sheet, and the liabilities go on the right. The total number for each column should be equal—hence the "balance" part of the title. You should generate a balance sheet at the end of every month, and at the end of the year.

FIGURE 6.2

A typical
balance sheet.

Balance Sheet

Assets		Liabilities	
Current Assets		**Current Liabilities**	
Cash	$12,453	Accounts Payable	$1,647
Accounts Receivable	$894	Interest Payable	$128
Inventories	$1,275	**Total Current Liabilities**	$1,775
Total Current Assets	$14,622		
		Long-Term Liabilities	
Long-Term Assets		Long-Term Notes Payable	$3,375
Equipment	$4,975	Taxes Payable	$563
Total Long-Term Assets	$4,975	**Total Long-Term Liabilities**	$3,938
		Equity (Net Worth)	$13,884
Total Assets	$19,597	**Total Liabilities and Net Worth**	$19,597

Here's a brief explanation of the most important asset items on the balance sheet:

- **Current Assets**. This category includes those items that can be converted into cash within the next 12 months. Typical line items would include Cash, Accounts Receivable, Inventories, and Short-Term Investments.

- **Fixed Assets**. This category (sometimes called *Long-Term Assets*) includes assets that are *not* easily converted into cash, including Land, Buildings, Accumulated Depreciation (as a negative number), Improvements, Equipment, Furniture, and Vehicles

- **Long-Term Investments**. This category includes any longer-term investments your business has made.

- **Total Assets**. This line reflects the value of everything your company owns. You calculate this number by adding together Current Assets and Fixed Assets.

The following are the key line items on the liabilities side of the balance sheet:

- **Current Liabilities**. This category includes any debts or monetary obligations payable within the next 12 months. Typical line items would include Accounts Payable, Notes Payable, Interest Payable, and Taxes Payable.

- **Long-Term Liabilities**. This category includes debts and obligations that are due to be paid over a period exceeding 12 months. Typical line items would include Long-Term Notes Payable and Deferred Taxes.

note

To make your balance sheet actually balance, the Total Liabilities and Net Worth number must equal the number for Total Assets.

- **Equity**. This line (sometimes called *Net Worth*) reflects the owners' investment in the business. Depending on the type of ownership, this line may be broken into separate lines reflecting the individual equity positions of multiple partners or the company's capital stock and retained earnings.
- **Total Liabilities and Net Worth**. This line (sometimes called *Total Liabilities and Equity*) reflects the total amount of money due plus the owners' value. You calculate this number by adding together Current Liabilities, Long-Term Liabilities, and Equity.

Software for Small Business Accounting

How do you put together all your business data and generate these financial statements? You have two practical options: hire an accountant or use an accounting software program. (You could also, I suppose, keep your books by hand, on oversized sheets of ledger paper—although hardly anyone does it that way anymore, in this computerized day and age.)

We'll look at accounting software first.

There are many different programs you can use to keep your business's books. The simplest of these programs are the personal financial management programs, such as Microsoft Money and Quicken. They may be able to do the job if your business is simple enough, but most small businesses will find them somewhat limited in functionality. A better choice for many eBay businesses is QuickBooks, which is a more full-featured small business accounting program—and is also available in an online version. If your business is big or unique enough, however, even QuickBooks might not be powerful enough; in that instance, you can evaluate other more powerful business accounting packages.

Quicken

The most popular financial management program today is Intuit's Quicken (www.quicken.com). Quicken comes in various flavors, only one of which has features of use to the small business: Quicken Premier Home & Business. In addition to its basic personal finance functionality, this version also lets you track your business expenses, record assets and liabilities, generate customer invoices, and create basic financial statements.

Microsoft Money

Microsoft Money (www.microsoft.com/money/) is a direct competitor to Quicken. Like Quicken, Money comes in various flavors; the version of interest to eBay businesses is Microsoft Money Small Business. This version offers similar functionality to Quicken Premier Home & Business, as well as basic payroll management.

QuickBooks

A better option for most small business owners is Intuit's companion package to Quicken, called QuickBooks (www.quickbooks.com). There are a number of versions of QuickBooks—Basic (shown in Figure 6.3), Pro, Premier, and Enterprise Solutions. For most eBay businesses, Basic is more than good enough.

You can use QuickBooks not only to do your monthly accounting and generate regular financial statements, but also to manage your inventory, track your sales, and do your year-end taxes. QuickBooks even integrates with PayPal, so you can manage all your PayPal sales from within the QuickBooks program.

FIGURE 6.3

One of the most popular small business accounting packages—Intuit's QuickBooks Basic.

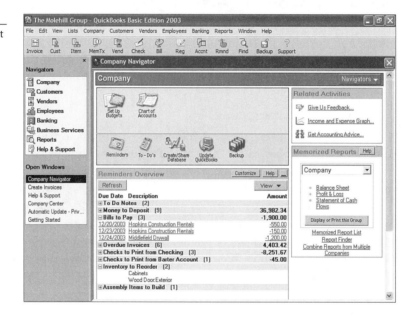

Intuit also offers a Web-based version of QuickBooks, called QuickBooks Online Edition, which you can access from the main QuickBooks Web site. This Online Edition keeps all your records online, so you can do your accounting from any computer, using nothing more than your Web browser. QuickBooks Online Edition isn't quite as robust as the standalone version, which makes it best for those eBay businesses with simpler needs. You'll pay $19.95 per month for this service.

Other Small-Business Accounting Packages

If QuickBooks doesn't satisfy your accounting needs, there are other small business accounting programs available. Some of these programs are more fully featured than QuickBooks, and more complicated to use. That might not present a problem if you're relatively numbers-savvy, but if accounting doesn't run in your blood, some of these programs might be more than you can handle.

Here are a few of these accounting packages to consider:

- Business Works (www.business-works.com)
- Cashbook Complete (www.acclaimsoftware.com)
- DacEasy (www.daceasy.com)
- MYOB Plus (www.myob.com)
- NetLedger Advanced Accounting (www.netledger.com)
- Peachtree Accounting (www.peachtree.com)

Working with an Accountant

Even if you use an accounting program like QuickBooks, you still might want to employ the services of a professional accountant—at least to prepare your year-end taxes. That's because an accountant is likely to be more experienced and qualified than you to manage your business's tax obligations.

Many small businesses use QuickBooks to generate their monthly financial statements, but then call in an accountant to prepare their quarterly estimated taxes and year-end tax statements. This is a pretty good combination; you can have QuickBooks print out just the right data that your accountant will need to prepare your taxes.

Of course, you can also use an accountant to handle *all* of your financial activities. This is a particularly good idea if (1) your business is generating a high volume of sales, and (2) you aren't particularly interested in or good at handling the books. You'll pay for this service, of course, but if your business is big enough, it's probably worth it.

Where do you find a reputable accountant? You should check with your local chamber of commerce or SBA office, as well as other local small business organizations. It wouldn't hurt to ask other small business owners; word of mouth is often the best way to find simpatico service providers.

In addition, you can use the Internet to search for small business accountants in your area. Check out these Web sites:

- 1-800-Accountant (www.1800accountant.com)
- CPA Directory (www.cpadirectory.com)
- eLance (www.elance.com)

■ The National Association of Small Business Accountants (www.
smallbizaccountants.com)

However you find an accountant, know up front that he'll need you to keep some
very specific financial records—like those we discussed earlier in this chapter. Your
accountant can't track your business unless you're tracking your business, so work
with your accountant to set up the best recordkeeping system for your business
needs.

THE ABSOLUTE MINIMUM

Keeping detailed records is essential to the running of any small business—including
an eBay business. When setting up your own recordkeeping system, keep these
points in mind:

■ The inventory management component of your system should track the date
purchased, date sold, cost, and sales price of each item you have for sale.

■ The customer management component of your system should track the
name, address, email address, and purchase history of all your customers.

■ You should document all the purchases and expenses associated with your
eBay business—and keep these receipts for as long as is practical.

■ All this sales and expense information ideally should feed into an accounting
system, and be used to generate income statements and balance sheets.

■ The easiest way to manage your finances is to use a small business accounting program, such as QuickBooks.

■ Even if you use QuickBooks, it's still a good idea to hire an accountant to
handle all your tax-related activities.

IN THIS CHAPTER

- Setting up your home office
- Setting up your packing center
- Managing your physical inventory

7

STEP FIVE: SET UP YOUR BACK OFFICE

Running an eBay business involves a lot of work—and a lot of *different* work. There's a fair share of bookwork involved, especially when it comes to managing your eBay auctions, which means working behind a desk or at a computer. Then there's the physical management of your inventory. And the packing and shipping of all the items you sell.

All of these back-office activities have to be done someplace. Assuming that you're running your eBay business out of your home, that means carving out space to run your business—space for your desk and computer, space for your inventory, and space for your "shipping department." That might mean appropriating a spare bedroom, or setting up shop in your basement, or even portioning off part of your kitchen or living room. Wherever you find the space, it's important to get your back office set up and running smoothly, so that you can perform your day-to-day eBay operations with a minimum of fuss and muss.

Setting Up Your Home Office

Let's start with the "white collar" part of your eBay operation—your home office. This is where you'll perform all your online operations and manage all your paper-work.

We'll look at all the parts of your home office separately, but let's start by going over a checklist of the major items you'll need:

Home Office Equipment Checklist

- ☐ Personal computer with monitor
- ☐ Microsoft Office and other computer software
- ☐ Accounting software
- ☐ Inkjet or laser printer
- ☐ Scanner
- ☐ Digital camera
- ☐ Internet connection
- ☐ Telephone
- ☐ Desk
- ☐ Chair
- ☐ Filing cabinet
- ☐ Storage for office supplies

Personal Computer

A decent personal computer system is a necessity for any eBay business. After all, you need the computer to get online and manage your eBay auctions!

How fancy a computer do you need? Fortunately, not too fancy. Your computing needs will be fairly modest, so you don't have to spend a lot of money on a state-of-the-art powerhouse PC. In fact, you can probably get by with one of the lowest-priced models available—or just use your existing PC, if you already have one.

What kind of PC are we talking about? Here are the minimum specs I'd consider if you're looking to buy a new PC:

tip

Remember, all of these expenses are tax deductible—so keep track of all your receipts.

- 1.5GHz Pentium or Athlon family micro-processor
- 256MB memory (RAM)
- 40GB hard drive
- CD-R/RW drive
- 17" CRT or 15" LCD monitor
- Windows XP Home Edition operating system

note

Learn more about buying a new PC—or upgrading your old one—in my companion book, *Absolute Beginner's Guide to Upgrading and Fixing Your PC* (Que, 2003).

In today's market, you can find a PC that fits these specs for well under $1,000. (And if you're an Apple fan, similarly featured Macintoshes are also easy to find.)

Naturally, you should also outfit your PC with the right type of modem for your Internet connection, which we'll discuss in a few pages. That means a traditional modem for a dial-up connection, a cable modem for cable broadband, or a DSL modem for DSL broadband.

If you have more than one PC in your business (or want to connect your business PC to another home PC), you might want to invest in the appropriate equipment to network your computers together. Your network can be either wired or wireless; the easiest solution is to buy an all-in-one networking kit that includes all the equipment you need to assemble and configure the network.

You can shop for a new computer in a number of places; just about every type of retailer carries computers these days, from Wal-Mart to CompUSA and everywhere in-between. You can even find good buys on brand-new (but often close-out) PCs from fellow eBay merchants.

That said, you should buy at a retailer with which you're comfortable. Look for a decent selection of models from a variety of manufacturers, good pricing (of course), knowledgeable salespeople (harder to find), and after-the-sale service and support.

Computer Software

You'll use your PC not only to access the eBay Web site, but also to manage all your auction transactions and your business's record-keeping. That means you'll need to install the appropriate computer software for your business needs.

" Mike Sez "

When it's time to go PC shopping, do yourself a favor and do a little homework. I recommend checking the professional equipment reviews at CNET (www.cnet.com) and the user reviews at Epinions.com (www.epinions.com).

What software do you need? Table 7.1 shows what I recommend:

TABLE 7.1   Recommended Computer Software

Function	Software	Web Site
Web browser	Internet Explorer	www.microsoft.com
Email	Microsoft Outlook *or* Outlook Express	www.microsoft.com
Letters, memos	Microsoft Word	www.microsoft.com
Photo editing	Adobe Photoshop Elements *or* Microsoft Picture It! Photo *or* PaintShop Pro	www.adobe.com www.microsoft.com www.jasc.com
Number crunching	Microsoft Excel	www.microsoft.com
Customer database	Microsoft Access *or* Microsoft Excel	www.microsoft.com
Accounting	QuickBooks *or* Quicken Premier Home & Business *or* Microsoft Money Small Business	www.quickbooks.com www.quicken.com www.microsoft.com

You should also consider a decent backup program, to create backup copies of all your important customer and accounting records. At a bare minimum, you can use Microsoft Backup (included with Windows) to regularly back up your data to CD-R/RW discs. If your backup needs are more sophisticated than what Microsoft Backup can achieve, check out Handy Backup (www.handybackup.com), NTI Backup Now (www.ntius.com), or Retrospect Backup (www.dantz.com). Or you can use an *online backup* service, which lets you back up your files online to a separate Internet site; this way, if your office burns down, your key files are safely stored offsite. Some of the more popular online backup services include @Backup (www.backup.com), Connected (www.connected.com), IBackup (www.ibackup.com), and Xdrive (www.xdrive.com).

Printer

One of the key components of your computer system is your printer. You'll be printing lots of invoices and labels, so there's no point spending the money on a color printer; buy a good black-and-white model that can handle a heavy printing load.

You'll need to choose between inkjet and laser printers. Inkjets are lower priced, but could end up costing you more in the long run; all those replacement ink cartridges add up, over time. Laser printers cost more, but are faster and better suited to heavy printing loads. If you think your eBay business will generate a high volume of sales, a laser printer is probably the way to go.

Digital Camera and Scanner

You might not think of these next items as absolutely necessary—but you'd be wrong. You need both a computer scanner and a digital camera to capture images of the items you'll be selling on eBay.

A scanner is good for flat items—CDs, books, small packages, and so on. A digital camera is needed to capture three-dimensional items. Both pieces of equipment save their images as digital files, which you download to your computer's hard disk. Once stored on your PC, you can edit the pictures with your image editing software, as you'll discover in Chapter 19, "Working with Photographs."

What kind of digital equipment should you buy? The scanner is relatively easy; go for a decent flatbed scanner, something in the $100–$150 range. Choosing the right digital camera is more complex. You can find models as low as $150 or so, or as high as $1,000 (or more!). Fortunately, your needs are modest. You don't need a camera with lots of megapixel resolution; the pictures you post on the Web will be low-resolution JPGs. Look for a model that's easy to operate and (especially if you plan on selling small-ish items) includes a macro or close-up focus capability. You can probably find what you need in the $200 range.

> **tip**
>
> If you think your business will need fax capability—or if you see the need to make copies of documents—then consider a combo printer/fax/copier/scanner machine. These units (sometimes called *all-in-one* machines) are very efficient, both in terms of cost and in desktop footprint. You can find combo units in both inkjet and laser varieties, starting from $250 or so.

Internet Connection

As you manage your eBay business on a day-to-day basis, you'll find yourself connecting to the Internet *a lot*. For that reason, you may not be happy with a traditional dial-up Internet connection. As you probably already realize, a dial-up connection is slow (56.6 kilobits per second) and cumbersome (you have to make a new connection every time you want to go online). For your new eBay business, something better might be in order.

That something better is a high-speed broadband Internet connection. A broadband connection can speed up your Internet access by 10 times

> **tip**
>
> While you're at the camera store, spend an extra $20 or so to buy a tripod. This is a small price to ensure rock-steady photographs of the items you intend to sell.

or more—plus it's always on, so you don't have to waste time dialing in to connect. Whenever you want to check your eBay auctions, just launch your browser and you'll be connected to eBay almost instantly.

tip

Learn more about all types of broadband Internet services and find a provider near you at Broadbandreports.com (www.broadbandreports.com).

Telephone and Fax

Your home office needs its own communication system—and that means more than just email. You'll need a separate phone for your office, even if that phone shares your home line. (You can choose to invest in a separate business phone line, but that's probably not necessary unless you generate a large volume of outgoing or incoming calls.) Consider a phone with a built-in answering machine or access to some sort of voice mail system, so that you won't miss any calls when you're away.

If you do decide to go with a separate business phone line, invest in a two-line phone. This way you can run both your home and business lines into the same phone, and use either line as necessary. You can find a good two-line cordless phone for less than $200.

Another option is to use your cell phone as your business phone. This is a good way to keep your business calls separate from your personal calls. This is also a good idea if you need to remain in contact with the outside world even when you're not in the office.

You may also have need of a fax machine. While a separate fax machine will work (and, with the proper devices, connect to your regular phone line), a better solution for many is the all-in-one printer/fax machine we discussed earlier. If nothing else, an all-in-one machine takes up less desk space than separate printer and fax machines.

Filing System

In the course of running your eBay business, you're going to generate a lot of records. Many of these records will be electronic, which are easy to deal with by using the appropriate software program. However, you'll also generate a fair amount of paper records, which you'll have to keep on file.

Short-term paperwork probably needs to stay on top of your desk. You can employ the "multiple pile" method of desktop filing, or go the more organized route and use a series of desktop baskets and organizers. I recommend the latter.

For your longer-term paper storage, nothing beats a good old fashioned filing cabinet. Go for either a two- or a four-drawer model, and keep things organized with the appropriate filing folders. You don't have to buy anything fancy, either; those low-priced metal filing cabinets work just as well as expensive wooden ones.

Furniture

The subject of filing cabinets brings us around to a bigger issue—office furniture.

The biggest and most obvious piece of office furniture you need is a desk. Your desk has to be big enough to hold your computer, printer, scanner, and other equipment, and still provide enough desk space to let you spread things out and do a little paperwork. That probably rules out using a folding card table—although some swear by the old wooden-door-laid-on-top-of-two-filing-cabinets approach. My personal preference is an L-shaped desk with filing-cabinet drawers on either end; I put my computer equipment on one side of the L, and use the other side for desk-based paperwork.

Another option is to go with a smaller desk and a separate computer stand. In any case, just be sure you have enough space for all the different kinds of office work you'll be doing.

Of course, you need a place to sit while you're doing all this work. Your office chair is maybe more important than your desk, in that it directly affects your physical comfort. Choose the wrong chair and you could end up either uncomfortable or in physical pain. And since we come in all different shapes and sizes, it pays to get a chair that adjusts to your own personal preferences—and to test-drive any chair before you buy it.

We already discussed filing cabinets, but you should also consider whether you need a bookshelf or two in your office. If you find yourself frequently referring to printed matter—like this book, for instance!—then by all means include a bookshelf in your office plans. Remember, your bookshelves can hold all types of books, from dictionaries to phone books to software instruction manuals. If you need one, get one.

Your local office supply store should have a good variety of furniture to choose from, at affordable prices. Also good are retailers like Ikea or traditional furniture stores. If you're on a tight budget, consider buying your furniture second-hand. Check out the "previously used" section at your local business furniture rental store, or keep an eye out for businesses that are going out of business. (A lot of entrepreneurs were able to snatch up fancier-than-normal furniture when all those dot-com companies went bust!) Naturally, eBay is also a good place to look for these kinds of bargains.

Office Supplies

Don't forget to stock your office with all the odds and ends you need to conduct your daily business. Your personal needs may differ, but here's a starter list of the office supplies you're likely to need:

tip

Don't skimp on your seating! If you have a few extra bucks to spend, invest in a really good ergonomic chair, like the (deservedly) popular Herman Miller Aeron chairs.

Office Supplies Checklist

- ☐ Note paper
- ☐ Letter paper (plain and letterhead)
- ☐ Envelopes (plain and letterhead)
- ☐ Labels
- ☐ Pens
- ☐ Paperclips
- ☐ Stapler and staples
- ☐ Rubber bands
- ☐ Post-It notes
- ☐ Ruler
- ☐ Scissors

You should find space in your immediate office for those supplies you'll be using on a regular basis. Additional quantities can be stored somewhere less convenient.

Configuring Your Space

Of course, you have to have enough space to put all this new equipment and furniture—and that space has to be conducive to actually working. It won't do to place your home office in the corner of a busy living room; you need to be able to separate your work life from your personal life. That might mean utilizing a separate room—preferably one with a door you can close.

How much space do you need? Think through all the equipment you'll have, then add an appropriate amount of clean desk space to write checks and spread out a few file folders. Make sure you have enough room to actually roll or walk around comfortably. Then take this total space—*and double it*. That's right, you'll always end up needing more space than you think, so you might as well plan for it from the start. Over the next several months you're bound to buy more computer equipment, add extra filing cabinets, or need to store *something* that you hadn't planned on. Plus, you might actually have visitors—and where will they stand or sit? Your home office has to be comfortable, so don't start out cramped. Whatever space you allocate, you'll end up filling it!

tip

Remember, your *dedicated* home office space is eligible for the home office tax deduction. Consult with your accountant for more details.

And where, pray tell, should this space be located? This is definitely a personal decision, and one that depends on what space you have available. I definitely don't recommend carving out space from a high-traffic public area. It's better to find a spare bedroom or area of your basement that you can partition off. Worse comes to worst, you can use a corner of your bedroom—assuming, of course, that it's a room that is otherwise vacant during working hours.

Another option, of course, is to rent office space outside your home. While this might sound appealing (especially if you want to get away from the kids while you work), it's expensive and not typically necessary. Still, if you can find affordable space nearby, it's worth considering.

After you stake out your space, make sure it has enough electrical outlets for your needs. Consider everything you'll be plugging in—your computer, monitor, external modem, printer, scanner, telephone, desk lamp, whatever—and make sure there's a plug for everything. And, while you're at it, make sure you have the appropriate phone and cable jacks for your telephone, fax, and Internet connections.

You should design your workspace with you in the center. Put your most important task—your computer—right in front of you, and everything else within reasonable reach. In this aspect, it pays to think *vertically*. That means incorporating a series of shelves above your desk, rather than spreading out sideways from your working area. There are lots of innovative storage options available that let you expand your workspace up instead of out.

Ergonomics are also important. You want everything in your office to be within comfortable reach. You should pay special attention to the relationship between your chair, computer screen, keyboard, and mouse. Consider one of those split ergonomic keyboards, such as the Microsoft Natural keyboard.

You should also pay attention to light. Your office needs to be well-lit—and that means more than a small desk lamp. Natural light is always good, if you have a window nearby, but appropriate artificial lighting is also necessary. Consider a combination of uniform and task lighting—which probably means both a floor or overhead lamp and a desk lamp. And you don't have to make do with flickering fluorescent lighting, either; you can upgrade both desk and floor lamps with full-spectrum bulbs that simulate sunlight.

Setting Up Your Packing Center

Your office is where you handle all your eBay-related paperwork and online activities. It is *not* where you store the items you have for sale, or where you pack them up for shipping. You'll need to set up separate areas for inventory storage and for packing.

We'll discuss inventory storage last. Right now, let's focus on setting up an efficient packing center for your eBay business.

Finding the Space

The first thing to consider is *where* you'll be doing your packing. This depends to some degree on what kinds of items you're selling. If you're selling relatively small items, you can get by with less space. If you're selling really large items, you'll need a lot of space. You'll have to do the math.

However much space you need, you'll want this space to be dedicated to the task at hand. If you're shipping out dozens (or hundreds) of items every week, you don't want to have to assemble and disassemble your packing area every time you sell an item. It's best to have everything set up and ready to go, permanently.

What type of space do you need? Well, you'll need a large flat area—some kind of tabletop or countertop, large enough for you to spread out your boxes or envelopes as you pack. You'll also need space to store your packing supplies, and additional space nearby for your packing boxes and envelopes. Then you'll need some sort of staging area to temporarily store your packed boxes until they're shipped. Again, depending on the size of what you're selling, this could amount to a fair amount of space.

Where should this space be? For most of us, it has to be someplace in the house. Many eBayers carve out a part of their garage for this operation. I use my kitchen. (I'm not much of a cook, so I might as well use my kitchen for something productive!) In any case, the space needs to be not only large but easily accessible for the task at hand.

Essential Supplies

Your packing center needs to include storage space for the supplies you use for packing your eBay items. You need to keep these basic packing supplies on hand, so that you're not constantly running off to the office supply store every time one of your auctions closes. These items should always be available and easily accessed.

What items are we talking about? Consider the following checklist:

Packing Supplies Checklist

- ☐ Packing tape (clear and brown)
- ☐ Bubble wrap
- ☐ Styrofoam peanuts *or* old newspapers
- ☐ Scissors
- ☐ Box cutter or similar kind of knife
- ☐ Postal scale
- ☐ Black magic marker
- ☐ Large shipping labels
- ☐ Return address labels
- ☐ Other necessary labels—Fragile, This End Up, and so on
- ☐ Labels or forms provided by your shipping service of choice
- ☐ Rate lists from your preferred shipping service(s)

Now for some explanations. I recommend clear tape because you can use it not just to seal the box but also to tape over the address label and make it somewhat waterproof. Brown tape can be used to tape over labels and logos when you reuse an old box. I prefer Styrofoam peanuts to newspapers because peanuts don't leave ink stains, and because of the weight factor; using newspapers as filler can substantially increase your package weight, and thus your shipping costs. (Of course, newspapers are free and peanuts aren't—but peanuts are cheaper than the added shipping costs you'll incur with newspapers.)

tip

Another item—not on the list—you may want to keep on hand is a rolling hand cart. This type of small, lightweight cart is particularly useful when transporting multiple items to the post office, or from one end of your house to the other.

Boxes and Envelopes

The other items you need to find space for are the boxes and envelopes in which you pack your items. Of course, what types of boxes and envelopes you need depends on what types of items you'll be selling.

Where do you find appropriate shipping containers? First, some boxes are free. If you're shipping via the U.S. Postal Service, you can get free Priority Mail and Express Mail boxes, envelopes, and tubes. Some post offices carry these free containers, or you can order in bulk (but still for free) from the USPS Web site at shop.usps.com and have them delivered direct to your home. (Click the Shipping Supplies link.)

note

Other carriers may or may not offer their own free shipping containers. FedEx, for example, offers certain sizes of envelopes and boxes for your (free) use, as does UPS.

Most post office locations also sell various types of boxes, padded mailers, mailing tubes, and other packing materials, although their prices tend to be a little on the high side. A better choice for high-volume shippers is your local office supply store, such as Office Depot, Office Max, or Staples—or a specialty box/shipping store.

Another good source of shipping supplies is eBay itself—or, more accurately, retailers who sell on the eBay service. There are several eBay Store sellers who specialize in packing supplies for other eBay sellers; go to www.stores.ebay.com and do a search for "shipping supplies" or "boxes." In particular, check out BubbleFAST (www.bubblefast.com), eSupplyStore.com (www.esupplystore.com), and ShippingSupply.com (www.shippingsupply.com).

note

Many eBay sellers recycle old boxes, shipping out their items in boxes that were originally shipped to them. While this works for low-volume sellers, it doesn't look very professional—and it's unlikely that you'll have enough old boxes sitting around to meet your high-volume shipping needs.

You'll definitely want to stock up on these boxes and envelopes. I like to keep at least a one-month supply on hand—and if you can get a good deal on a larger quantity, go for it! Of course, you have to find a place to store all those boxes. One good approach is to keep a week's supply in your in-house packing center, and store your extra boxes someplace less central—in your garage or basement, in a shed, or even in a rented storage bin. You can then transfer supplies of boxes as needed to your packing center.

Managing Your Physical Inventory

Now we come to the big space hog—your product inventory. That's right, you need someplace to store all the items you plan to sell.

Again, if your items are small, your storage needs are simpler. If you sell baseball cards, for example, it's easy to find space for a lot of small flat items. If you sell basketballs, on the other hand, you'll need a lot more physical volume for storage.

Where should you store your inventory? Here are some suggestions:

- A spare closet
- Your garage
- Your attic
- Your basement
- A friend's garage (or attic or basement)
- A spare room
- A storage shed
- A rented storage bin
- Rented warehouse space

note

Here's another option—don't stock anything for sale. That's right, depending on what you sell, you might not have to carry your own inventory. You may be able to employ the services of a fulfillment company; you make the sale (via eBay), but the fulfillment company carries the inventory and ships directly to your customers. A variation on this is to become an authorized dealer for a particular brand or product, and let the manufacturer handle the inventory and shipping. Learn more in Chapter 8, "Step Six: Find and Manage Your Inventory."

Naturally, the first few options are less expensive than the last few. If you absolutely positively have to rent storage space, make sure you figure those costs into your business plan. For most eBay businesses, however, you'll want to minimize your storage costs—which means minimizing your space needs, as much as possible. That means either keeping less stock on hand, or selling physically smaller items. (In this fashion your storage capacity can help determine the types of items you intend to sell.)

Finding the space is only part of the equation. If you're selling smaller items, you may need to install some sort of shelving to help organize your inventory. Consider the type of inexpensive plastic or metal shelving that you can find at your local hardware or home store. You might also need some sort of container to hold your really small items. Think about plastic drawers or bins, or even clear plastic bags. Again, home stores and office supply stores should stock what you need.

If you have a variety of items in your inventory, you'll also need some way to identify what you have on hand. That means some sort of labeling system, which can be as simple as handwritten pieces of paper or cards. If you really have a *lot* of different items, consider creating some sort of plan-o-gram or map to help you remember where you put what.

How much inventory should you stock? Not too much—especially if space is at a minimum! I like to have no more than a few weeks' worth of inventory on hand; anything more than that and you're at risk if sales suddenly turn downward. On the other hand, you may need to buy larger quantities to get an attractive discount, or perhaps you may only be able to buy your items in large lots. In any case, the less stock you can keep on hand the better—and the easier it will be to find space for.

Of course, you don't have to stock all your inventory where it's easy to get to. Just as with your shipping boxes, you can store a certain amount of inventory where it's convenient for immediate shipping, and store the rest off-site until you need it. Just make sure you can get your hands on enough items to fulfill the sales you make—the last thing you want to do is sell something that doesn't exist!

THE ABSOLUTE MINIMUM

When it comes to physically setting up your eBay business, keep these thoughts in mind:

- To keep your costs at a minimum, find a way to carve out space in your house or apartment—but keep that space separate from your normal living space.
- Invest in a low-priced computer system with black-and-white printer—but make sure you have a high-speed Internet connection.
- You should also purchase a digital camera and scanner, to capture images of the items you intend to sell.
- You'll need an uncluttered, well-lit space to set up your home office—big enough for a desk, filing cabinet, and comfortable chair.
- In addition to your office space, you'll also need a packing center and a place to store your inventory for sale.

IN THIS CHAPTER

- Where to find merchandise to resell
- Managing your inventory levels

8

STEP SIX: FIND AND MANAGE YOUR INVENTORY

A successful eBay business involves the selling of large quantities of merchandise. To sell that merchandise, you first have to obtain the merchandise—which means finding a steady supply of items to sell. These items become your business's inventory.

Managing your inventory sounds simple on paper. You identify items you want to resell, purchase those items (at as favorable a price as you can negotiate), store those items until they're sold, and then sell and ship them to your customers. When you run low on inventory, you order more. Hopefully you don't order more merchandise than you can actually sell. And hopefully you can sell your inventory for a higher price than what you paid for it—and enough higher that you can pay all your other expenses (and make a little profit) from the difference.

This chapter looks at the entire inventory issue—how you find items to sell, and how you manage that inventory in the day-to-day running of your business.

Where to Find Merchandise to Resell

When you put together your business plan, you indicated the type of business that you wanted to conduct. If you planned your eBay business around merchandise that you currently own or create yourself, you can skip this section. But if you planned your business around the resale of new or used merchandise, then you have to find a source for the items you want to sell.

Sourcing your inventory is one of the toughest tasks for high-volume eBay sellers. While the average eBay seller typically finds items in their own home or in garage sales, high-volume sellers have to find a constant supply of new merchandise. In essence, high-volume sellers are *resellers*, as they purchase merchandise from wholesalers or other sources and then resell that merchandise to their customers via eBay auctions.

Where can an individual find a source for merchandise to resell on eBay? There are several options, all of which involve buying items in bulk. That means laying down the cash upfront to buy large quantities of items, and then making your money back later, one sale at a time. This is one reason why a budding eBay business needs a source of funding; purchasing your starting inventory can tie up a lot of cash. (Learn more about obtaining funding for your business in Chapter 4, "Step Two: Evaluate Your Funding Needs.")

Whatever type of merchandise you choose to resell, you should always make sure you're buying from a reputable supplier. That means passing up those companies that have a Web site but no published phone number, or a post office box but no physical address. Even better, research the business on the Better Business Bureau Web site (www.bbb.org), or check the company's ratings at Dun & Bradstreet Small Business Solutions (sbs.dnb.com) or Hoover's (www.hoovers.com). You can also pick up the phone and give the company a call; you can tell a lot from a simple conversation.

Read on to learn about the many different sources of resellable merchandise.

> **tip**
>
> Another strategy is to go directly to the manufacturer for information (and, sometimes, product). The Thomas Register (www.thomasregister.com) is the definitive directory for finding products and companies in the U.S.

Wholesale Distributors

The way traditional retailers do business is to purchase merchandise from a wholesale distributor. The distributor purchases their merchandise direct from the manufacturer, who in many cases doesn't deal directly with retailers. The distributor, then, is a middleman who provides a variety of services to the retailer, not the least of which is warehousing the large quantities received from the manufacturer.

tip

Search for trade shows of interest at the *Tradeshow Week* magazine Web site (www.tradeshowweek.com).

If you want to be an "official" reseller of many types of products, you'll have to deal with the product's authorized distributor. There are thousands of wholesalers out there, most specializing in specific types of merchandise. Most wholesalers are set up to sell in quantity to legitimate retailers, but many also handle smaller orders and smaller buyers, making them ideal for eBay sellers. Many of these distributors operate over the Internet, which makes the process even easier for you.

How do you locate a wholesaler? One way is to attend an industry trade show or conference. Most distributors attend or exhibit at these shows; you can also find out about new products and (sometimes) get special tradeshow pricing. You can also contact the manufacturer directly; most will be glad to direct you to the distributor in your region.

If you live in a major metropolitan area, there may be a trade or merchandising mart where multiple wholesalers may be found. For example, Atlanta's AmericasMart is home to hundreds of specialized distributors, as is Chicago's Merchandise Mart. Check with your local chamber of commerce to see what's available in your area.

In addition, you shouldn't be afraid to ask other retailers (online or local) who they buy from. Most merchants are quite helpful, as long as they don't perceive you as a direct competitor.

You'll have to conduct your own search for a wholesaler that specializes in the particular type of merchandise you're interested in selling. I'll list a

note

One advantage of dealing with an official wholesaler is that, if you do enough business (and your credit rating is strong enough), you may be able to establish credit terms for your purchases. Instead of paying cash on the barrelhead, you may not have to pay until 15, 30, or even 60 days after you receive your merchandise. Check with your wholesaler to see what terms are offered.

few sites that function as directories or search services of wholesale distributors, but it's hard to beat a targeted Google search—just make sure you put the words "wholesale" or "distributor" in your query.

Wholesale411

Wholesale411 is one of the best search directories for wholesale and closeout merchandise. Wholesalers and liquidators list their merchandise and services on the Wholesale411 site, which then organizes the available merchandise into a variety of product categories, as shown in Figure 8.1. You can also search the site for specific types of merchandise.

FIGURE 8.1

Browse through the categories or search for specific types of wholesalers at Wholesale411.

Buylink

Another place to find vendors of different products is the Buylink site (www.buylink.com). You have to register as a retailer to search the Buylink marketplace, but then you can search for specific products or vendors.

Wholesale Central

Wholesale Central (www.wholesalecentral.com) is another leading directory of merchandise wholesalers. You can browse for vendors by category, or search for vendors of specific products.

Merchandise Liquidators

Liquidators are companies that purchase surplus items from other businesses, in bulk. These items might be closeouts, factory seconds, customer returns, or overstocked items—products the manufacturer made too many of and wants to get rid of. Liquidators help manufacturers and retailers dispose of this unwanted merchandise to the secondary market.

Just as liquidators purchase their inventory in bulk, you also buy from them in bulk. That means buying ten or twenty or a hundred units of a particular item. You get a good price for buying in quantity, of course, which is part of the appeal. You also have to manage that large inventory—and inventory storage can be both a lot of work and somewhat costly, as you learned in Chapter 7, "Step Five: Set Up Your Back Office."

caution

Just because you can buy bulk merchandise cheap doesn't make it a good deal. Remember, there's probably a reason why an item is being liquidated. It may be last year's model, it may be factory seconds, it may be used or returned, or it may just be something that no one wanted to buy. If it didn't sell well originally, there's no guarantee that it will sell well (at a lower price, of course) in an eBay auction.

When you buy surplus merchandise, check the warranty terms. Unlike the new merchandise you purchase from traditional wholesalers, most liquidators sell their goods "as is." That means if it's bad, you have to eat it—unless you also sell your goods with no warranty to your eBay customers.

Here's a short list of liquidators that can supply you with merchandise for your eBay auctions.

Liquidation.com

Liquidation.com (www.liquidation.com) is one of the largest and most reputable online liquidation services. The Liquidation.com Web site, shown in Figure 8.2, offers a steady stream of surplus, close-out, and returned merchandise in a variety of categories.

What kind of merchandise are we talking about? How about a lot of 500 Gap jeans, or 120 Panasonic cordless phones, or 1,000 units of *The Addams Family* TV show on VHS tape, or 4 huge pallets worth of assorted returned consumer electronics items—just for a start. Pricing is pretty good, if you can take the quantities. For example, those *Addams Family* tapes went for less than 50 cents apiece at a total lot price of $485. The key here is to pick an item that you know you can move in bulk over a period of weeks or months.

FIGURE 8.2

Buy surplus
items in bulk at
Liquidation.com

Note that Liquidation.com actually serves as a middleman between sellers (the original manufacturer or retailer) and buyers (you). Goods are sold in an online auction format, so you'll find yourself bidding on items just as you would in an eBay auction; all auctions start at $100, with no reserve. You can even pay for your merchandise with PayPal.

American Merchandise Liquidation

American Merchandise Liquidation (www.amlinc.com) handles closeouts, overstocks, customer returns, and salvaged merchandise in a variety of categories.

AmeriSurplus

AmeriSurplus (www.amerisurplus.com) sells salvage merchandise by the pallet from their warehouses in South Carolina and New Jersey. Products offered include automotive supplies, groceries, small appliances and electronics, sporting goods, and toys.

Bid4Assets

Bid4Assets (www.bid4assets.com) is an online auction site offering merchandise obtained from bankruptcies, private companies, and the government. This site offers primarily high-ticket items, including artwork, computer equipment, jewelry, vehicles, and even real estate. The items offered are typically single quantity, not bulk.

Luxury Brands

Luxury Brands (www.luxurybrandsllc.com) offers higher-end surplus merchandise than you find at other sites. Items include luxury branded European clothing, accessories, and gift items. Even though this is surplus merchandise, you might recognize some of the brands—including Giorgio Armani, Ralph Lauren Polo, Givenchy, Gucci, and Burberry. The company purchases large mixed parcels of European merchandise, typically end-of-season merchandise, and then imports it for sale in the U.S. You can purchase product in lots of 25, 50, 100, and so on.

My Web Wholesaler

My Web Wholesaler (www.mywebwholesaler.com) sells box lots, pallets, and truckloads of merchandise obtained from major department store returns, closeouts, overstocks, and liquidations. Categories carried range from As Seen on TV and Automotive to Toys and Watches.

OverstockB2B.com

OverstockB2B.com (www.overstockb2b.com) offers surplus merchandise from a variety of manufacturers. Merchandise categories include Apparel & Accessories; Bed, Bath & Linens; Computer & Home Office; Electronics & Cameras; Gifts, Gadgets & Toys; Global Designs; Home and Garden Décor; Housewares & Appliances; Jewelry & Watches; Luggage & Business; Movies, Books & Music; and Sports Gear.

Salvage Closeouts

Salvage Closeouts (www.salvagecloseouts.com) offers liquidated merchandise and department store closeouts in a wide variety of categories, from Apparel and Appliances to Tools and Toys. They also offer a variety of pallet and truckload specials, and have a special eBay Recommendations category.

TDW Closeouts

TDW Closeouts (www.tdwcloseouts.com) is another distributor of department store returns and closeout merchandise. They offer liquidated, salvage, overstock, and surplus items in a variety of categories, from Apparel to Toys.

Ándale Sourcing

If you're not sure where to find specific types of merchandise, you're in luck. Ándale Sourcing (www.andale.com) is a free service that helps you find suppliers of various types of merchandise for resale. It does a good job of matching resellers with suppliers, by keeping a big database of both.

When you sign up for Ándale Sourcing (it's free, remember), you fill out the sourcing profile shown in Figure 8.3. Select the categories of merchandise in which you're interested, and Ándale Sourcing will automatically match you with suppliers who match your criteria.

FIGURE 8.3

Use Ándale Sourcing to look for merchandise suppliers by category.

You can choose to receive your leads by email or via the Leads Dashboard; you can also opt to put a link in all your eBay item listings to generate sales leads. (The link asks: "Have one to sell?") The Leads Dashboard lists suppliers (companies and individuals) that have goods for sale in the categories you selected. Each listing includes the supplier's location and eBay feedback rating, so you can judge their trustworthiness. Click the supplier's name to display a detailed Sourcing Profile, which includes the supplier's phone number and email address. You can then contact the supplier at your discretion.

Other Sources of Merchandise

If you're less interested in bulk and more interested in variety, there are other sources available that can supply you with merchandise for your eBay auctions. I'll list some of the more popular ones next.

Garage Sales

Many eBay sellers got their start by reselling merchandise they picked up at local garage/yard/tag/rummage sale sales. While this can certainly be a source of merchandise, I don't really recommend it for high-volume sellers, for a number of reasons. First, the merchandise you buy isn't limited to a specific category, and it's tough to deal with such a large variety of items. Second, it's not a guaranteed supply; you might stumble across a great deal one week, but then go dry the next. Finally, this source looks to be getting tapped, as more people choose to sell their old stuff on eBay rather than putting it out in their front yards. Take a gander, but don't be disappointed if it doesn't pan out.

Flea Markets

Flea markets offer similar merchandise to what you find in garage sales, although you can sometimes find surplus items in bulk. If you keep your eyes peeled, you might find the occasional bargain that can supply your eBay auctions for an extended period of time.

Estate Sales/Auctions

Not to be insensitive, but dead people provide some of the best deals you can find. It's the equivalent of raiding somebody else's garage or attic for old stuff to sell. Check out the weekly estate sales and auctions in your area, be prepared to buy in quantity, and see what turns up.

Traditional Auctions

Real-world auctions (not the eBay kind) remain a good source of inventory for many eBay sellers. Many auctions feature large lots or bulk quantities, which are perfect for ongoing eBay sales. Make sure you inspect the merchandise before the auction, and don't get caught in a bidding frenzy; set your maximum price beforehand, and don't exceed it. The IAL Auction Calendar keeps a list of ongoing auction events by date and location; check out the Web site at www.internetauctionlist.com.

Vintage and Used Retailers

You can often pick up some decent collectible merchandise at your local "vintage" or used merchandise retailer—although you may have to haggle a little to get down to a decent price. The big drawback is that you're typically buying onesies and twosies; this isn't a good source for large lots.

Thrift Stores

Think Goodwill, Salvation Army, and similar stores here. You can typically find some decent merchandise at low cost—and help out a nonprofit organization, to boot. This approach has the same drawback as buying from a vintage retailer, however; large lots are rare.

Dollar Stores

These "big lot" retailers are surprisingly good sources of eBay-ready merchandise. Most of these retailers carry overruns and closeouts at attractive prices. You can often pick up items here quite cheap—and enough of them to feed your auction activity for awhile. Some of the larger dollar-store chains include 99¢ Only (www.99only.com) and Big Lots (www.biglots.com).

Warehouse Clubs

You'd be surprised what deals you can find at your local Sam's Club (www.samsclub.com) or Costco (www.costco.com). Buy something cheap enough here, and it's not to hard to resell it at a decent markup on eBay. Just remember that the clubs' product mix is continually changing, so you'll need to visit often to find the latest deals.

Closeout Sales

You don't have to shop at a cheap retailer to find a good deal. Many mainline merchants offer terrific deals at the end of a season or when it's time to get in next year's merchandise. If you can get enough good stuff at a closeout price, you have a good starting inventory for your eBay sales.

Going Out of Business Sales

Even better, look for a merchant flying the white flag of surrender. When a retailer is going out of business and says "everything must go," that means that bargains are yours to be had—and don't be afraid to make a lower-priced deal, if you can.

eBay

This leads us to the final place to look for items to sell on eBay—eBay itself! Yes, it's possible to make money buying something on eBay and then turning around and selling it to someone else on eBay at a later date. The key is timing. Remember, you have to buy low and sell high, which means getting in at the start of a trend. It's possible—although it takes a lot of hard work, and not a little skill.

One way to find goods for resale is to use eBay's search feature. Make sure you include the words "case," "closeout," "lot," or "surplus" in your query.

Another option is to go directly to eBay's Wholesale Lots category (pages.ebay.com/catindex/catwholesale.html). As you can see in Figure 8.4, this page lists eBay auctions of surplus merchandise in almost all of eBay's major categories. Just click through to bid on merchandise ideally suited for resale.

FIGURE 8.4

Sourcing surplus merchandise on eBay's Wholesale Lots page.

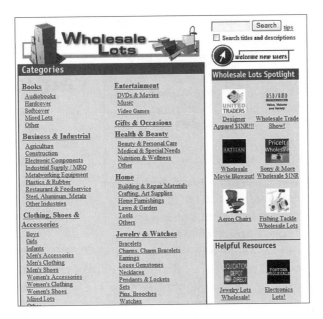

Managing Your Inventory Levels

Once you find a source for merchandise, you now have the challenge of managing your newfound inventory. That means determining how much to buy and when to reorder.

Ordering the Right Quantity

It's tough to establish how much merchandise to order, especially when you're first starting out. The problem is amplified when you have to order large quantities of an item, or qualify for a larger discount the more you order. It's tempting to shoot the moon to get the best possible price, but that's sometimes a dangerous strategy. It's also problematic if your storage space is at a premium; you certainly don't want to order more stuff than you have room for!

The best strategy is to research similar auctions on eBay, as discussed in Chapter 3, and make an educated guess as to how many items you can sell in a typical week. Multiply that by 4, and round off a little to come up with a *conservative* estimate of your first month's sales. When you're first starting

"Mike Sez"

When you're dealing with a commodity product for resale, it's better to order too few than too many. If your business is an overnight success, you can always order more.

out, keeping a month's worth of inventory on hand is a safe way to go. If your guess is off by 50% either way, you're still okay; you'll either have two weeks' or two months' worth of inventory on hand, either of which you can handle. If, on the other hand, you order two months' worth of inventory, then if you're off by 50% you're either out of stock in a week or stuck with four months' worth of stuff—neither of which is that attractive.

caution

It's worth repeating—when it comes to ordering inventory, don't bite off more than you can chew. It's better to pay a higher price for a smaller quantity than to get stuck with a garage full of unsold merchandise!

In addition, when you place an order for a large quantity of merchandise, you need to make sure that there is a sufficient long-term demand for that product. Fads and fashions change over time; don't order six months' worth of inventory if the current fad looks to burn itself out in three. It may be more prudent to pay a higher per-item price for a lower quantity than risk not selling a substantial portion of a larger-quantity order. (And remember—you have to store all those items somewhere.)

Managing Your Reorders

Once you start selling, you need to keep track of how much inventory you have on hand. That's where your inventory management system (see Chapter 6, "Step Four: Set Up a Record-keeping System") comes into play. You have to subtract every item you sell from the quantity you initially had on hand. When your inventory drops to a specified level, it's time to reorder more.

Of course, this situation poses two questions: At what level should you set your reorder point, and what quantity should you reorder?

To the first question, your reorder point should be based on how long it takes you to receive any order you place from your supplier. For example, if your supplier ships within a week of you ordering, you can safely set your reorder point at a week's worth of inventory. Let's say you're selling 20 units per week, and your supplier reliably ships within a week of your order. Set your system to alert you when your inventory drops to 20 units. Place your reorder immediately, and you'll have your new stock arrive just as the last of your old stock runs out.

caution

Don't wait until your inventory drops to zero to reorder—you'll be stuck with nothing to sell, and no income coming in. Better to reorder before you run out, so your auctions can continue uninterrupted.

Naturally, if your supplier ships more slowly, you should set your reorder point higher. Let's say your supplier takes two weeks to fill an order. If you're selling 20 units a week, you should set your reorder point at 40 units—two week's worth of inventory.

As to how much you should reorder, this is dependent on how many units you're selling per week, how long you expect sales to stay at this rate, how much inventory you feel comfortable with, and what discounts are available for larger orders. If you're fairly confident that sales will continue at current levels for the next two months, and you get an extra discount for larger quantities, then go ahead and order two months' worth. (Assuming you have the space to store it, of course.) On the other hand, if you think sales will slow (because of changing fashions, or seasonal trends, or whatever), then don't go out on a limb—order another few weeks' or at most a month's supply. Order the quantity you feel comfortable with—you're the one who has to assume the risk.

> **tip**
>
> When you're factoring the cost of your merchandise, don't forget to include warehousing costs. This might be zero if everything fits in your garage (and you don't mind parking outside), but could add up if you have to rent a storage bin or warehouse. You might think that large-quantity discount is worth it—until you have to pay through the nose to store all those boxes somewhere.

Deciding to Drop Ship

This is as good a place as any to discuss the issue of *drop shipping*. This is the practice of selling an item that you don't physically have in stock. You make the sale (via eBay), and then notify your supplier of the purchase. Your supplier then drop ships the merchandise directly to your customer, billing you in the process.

While drop shipping might sound attractive from an inventory management standpoint (you have none to manage), it might not always be the best deal for your customers—especially if your supplier isn't always a speedy shipper. Remember, your customers hold you responsible for shipping the products they purchase, and if a drop shipment isn't prompt, you are the one who'll get the complaints (and the negative feedback). If, for whatever reason (like they're temporarily out of stock), your supplier drops the ball and never ships the merchandise, you're on the hook. If this happens too often, you could get the boot from eBay.

While not all distributors offer drop ship services, many do. Check with your wholesaler to see what services are available.

In addition, a good source of drop-shipped merchandise is All Drop Ship (www. alldropship.com). This site offers merchandise from a variety of wholesalers, and then serves as a middleman to provide drop ship service to your customers.

Also useful is the Worldwide Brands Drop Ship Source Directory (www.info1.mydssd.com/wwb/). For a fee ($69.95 for the first six months—pricey!), you can search from thousands of companies that drop ship a variety of different merchandise; you can search by either brand name or product type.

THE ABSOLUTE MINIMUM

Finding merchandise to sell and managing your inventory is one of the tougher tasks for an eBay business. Keep these points in mind:

■ There are lots of different places to find merchandise to resell on eBay; two of the most popular sources for cheap merchandise are wholesale distributors and liquidators.

■ You can also find merchandise for resale in eBay's Wholesale Lots category, or use Ándale Sourcing to locate products to sell.

■ When you're first starting out, go easy on the inventory; a month's worth of inventory is plenty until you get a feel for how sales are going to go.

9

STEP SEVEN: RESEARCH OTHER EBAY AUCTIONS— AND SET A PRICING STRATEGY

The next step in preparing to launch your eBay business is to do a little research. In particular, you need to research the products you intend to sell—to find out how well those products are likely to sell for you, and to figure out at what price you should sell them. This research, then, will help you determine the pricing strategy for your eBay auctions.

By the way, this type of research is also useful in determining which types of items to sell on eBay. Pick a product category and research the auction close rate and average selling price; avoid those categories that don't meet your criteria, and target those categories that do.

Why Researching Pricing Is Important

Let's back up a minute. How important can pricing be when all items are sold to the highest bidder? It's simple, really. First, the initial bid price you set for an item will determine how many bidders you attract. Set the initial price too high and you drive away potential buyers; set the price too low, and the auction might not hit the final selling price you want.

Second, you have the option of using eBay's Buy It Now option, which lets buyers purchase an item without going through the entire auction process. Buy It Now is great when you have large quantities of items to sell, and lets you generate income independent of the normal auction closing schedule. But to set a Buy It Now price, you have to determine the correct selling price for the item. (With no auction bids, the price won't rise to the market level by itself.)

Third, if you know what items similar to yours sell for, on average, you can do a better job of projecting your auction revenue. And, of course, this also helps you determine what types of items you want to sell.

So it's key that you research item sales pricing before you start into high-volume selling. But how do you do it?

How to Research Other eBay Auctions

Here's something all high-volume eBay sellers know—you should never sell without doing your homework first. You need to make sure you know the true value of an item before you put it up for auction.

That means that before you price your item, you should research similar items that have already sold on eBay. What was the starting bid price? What was the final selling price? How did the starting price affect the final price—and the likelihood of that item to actually sell?

For example, in a recent six-week period in mid-2003, I discovered that there were 3,270 auctions for Olympus digital cameras on eBay, and that 63% of those auctions closed successfully, at an average selling price of $258.62—definitely a hot category. On the other hand, during the same period there were 480 auctions for men's golf shirts, of which only 48% closed successfully, at an average selling price of $16.14; a less-exciting category, by all measurements. If I had to choose between these two products to sell, I'd be a lot more interested in those digital cameras.

tip

You can also research the price of similar items offline; sometimes you can get a feel for relative value if you compare your item to similar items sold in bricks-and-mortar stores.

How did I get this information? Read on and discover the many ways to research prior sales on eBay.

Searching Closed eBay Auctions

The cheapest (but not necessarily the easiest) way to research auction pricing is to do it yourself, using eBay's search feature. The downside to this method is that it's labor intensive; you'll have to perform a number of manual searches, and then crunch all the numbers yourself. The upside is that the only cost is your time.

tip

You can limit your search to specific product categories by making a selection from the Category list.

Assembling the Data

Here's how to research pricing manually:

1. From the eBay Navigation Bar, click the Search button.

2. When the Search page appears, select the Advanced Search tab.

3. When the Advanced Search page appears, as shown in Figure 9.1, enter one or more keywords for a specific type of item into the Search box.

FIGURE 9.1

Use eBay's Advanced Search page to list auctions of specific merchandise.

4. Check the Completed Items Only option (in the Refine Your Search section).

5. Click the Search button to start the search; eBay displays your results on a separate Items Matching page.

The key point here is to search for *completed auctions only*. You don't want to list in-process auctions, because you don't know what the final selling prices will be until the auction closes. When you list completed auctions, you'll have all the information you need—including the final selling price.

When the Items Matching page appears, it's time to get your fingers dirty. You'll need to click through each of the auctions listed and write down the following:

■ Starting price
■ Final selling price
■ Number of bids

It's best to enter this information into an Excel spreadsheet, with one row for each completed auction and a column for each of the parameters. If the auction ended without a sale, enter "0" for both the final selling price and number of bids.

Analyzing the Data

Once you've gathered your data, it's time to analyze it. Here are some things to look at:

■ Look at the range of prices by sorting the list in order of highest selling price
■ Add a new column to calculate the ratio of final selling to starting price; fill the column by dividing the final selling price column by the starting price column
■ Calculate the closing percentage by manually counting the number of auctions that had a winning bid and dividing by the total number of auctions

Fun, eh? Well, it gets better. The search you just did only captures auctions that closed in the past 15 days. (That's the longest eBay keeps this information for public consumption.) You'll want to supplement this data with more recent auctions, so you should repeat this search on a weekly basis. This way you can capture any pricing trends over time.

Using Research Tools

All that manual number crunching seem like a lot of work? Then let somebody else do it for you! There are a handful of pricing research services and programs available that perform all sorts of analysis on eBay auction trends. The good news is that these services greatly simplify this process, and provide highly detailed (and very professional) analysis. The bad news is that you have to pay for what you get.

That said, let's look at three of the best pricing research products—Ándale Research, AuctionIntelligence, and DeepAnalysis.

Ándale Research

Ándale Research (www.andale.com) is one of the most versatile eBay research services available. For a fee of $2.95 per month (cheap!), you can use Ándale Research to generate pricing reports by category or specific product, and thus take some of the guesswork out of your eBay item pricing. Ándale Research will help you determine the best category in which to list your product, the best time of day (and day of week) to list, the most profitable starting price, which listing features generate the most sales, and the average selling price. You can even compare your sales rates and prices with eBay averages. The service is easy to use, and the reports are presented in an extremely easy-to-understand format.

To research the pricing for an item, enter the keyword(s) for the item into the Item Search box, then click the Search button. Alternatively, click the Advanced Search link to search for items within a specific price range or category.

The Search Results page, shown in Figure 9.2, includes several different sections, each displaying a specific bit of information, as follows:

- **Summary**. This section shows you the average selling price, the range of final prices, the number of items listed and sold, and the percent of successfully completed auctions (success rate).

- **Ándale Recommends**. This section tells you exactly what you want to know to maximize your sales results, based on Ándale's analysis of this selling data: what category to list in, where you should set your initial price, what day and time you should list, and what special listing features you should incorporate. Follow this advice for best results.

"Mike Sez"

In my personal opinion, Ándale Research is the single most useful eBay research tool I've found. To me, it's well worth the monthly cost to find out which prices and listing options generate the best results.

- **Category**. This section provides the details (including a cool bar chart) of the different categories in which this type of item has been listed. You'll see what percent of auctions utilized each category and the average price and success rate for each category.

- **Pricing Options**. This section details the results (selling price, success rate, and so on) for four different types of auctions: Regular (no reserve), Reserve, Buy It Now (BIN), and Fixed Price. This will help you decide what type of auction to run.

- **Scheduled Start Day**. This section provides auction results by day the auction launched; all you have to do is look at the bar chart to see which day of the week produced the highest selling prices.

- **eBay Marketing Features**. This section details the results for auctions utilizing eBay's various listing enhancements: Bold, Highlight, and Gallery (and None, of course).

- **Successfully Completed Auctions**. This section lists a sampling of the auctions were used for Ándale's analysis; click the item link to view the listing page for a specific auction.

FIGURE 9.2

View pricing and sales data on the Search Results page.

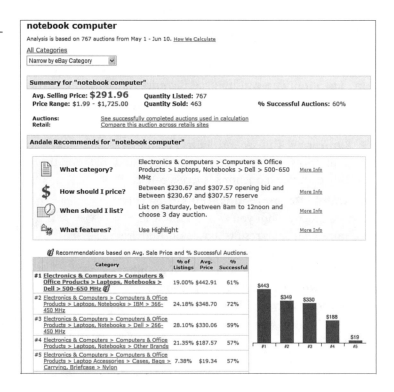

To save a specific research report, click the Save Search to My Portfolio button at the bottom of the page. Your saved searches are displayed on the My Portfolio page. Going forward, you can choose to view a Snapshot of your research (which runs the entire report anew, using the most recent data), or a Charted Report of new listings since your last report.

AuctionIntelligence

AuctionIntelligence (www.certes.net/AuctionIntelligence/) is an auction analysis program available on a subscription basis. Downloading the software is free; you have to pay $9.99 per month to use it.

This program lets you search eBay by category or keyword; after it retrieves all matching auctions, you can generate a wide variety of sophisticated reports just by clicking the name of the report in the Reports list. Available reports include

- Search Summary
- Price Over Time
- Bid and Price Trend
- PayPal Effects
- Feedback Effects
- Duration Effects
- Premium Features
- Category Distribution
- Frequent Sellers
- Frequent Bidders
- Raw Search Results
- Common Words in Title (by Price)
- Common Words in Title (by Bids)

For example, Figure 9.3 shows the Price Over Time report. This report is a good way to discover the pricing trends for a particular item, whether the average selling price is going up or down.

AuctionIntelligence is an extremely full-featured research program, although it's somewhat technically demanding (it requires the installation of a Microsoft SQL Server 2000 or MSDE 2000 database before it can run) and not the easiest program in the world to use. Given these caveats, AuctionIntelligence can generate some extremely valuable research reports.

FIGURE 9.3

Track pricing
trends with the
AuctionIntelligence
Price Over Time
report.

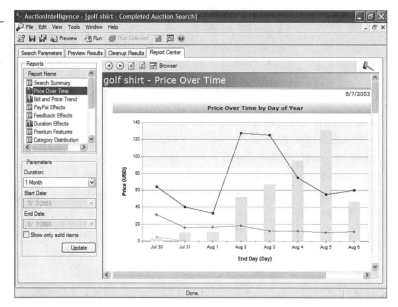

DeepAnalysis

DeepAnalysis is a software program from HammerTap (www.hammertap.com) that performs basic auction sales analysis. It's a tad pricey at $179, although there's no monthly subscription fee (and there is a 30-day free trial). DeepAnalysis provides fundamental information about any category or specific product, including the number of auctions in the past 30 days, the number of bids for each auction, percentage of items sold, average selling price, and so on.

You start out on the DeepAnalysis main screen. Click the Category button to enter a category number you're interested; if you don't know the number, click the Category List button to open eBay's Category Overview page in your Web browser. To research a particular type of product, click the Keyword button and enter your query in the Keywords box. Remember to select the Completed Auctions option for best results, and to pull down the Analyze list to select how many auctions to analyze; click the Start Analysis button to continue.

Search results are shown in the bottom part of the window; you can display the results by seller (select the Sellers tab) or item (select the Items tab). You can also view overall selling data by selecting the Statistics tab. You'll see:

- Number of auctions—including number of regular, reserve, and Dutch auctions
- Number of auctions resulting in a sale (both number and percentage of total)
- Average number of bids per auction

- Average high bid and average sale price
- Total value of all high bids, and total actual sales for that category or product

You can save individual searches by selecting File, Save Report. You can also export your results to both spreadsheet and database formats, by selecting File, Export Report.

Working with Grading, Authentication, and Appraisal

Sometimes the proper pricing for an item can be determined by means other than looking at completed auctions. Naturally, if you're selling new merchandise, you can compare your pricing to that of a typical retail store. And if you're selling certain collectible items, there are established price guides available to determine both the condition and the market value of your item.

caution

I evaluated several other research programs, but found a disturbing number of technical problems when trying to use the software. You should definitely avail yourself of any free trial offers before you lay down your hard cash—just to make sure the programs actually work on your PC.

Understanding Grading

The process of setting a market value based on age and condition is called *grading*. Collectors use these grading scales to help evaluate and price items within a category. If you know the grade of your item, not only can you better determine the ideal selling price, you can also include the grade in the item's title or description, and thus more accurately describe the item to potential bidders.

Every type of collectible has its own grading system; there's no such thing as a "universal" grading system for all items. For example, trading cards are graded from A1 to F1; stamps are graded from Poor to Superb.

That said, many collectible categories use a variation of the Mint grading system, as shown in Table 9.1.

TABLE 9.1   Mint System Grading

Grade	Abbreviation	Description
Mint	MT, M, 10	An item in perfect condition, without any damage or imperfections.
Very Fine	VF	Similar to mint.
Near Mint	NM, 9	An item with a very minor, hardly noticeable flaw. Sometimes described as "like new."

Table 9.1 (continued)

Near Fine	NF	Similar to near mint.
Excellent	EX, 8	An item considered above average, but with pronounced signs of wear.
Fine	F	Similar to excellent.
Very Good	VG, 7	An item in average condition.
Good	GD, G, 6	An item that has clear indications of age, wear, and use.
Fair	F	An item that is heavily worn.
Poor	P, 5	An item that is damaged or somehow incomplete.

Degrees between grade levels are indicated with a + or −. (For example, an item between Fine and Very Fine would be designated as F+.) Naturally, the definition of a Mint or Fair item differs by item type.

Getting Graded

If you're not sure what grade an item is, you may be able to utilize a professional grading and authentication service. These services will examine your item, authenticate it (confirm that it's the real deal), and give it a professional grade. Some services will even encase your item in a sealed plastic container or bag.

Where can you get your items graded? Table 9.2 lists some popular Web sites for grading and authenticating collectible items:

Table 9.2 Grading and Authentication Services

Collectible	Site	URL
Autographs	OnlineAuthentics.com	www.onlineauthentics.com
	PSA/DNA	www.psadna.com
Beanie Babies	Peter Gallagher Enterprises	www.beaniephenomenon.com
Books	PKBooks	www.pkbooks.com
Coins	American Numismatic Association Certification Service	www.anacs.com
	Numismatic Guaranty Corporation of America	www.ngccoin.com
	Professional Coin Grading Service	www.pcgs.com
Comic books	Comics Guaranty	www.cgccomics.com
Jewelry	International Gemological Institute	www.e-igi.com

Collectible	Site	URL
Sports cards	Professional Sports Authenticator	`www.psacard.com`
	Sports Collectors Digest Authentic	`scda.krause.com`
	Sportscard Guarantee Corporation	`www.sgccard.com`
Stamps	American Philatelic Society	`www.stamps.org`
	Professional Stamps Experts	`www.psestamp.com`

The cost of these authentication services varies wildly, depending on what you're authenticating, the age or value of the item, and the extent of the service itself. For example, Professional Sports Authenticator rates range from $5 to $50 per sports card; Professional Stamps Experts rates range from $15 to $85 per stamp. Make sure the item you're selling is worth it before you go to this expense.

Working with Appraisals

Similar to grading is the process of having an item's value appraised. Professional appraisal services will examine your item and pass judgment on its approximate market value. Appraisal is often recommended for high-value art and antique items.

You can locate an appraiser in your area by searching the International Society of Appraisers Web site, at `www.isa-appraisers.org`.

Setting a Pricing Strategy

Now that you have some idea as to what an item is worth, how should you price it at auction? If you set your minimum price too high, you might scare off potential buyers. If you set your minimum price too low, you'll probably get more interested bidders, but you might end up selling your item for less than you want or than what it's worth.

So what's the right starting price? It all depends on your pricing strategy.

Set It Low Enough to Be Attractive...

To a customer, a lower price is more desirable than a higher one. Think about it; if you see two similar items and one is priced a dollar lower than the other, you're going to be attracted to the lower-priced item.

tip

eBay provides a page of links to "authorized" authentication services at `pages.ebay.com/help/community/auth-overview.html`.

For that reason, I like setting a price that's low enough to get some interested initial bidding going. That could be as low as 99 cents, or at the very least competitive with the lowest starting bids on similar merchandise also for auction on eBay.

On the other hand, you shouldn't set the initial price so low that it won't eventually rise to the final price you think the item can really sell for. If you think the final selling price will be $100, setting the initial bid at a penny might leave too large a gap to be bridged.

...But Don't Set It So Low That It's Not Believable

A low initial price is good, but it's possible to actually set the starting price for an item *too* low. That's because if you set too low a minimum bid, some potential bidders might think that something is wrong with the item. (It's the old "if it's too good to be true, it probably is.") Although you might assume that bidding will take the price up into reasonable levels, too low a starting price can make your item look too cheap or otherwise flawed. If you start getting a lot of emails asking why you've set the price so low, you should have set a higher price.

With an ultra-low starting price, you also run the risk of the final selling price not making it up to the level you'd like to hit. Sometimes the difference between here and there is just too great for your bidders to distance.

...And Not So High You Pay Too High a Listing Fee

Of course (and there's always another "of course"), if you set a higher starting price, you'll pay a higher insertion fee. Here's where it helps to know the breaks—in eBay's fee schedule, that is. Table 9.3 shows the fee breaks as of summer 2003:

Table 9.3 eBay's Insertion Fee Breaks

Price Point	Fee
$0–$9.99	$0.30
$10.00–$24.99	$0.55
$25.00–$49.99	$1.10
$50.00–$199.99	$2.20
$200.00 and up	$3.30

Let's think about what this means. At the very least, you want to come in just below the fee break; coming in *above* the fee break will cost you an unnecessarily higher fee. For example, you probably want to list at $9.99 (which incurs a 30-cent fee) and not at $10.00 (which incurs a 55-cent fee). That extra penny could cost you 25 cents!

Obviously, it's in your best interest to minimize any and all fees you have to pay. If you're almost positive (based on completed auction activity) that your item will sell in the $20 range no matter what you price it at, price it as low as is reasonable. And remember—if you set the starting price for anything under $10, you only pay a 30-cent listing fee!

Using Reserve Pricing

You learned about reserve price auctions back in Chapter 1, "Reviewing eBay Basics." In a nutshell, in a reserve price auction the initial bid price you set *isn't* the lowest price you agree to accept. Your lowest acceptable price—which is hidden from all bidders—is called your reserve price. You use reserve pricing to get bidding started at an attractive initial price, while reserving the right not to sell unless the final price reaches the (higher) level you really want to get.

That might mean starting bidding at a penny, but setting a reserve price of $10 or so. Bidders will get excited about the one-cent starting price, and (hopefully) bid the price up to where you want it. Once the bidding reaches $10, you're home free. If the bidding doesn't get there, the auction closes without a winner and you're not out anything. (Except your listing fees, of course.)

The only problem with reserve price auctions is that you run a very real risk of scaring away some viable bidders. That's because many new or inexperienced eBay users are confused by the whole reserve price process, and when potential buyers are confused, they just don't bid. If you want to run that risk, fine; reserve auctions do let you get bidding started at a very attractive level, while protecting you if bids don't rise to the price you're looking for.

You activate reserve pricing on the Sell Your Item page. Just enter a value into the Reserve Price field, and this option will automatically be added into your auction.

Using Buy It Now

A better option might be using eBay's Buy It Now (BIN) feature, which enables you to add a fixed-price option to your auction listings. With BIN, you indicate both an initial starting price and a fixed Buy It Now price; if a user bids the BIN price, the auction is automatically closed, with that user the high bidder.

BIN is a great option if you have a lot of auctions featuring the same item—especially if that item is somewhat of a commodity, with an easily predictable selling price. For example, if *Star Wars* DVDs consistently sell for $12, and you plan on running a hundred of them for auction over the next month or so, you would set a BIN price of $12 on your item. When a buyer finds your auction, he or she can purchase the item immediately (without waiting a week or so for the auction to close) by choosing the Buy It Now option. The advantage to you is that you generate revenue faster than if you had to wait for the full auction cycle to run.

When is BIN *not* a good idea? When you have a rare or collectible item of which you're not sure of its true market value. Set the BIN too low and you cheat yourself out of potential revenue; in this situation, it's better to let the auction run its course and see where things end up.

You activate BIN on the Sell Your Item page. Just enter your BIN price into the Buy It Now Price box. And remember—your BIN price should be higher than your starting price.

note

The BIN price is active only until the first bid is placed (or, in a reserve price auction, until the reserve price is met); if the first bidder places a bid lower than the BIN price, the BIN price is removed and the auction proceeds normally.

THE ABSOLUTE MINIMUM

When it comes to determining item pricing, keep these points in mind:

- When you do your research, you'll better know what starting price at which to list your products—and a have a pretty good idea of the final selling price, as well.

- The cheapest way to research item pricing is to search eBay for completed auctions of similar items.

- There are a number of paid services and software that generate sophisticated research reports; the most popular of these are Ándale Research, AuctionIntelligence, and DeepAnalysis.

- Your pricing strategy determines the initial bid price for your item—set too high a starting price, and you'll turn off potential customers.

- You always have the option of setting a low initial bid price and a higher reserve price—or of letting customers purchase your item at a fixed Buy It Now price.

IN THIS CHAPTER

- Creating an eBay seller's account
- Arranging to pay your fees
- Building your reputation—with positive feedback

10

STEP EIGHT: ESTABLISH YOUR EBAY PRESENCE

You've done all your homework. You've created a business plan, set up a record-keeping system, made space for your office and shipping operation, and even researched other eBay auctions and obtained items to sell. Now it's time to put it all together and start selling.

Before you can sell on eBay, however, you first have to register with eBay—and establish yourself as a trustworthy eBay member. Now, you may already know how to do this; you may, in fact, already be selling to some degree on eBay. If so, feel free to skip some of the information on this chapter and proceed to more advanced material later in this book. If you're just getting started, however, you'll want to carefully read this chapter and follow the steps within—and you'll have your eBay business up and running in no time!

Creating an eBay Seller's Account

Anyone who wants to buy or sell merchandise on eBay has to establish an account with eBay. Fortunately, this registration is free, easy, and relatively quick. But before you register, you need to prepare some key information, as detailed in the following checklist:

Checklist: Before You Register

- ☐ Your name
- ☐ Your street address
- ☐ Your email address
- ☐ Your phone number
- ☐ Your date of birth
- ☐ Your credit card or checking account number

With this information at hand, you register as an eBay user by following these steps:

1. From eBay's home page, click the Register Now button.

2. When the eBay Registration page appears (as shown in Figure 10.1), enter the following information:
   - ■ First name and last name
   - ■ Street address (including city, state, ZIP code, and country)
   - ■ Telephone number
   - ■ Email address

3. Still on the same page, create and enter a user ID into the Create Your eBay User ID box.

4. Create and enter a password (at least six characters long, with no spaces) into the Create Password box.

5. Select a question from the Secret Question list, and then enter your answer in the Secret Answer box. (This is used if you ever forget your password.)

note

Even if you've already registered for eBay as a buyer, you'll need to revise and supplement your information when you want to start selling. In particular, you'll need to choose some sort of payment method; as a buyer you didn't have to pay any eBay fees, but as a seller you will!

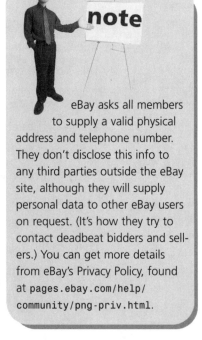

note

eBay asks all members to supply a valid physical address and telephone number. They don't disclose this info to any third parties outside the eBay site, although they will supply personal data to other eBay users on request. (It's how they try to contact deadbeat bidders and sellers.) You can get more details from eBay's Privacy Policy, found at `pages.ebay.com/help/community/png-priv.html`.

6. Enter your date of birth, and then click the Continue button.

7. eBay now displays its user agreements. Read these agreements (if you want), check each of the I Agree boxes, and then click the I Agree to These Terms button.

8. eBay now verifies your email address and sends you a confirmation message. Click the Web page link in the confirmation email message to continue.

9. eBay now displays a congratulations page, along with a pop-up window that asks you to enter more (optional) information about yourself. This information is used for marketing purposes; you can choose to fill in the blanks or close the window and click the Home link to go directly to eBay's home page.

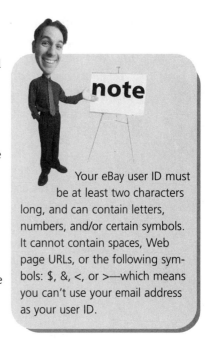

Your eBay user ID must be at least two characters long, and can contain letters, numbers, and/or certain symbols. It cannot contain spaces, Web page URLs, or the following symbols: $, &, <, or >—which means you can't use your email address as your user ID.

FIGURE 10.1

Enter the first page of your registration info.

Arranging to Pay Your Fees

If you intend to sell items on eBay, you'll have to pay eBay for that privilege. In particular, eBay charges a listing fee when you post an item for auction, and a final value fee when you sell an item. These fees are charged automatically to your account—which is why you have to choose an appropriate method of payment when you create your eBay seller's account. In particular, you need to provide eBay with either your credit card or checking account number for direct withdrawal of all your eBay fees. You can also choose to pay your eBay fees by check or money order, although it's somewhat of a hassle and not encouraged.

To activate payment via credit card, follow these steps:

1. Go the eBay Site Map page and click Place or Update my Credit Card on File with eBay (in the Seller Accounts section of the Services section).

2. When the credit card submission form appears (see Figure 10.2), enter your user ID or email address, password, and credit card billing information, then check the I Would Like to Use This Credit Card to Pay Seller Fees option.

3. Click the Submit button when done.

To activate payment via automatic checking account withdrawal, follow these steps:

1. Go to the eBay Site Map page and click Sign Up/Update eBay Direct Pay for Seller Fees (in the Seller Accounts section of the Services section).

2. When the Direct Pay submission form appears, enter your name, your bank's name, your bank's routing number, and your checking account number.

3. Click the Submit button when done.

Your payment information will be applied to your eBay account within 12–24 hours.

Building Your Reputation—with Positive Feedback

Now that you're signed up for eBay, you're ready to start selling, right?

note

If you ever move, you'll need to change the address and phone number information eBay has on file. Just go to the Site Map page, scroll to the My eBay section, and click the item you want to change: User ID, Password, Registration Information, E-Mail Address, and so on.

"Mike Sez"

I recommend you go with credit card billing. I don't like the idea of eBay (or any other company) having automatic access to my checking account; who knows if I'll have enough funds on tap the day they decide to make the automatic withdrawal? Credit card payment is easy and just as automatic, with few (if any) hassles.

FIGURE 10.2

Entering credit
card information
for your eBay
seller's account.

Enter Your Credit Card /debit Card Information

Credit card /debit card number	Credit Card: Visa, MasterCard , American Express, Discover; Debit Card: Visa, MasterCard
	eBay Welcomes **VISA**
Expiration date	Month: -- ∨ Day: -- ∨ Year: -- ∨
	Leave day as --, if day on credit/debit card is not listed
Your name on card	

Please enter your billing address as it appears on your credit card bill statement:

Billing address	
City	
State/province	
Zip/postal code	
Country	United States ∨

☐ **I would like to use this credit card to pay seller fees.**
If approved, eBay will bill your credit/debit card each month for your previous month's fees. For more payment options, visit Payment Terms section.

Submit

Well, not quite. Before you can achieve high-volume seller status, you first have to establish your reputation with other eBay users. As you learned in Chapter 2, "Using eBay's Advanced Features," your reputation is tracked via eBay's feedback feature. The better your feedback (the higher the feedback number), the most trustworthy you are. Potential buyers are less likely to deal with you if you have a zero or low feedback number, so you have to do a little groundwork to establish positive feedback before you enter the big leagues.

The easiest way to establish positive feedback is not as a seller, but as a buyer. That's right, before you start selling, you need to go online and buy some stuff.

Here's what you need to do. You need to identify a handful of auctions that meet the following criteria:

■ Feature merchandise that you actually want to buy

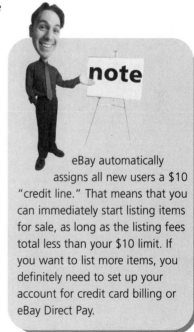

note

eBay automatically assigns all new users a $10 "credit line." That means that you can immediately start listing items for sale, as long as the listing fees total less than your $10 limit. If you want to list more items, you definitely need to set up your account for credit card billing or eBay Direct Pay.

■ Incorporate the Buy It Now feature

■ Have relatively low prices

That's right—you want to find auctions that are quick and fast. By using Buy It Now, you can end the auction immediately; you don't have to wait a week for the auction to close, or risk being outbid. Most sellers will leave positive feedback for you soon after you pay, so if you play your cards right you'll have a positive feedback number within a day or two. Repeat this procedure until you build your feedback to 10 points or more, and then you'll look like a trustworthy user—and be ready to start selling for real.

tip

Know that not all sellers leave feedback, and those that do don't always do so immediately—so you may need to buy 10 items to get 5 positive feedbacks.
Alternatively, you can email the seller and ask them to provide feedback ASAP, so you can get your feedback rating up faster.

THE ABSOLUTE MINIMUM

When you're ready to sign up for an eBay account, keep these points in mind:

■ All users have to have an eBay membership before they can buy or sell on eBay.

■ eBay membership is free—but you have to arrange for credit card payment or automatic checking account withdrawal to pay your seller fees.

■ Before other users will trust you, you need to establish a positive feedback rating—which you can do by some targeted eBay purchases.

PART III

Managing Your Day-to-Day Business

11

CREATING ITEM LISTINGS

You've made your plans and have your merchandise ready to sell. Now it's time to get your auctions started—which is what this section of the book is all about.

The next few chapters deal with all the ins and outs of day-to-day eBay selling. Of course, the whole process starts with listing an item for sale, which is the topic of this particular chapter.

Creating an auction item is a relatively straightforward process, as you'll see. That doesn't mean, however, that there aren't subtleties that you can take advantage of to increase your chances of having a successful auction. So it's worth your while to not only learn the mechanics of creating item listings, but also discover the ins and outs of creating *great* listings—and lots of them.

So if you've never sold anything on eBay before—or even if you have—this is the chapter for you!

Before You List

Remember that before you can list an item for sale, you have to be a registered eBay user. So if you haven't registered yet, turn back to Chapter 10, "Step Eight: Establish Your eBay Presence," and follow the instructions there.

Even after you've registered, there's a bunch of other stuff you need to do before you actually create your item listing. We'll cover them all over the course of the chapter, but for now you can see what's ahead by taking a look at the following checklist.

Before You List Checklist

- ☐ Make sure the item exists and is ready for sale. (The exception is if you're arranging drop-shipping for this item, as described in Chapter 8, "Step Six: Find and Manage Your Inventory.")

- ☐ Take a picture or a scan of the item and prepare a JPG-format file for uploading. (See Chapter 19, "Working with Photographs," to learn more.)

- ☐ Determine what you think the final selling price will be, and then choose an appropriate minimum bid price.

- ☐ Determine what listing options you might want to purchase—such as boldfacing the title or placing the item in the Gallery.

- ☐ Think up a catchy yet descriptive headline for the item.

- ☐ Write out a detailed description of the item.

- ☐ Determine what payment options you'll accept. (If you haven't yet signed up with PayPal, now is the time.)

- ☐ Determine how you want to ship the item.

- ☐ Weigh the item, and then try to determine the actual shipping costs. Use that information to set an upfront shipping/handling charge, if you want.

- ☐ If you haven't yet registered as an eBay user and entered your credit card information, do that now.

- ☐ Determine what day of the week—and what time of the day—you want your auction to end. (If you're not sure about this, check out the tips in Chapter 18, "Making Your Auctions More Effective.")

- ☐ Determine whether you want to use eBay's Checkout feature—and if so, change your selling preferences to activate Checkout. (See the following section for details.)

We'll cover the most important of these little pre-listing details next. But if you want a more detailed introduction to eBay selling, I suggest you pick up a copy of my companion book, *Absolute Beginner's Guide to eBay*—it goes over this entire process in much more depth.

Understanding eBay's Fees

If you're going to be a successful seller, you'd better get used to paying eBay. That's because they get their cut every time you list or sell an item. *Every time*. It may be a few pennies here and a few pennies there, but eBay's fees add up quite rapidly—and become a significant expense if you're selling a lot of items each month.

For that reason, you need to understand the costs involved before you put any items up for auction. eBay charges two main types of fees to sellers:

- **Insertion fees** (I prefer to call them *listing* fees). These are what you pay every time you list an item for sale on eBay. These fees are based on the minimum bid or reserve price of the item listed. These fees are nonrefundable.
- **Final value fees** (I prefer to call them *selling* fees, or *commissions*). These are what you pay when an item is actually sold to a buyer. These fees are based on the item's final selling price (the highest bid). If your item doesn't sell, you aren't charged a final value fee.

eBay also charges a variety of fees for different types of listing enhancements, such as bold and highlight. You can view all of eBay's fees at `pages.ebay.com/help/sell/ fees.html`.

As you might expect, there's all manner of fine print associated with these fees. The most important to keep in mind are the following:

- Insertion fees are nonrefundable.
- You will not be charged a final value fee if there were no bids on your item or (in a reserve price auction) if there were no bids that met the reserve price— in other words, if your item didn't sell, you don't pay a final value fee.
- It doesn't matter whether the buyer actually pays you; you still owe eBay the full final value fee, even if you get stiffed.

Invoicing on your account occurs once a month, for the previous month's activity. You'll get an invoice via email detailing your charges for the month; if you've set up your account for automatic credit card billing or checking account withdrawal, your account will be charged at that time. (If you prefer to pay via check, now's the time to get out the old checkbook.)

Creating a Basic Auction Listing

Assuming you've worked through the Before You List Checklist, you're ready to take the next step—creating an item listing. There are a number of ways to create an item listing, the easiest of which is to use eBay's standard Sell Your Item pages. If you've ever sold anything before, this is probably how you did it.

You typically use the Sell Your Item pages to create basic one-off item listings—which is fine if you only have a few items to sell. If you have a *lot* of items for sale, however, you need to think about bulk listing your auctions; we'll cover that in the "Listing in Bulk" section, later in this chapter.

By the way, if you're already familiar with eBay's basic listing process, feel free to skip this section. But if this is truly your first time around, read on to learn how to do what you need to do to create basic one-off listings—step by step.

Step 1: Get Ready to Sell

This is the easiest thing you'll do in the whole process. All you have to do is click the Sell button in the eBay Navigation Bar.

Step 2: Choose the Type of Auction

eBay now displays the Choose Selling Format page. You can choose from three different types of selling formats:

- **Sell Item at Online Auction**. This is the option you want for a traditional eBay auction. (You also choose this option if you want to run a reserve or Dutch auction, or utilize the Buy It Now option.)

- **Sell at a Fixed Price.** This option isn't for auctions, but rather for strictly fixed-price sales. (If you want to run a regular auction with the Buy It Now option, choose the Sell Item at Online Auction option, instead.)

- **Advertise Your Real Estate**. Select this option if you want to create a real estate listing.

Assuming you want to create a normal auction listing, choose the Sell Item at Online Auction option, then click Continue.

Step 3: Choose Your Category

If this is your first time selling, you'll see a Select Category page that asks you to select a top-level category for your item. Select a category and you're shown a more detailed Select Category page, as shown in Figure 11.1, where you can drill down and choose the specific subcategory for your item. (If you're a seasoned seller, you go directly to the second Select Category page.)

Start by selecting a major category in the 1) list; when you select a category, eBay displays available subcategories in the 2) list. Select a subcategory and eBay displays more subcategories (if available) in the 3) list, and so forth. Make your selections in each list, then click Continue.

FIGURE 11.1

Select the category—subcategories—for your item.

If you're not sure what category is best for your particular item, take advantage of eBay's Find Suggested Categories feature. Click this link and you can look up what category other sellers have used for similar items. It's a great way to find the right category without doing a lot of reinventing the wheel on your end.

If you want to list your item in more than one category, scroll down to the Choose a Second Category section and repeat this whole procedure. Remember that you'll pay a double listing fee to list in two different categories—although you'll still pay a single final value fee when the item sells. (Since you can't sell the item twice, eBay can't charge you twice!)

tip

If you know the specific number for a category, you can enter it in the Main Category # box instead of making selections in the lists. You can also choose a category you've previously used by making a selection from the Previously Used Categories list.

Step 4: Describe Your Item

When the Describe Your Item page appears, as shown in Figure 11.2, it's time to draw on all your writing skills and get ready to create some sell-oriented copy. You start with the item's title, which you enter into the Item Title box. (The title must be 45 characters or less.) You can then enter a description—of any length—into the Item Description box.

note

Not sure what to write? Then turn to Chapter 18, "Making Your Auctions More Effective," to learn how to write more powerful item titles and descriptions.

Your item title can only contain plain text, although your item description can include HTML code. You'll learn more about HTML in Chapter 18, but for now know that this is how you add fancy text effects and colors to your listing. You can either add HTML codes manually, or click the HTML Text Editor link to display eBay's easy-to-use HTML editor, which works a little like the WYSIWYG text formatting buttons in a word processor.

FIGURE 11.2

Provide a description for your item.

Sell Your Item: Describe Your Item				
1 Category	② Title & Description	3 Pictures & Details	4 Payment & Shipping	5 Review & Submit

Item title ✱
Enter title here
No HTML, asterisks, or quotes. 45 characters maximum.

✱ = Required

Learn how to write a good item title.

Item description

◆ **Need help formatting your description?**
◆◆ Use our new html text editor for free.

Description ✱   Enter either plain text or HTML.
Enter your description here.

Enter plain text or add simple HTML tags to change font size, create paragraphs or bulleted lists, add images, and more.

HTML Tip:
Enter <p> to start a new paragraph.

Pictures and themes may be added to your listing on the next page.

Click Continue to proceed.

Step 5: Fill in the Details

When the Provide Pictures & Item Details page appears, shown in Figure 11.3, you have a lot of entering to do. This is the page that determines all the mechanical details of your auction, as well as which listing enhancements you want to pay for. You'll need to provide the following information:

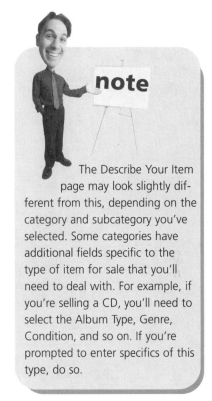

- Duration
- Start Time
- Quantity
- Starting Price
- Reserve Price
- Buy It Now Price
- Private Auction
- City, State
- Region
- Country
- Add Pictures
- Listing Designer
- Gallery Picture
- Listing Upgrades
- Gift Services
- Free Page Counter

note

The Describe Your Item page may look slightly different from this, depending on the category and subcategory you've selected. Some categories have additional fields specific to the type of item for sale that you'll need to deal with. For example, if you're selling a CD, you'll need to select the Album Type, Genre, Condition, and so on. If you're prompted to enter specifics of this type, do so.

Click Continue when you're done making your selections.

Step 6: Enter Payment and Shipping Info

When the Enter Payment & Shipping Page appears, as shown in Figure 11.4, you have to select how you want to get paid. This should be fairly cut and dried, assuming that you've already determined which payment methods you'll accept. You can opt for payment by PayPal, Money Order or Cashiers Check, Personal Check, COD, or Other Online Payment Services. You can also leave all the other options unchecked and select See Item Description instead; if you choose this option, make sure you describe your payment options in the description section of your item listing.

FIGURE 11.3

Select all man-
ner of listing
options.

Sell Your Item: Provide Pictures & Item Details

1 Category	2 Title & Description	③ Pictures & Details	4 Payment & Shipping	5 Review & Submit

Title	Enter title here		★ = Required

Pricing and duration

Duration ★	7 days	
	Note: Some durations have additional fees.	

Start time	⦿ Start listing when submitted (Free)	Learn more about scheduled
	○ Schedule to start on:	listings and eBay Time.
$0.10 fee applies for scheduled listings	Date Time ▾ PDT	

Quantity ★	1	Learn more about Multiple Item Auctions (Dutch Auctions)

Starting price ★	$	Learn more about starting price.

Reserve price (optional) Variable fee applies	$	A reserve price is the lowest price you're willing to sell the item for. Learn more.
	Note: You can't use Reserve Price if you sell a quantity greater than 1.	

Buy It Now price (optional) $0.05 fee applies	$	Sell to the first buyer who meets your specified price. Learn more.
	Note: You can't use Buy It Now if you sell a quantity greater than 1.	

☐ Private Auction		When to use Private Auctions.
Keeps bidders' User IDs from being displayed to others.		

Item Location		Minimize ☒

City, State ★	Carmel, IN	
Region ★	IN-Indianapolis ▾	Increase your exposure for free by listing locally. Learn more.
Country ★	United States [edit]	

By the way, you can choose to accept payment via PayPal even if you don't currently have a PayPal account. Just enter your email address in the Payment Will Go
To box, and PayPal will contact you if the buyer chooses to pay via PayPal. At that
point PayPal will walk you through creating a PayPal Premier account, so you can
receive your funds.

If you already have a PayPal account, enter the email address you use for that
account into the Payment Will Go To box. (PayPal
identifies members by their email addresses.) With
this information entered, eBay can route any
credit card payments to the correct PayPal
account—*yours*.

Next up on the page is the Shipping Costs section. Start by selecting who will pay shipping
costs—which should be the Buyer.

Next up are the shipping costs themselves. If
you plan to charge a flat shipping rate (and
know what it is), click Flat Shipping Rates and
then enter the numbers for Shipping &
Handling, Shipping Insurance (if you offer it),
and Sales Tax (if you charge it).

Learn more about
PayPal and other payment
methods in Chapter 13, "Managing Customer Payments."

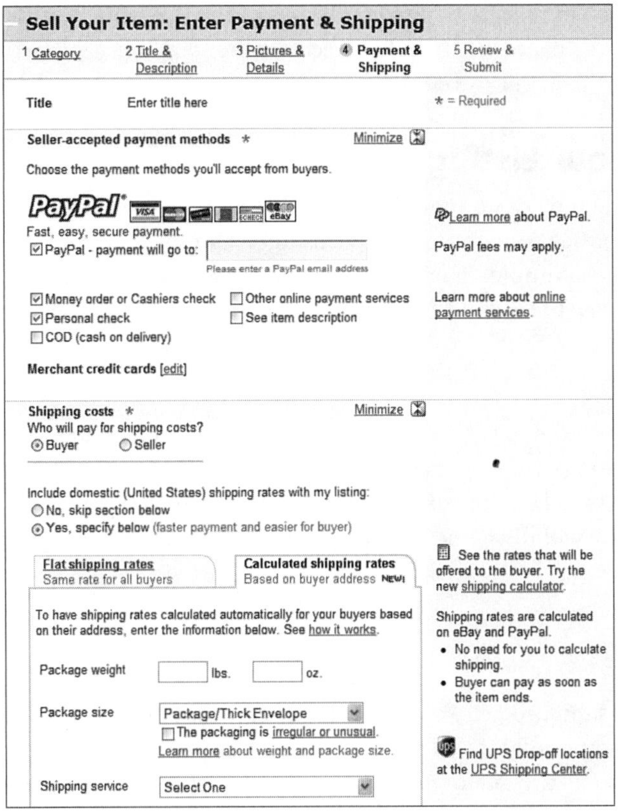

FIGURE 11.4

Choose your
payment and
shipping
options.

If your shipping costs depend on where the buyer lives, you can use eBay's Shipping Calculator in your listing. Just click Calculated Shipping Rates and then enter the package weight and size, what shipping service you plan to use, and your ZIP code. Also add any handling fee you want to charge over and above the actual shipping rate (a buck is good), and your buyers will be able to figure their own shipping charges right on the item listing page.

If you don't want to include any up-front shipping rates, select the No, Skip Section Below option.

Now you can enter any specific payment instructions into the Payment Instructions box. If your Checkout preferences did not include your payment address, you'll also see a Payment Address section; enter your address here. If your Checkout preferences *did* include your payment address, there won't be a Payment Address section on this page.

Next, you need to select whether you'll ship to the U.S. only, worldwide, or to the U.S. and specific countries. Finally, select whether you'll accept escrow payments for this item, and then click Continue.

Step 7: Preview Your Listing

The next page provides a preview of your listing page and the options you've selected. If you see something that needs to be changed, click the Edit link next to that item. (For example, to edit the title you'd click the Edit Title link.) If everything looks right, click the Submit Listing button.

You're Done!

When you're all done, eBay displays the Congratulations page. This page confirms your listing and presents you with important details about your auction—including your item listing's URL, in case you want to publicize your auction elsewhere on the Internet. (eBay will also send you a confirming email containing this same information.)

Listing in Bulk

Using eBay's standard Sell Your Item pages isn't that hard, really, but it is time-consuming—especially if you have a lot of items to list all at once. Going through that cumbersome procedure for a dozen or more items isn't very appealing; trust me.

A better solution for high-volume sellers is to use a bulk listing program or service. These tools let you create a large number of item listings in advance, and even reuse saved listings—great if you run multiple auctions for similar items. You then schedule your auctions to launch at the time of your choosing, and you're done with it.

There are a number of these bulk listing tools available; I'll discuss some of the most popular ones next. Which of these should you choose? That's entirely up to you, of course; they all offer many of the same functions. One of the big differences is price; they range in cost from free (eBay Turbo Lister) to 25 cents or more per listing—and some even charge a final value fee on top of that! Fortunately, most of these services provide free trials, so you can try them out before you commit.

note

Most of these bulk listing programs/services also enable you to create sophisticated HTML-enabled listings—which you'll learn more about in Chapter 18.

Pick the tool that works best for you, with a cost you can live with. Remember—all these individual fees can really take a cut out of your profits, so make sure you factor the costs into your overall financial plan.

eBay Turbo Lister

eBay offers its own bulk listing software, called eBay Turbo Lister. To download the Turbo Lister software, go to pages.ebay.com/turbo_lister/. The program is free, and there are no monthly subscription fees—which makes it the program of choice for cost-conscious sellers.

note

For years, eBay offered the Mister Lister bulk listing software. Turbo Lister is the replacement for Mister Lister, with many new features.

Turbo Lister lets you create your item listings offline, at your leisure. (It also offers HTML-based templates you can use to spruce up your item listings—although these are pretty much the same templates found in the Listing Designer section of the Sell Your Item page.) Then, when you're ready, it uploads all your listings at once, with the click of a button. Creating multiple auctions couldn't be easier.

Creating a Listing

The Turbo Lister software is quite easy to use. It uses a series of forms to request information about your listings, as well as a WYSIWYG editor for creating great-looking listings. Here's how it works:

1. From the main Turbo Lister screen, click the Create Item button.

2. When the Create a New Item screen appears, select the country you're selling in and your preferred auction format. Click Next to proceed.

3. When the next screen appears, enter your item title and select a category. Click Next to proceed.

4. When the Design Your Listing screen appears, as shown in Figure 11.5, select a visual theme; select a layout; enter your description text; and upload your listing photo(s). You can do all this from either the Design View or HTML View tabs; select the Preview Tab to see how your listing will look. Click Next to proceed.

5. When the Format Specifics screen appears, as shown in Figure 11.6, enter the remaining details of your item listings.

FIGURE 11.5

Use Turbo Lister's Design View to design great-looking item listings.

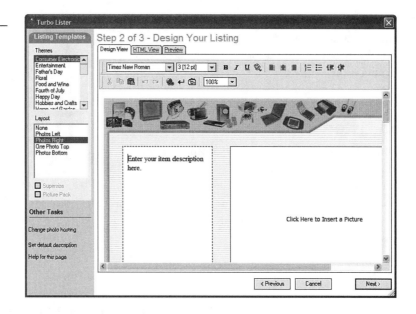

FIGURE 11.6

Enter listing details on the Format Specifics page.

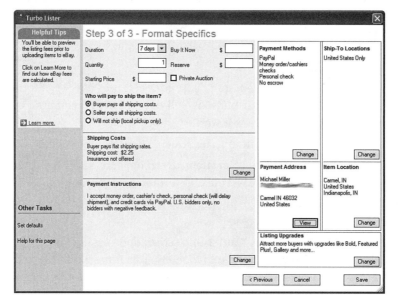

6. Click the Save button to save this listing.

This item is now added to your item inventory. You use this inventory to upload individual listings to eBay.

Uploading Your Listings

To view the items you've added to your inventory, click the Item Inventory tab. This screen lists all the items you've created; from here you can edit, delete, or create duplicate items.

When you have an item that you want to list on eBay, select the item and click the Add to Upload button. You can see all the items in your upload queue by clicking the Listings Waiting to Upload tab. This page shows all items waiting to be uploaded. While they're waiting, you can calculate listing fees and change the start time for any specific auction.

Uploading your pending auctions is as easy as clicking the Upload All to eBay button. Listings set to start immediately do so, and items with a future start time are sent to eBay's Pending Listings section. These auctions will go live at the time(s) you previously scheduled.

Ándale Lister

If you've read this far in this book you already know that I'm a fan of Ándale's auction-management tools. Ándale Lister is the company's primary bulk-listing tool, and I like it.

Ándale Lister lets you create good looking listings, using a variety of professionally created ad templates. You create your ads in bulk, then upload them according to your designated timetable. (You can even program a series of listings to launch on a regularly occurring schedule—or until your inventory runs out.)

Like most of the other third-party bulk listing tools (but unlike eBay Turbo Lister), Ándale Lister isn't free. Table 11.1 details Ándale's rather complex fee schedule for this service:

Table 11.1   Ándale Lister Fees

Monthly Fee	Listings Included	Each Additional Listing
$2.00	10	$0.20
$7.50	40	$0.18
$16.95	110	$0.15
$33.95	275	$0.12
$56.95	550	$0.10
$89.95	1,100	$0.08
$149.95	2,750	$0.05
$224.95	5,600	$0.04

When it comes to creating your auction listings, Ándale gives you a choice. You can create your listings online, using their One-Step Lister, or offline, using their Ándale Lister Pro software. The software is free (although Ándale still charges their fees for all listings you upload) and provides the option of creating all your ads offline, at your leisure.

We'll look at how to use the Lister Pro software, as it's the best way to bulk list large numbers of items; the Web-based One-Step Lister operates similarly.

Creating a Listing

Before you can create a listing, you first have to create a "market profile" and a "checkout profile," which tell Ándale what key details to insert into your item listings. You do this by selecting Tools, Manage Profiles, and then selecting the profile you want to edit.

Now you have to enter an item into inventory and create your item listing. You do this by following these steps:

1. Click the New button on the toolbar.

2. When the Inventory Item dialog box appears, select the Item Information tab (shown in Figure 11.7) and enter the following details about your item:

   - SKU (a unique item number)
   - Ad Name
   - Quantity in Stock
   - Cost Price
   - Market (select eBay)
   - Auction Type (select Auction)
   - On Market Title (listing title)
   - Category1 and Category2 (optional)
   - Quantity
   - Minimum Bid
   - Reserve Price (optional)
   - Duration
   - Buy It Now price (optional)
   - Market Profile (select from the list, or click Create New to create a new profile)

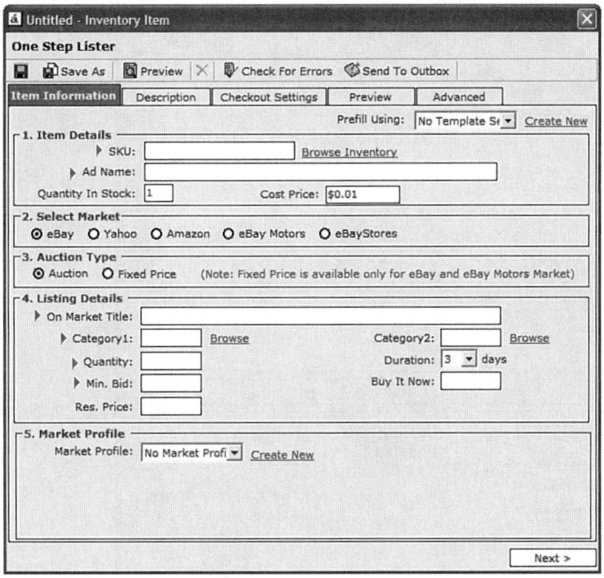

FIGURE 11.7

Entering a new item into inventory with Ándale Lister Pro.

3. Click Next to continue, or select the Description tab (shown in Figure 11.8), then enter the item description.

4. To add photographs to your listing, click the Add Images button and follow the onscreen instructions.

5. Select a layout and theme from the appropriate lists, then select what type of counter you want.

6. Click Next to continue, or select the Checkout Settings tab, then select a Checkout Profile, choose a Checkout Notification method, select whether to display a Checkout Link in your listing, and then enter the item's shipping weight and packing information.

7. Click Next or select the Preview tab to view a preview of your item listing, or select the Advanced tab to enter further details about the item and its condition.

8. When you're finished entering information, click the Save As button, enter a name for this listing, then click OK.

FIGURE 11.8

Entering listing
information into
Ándale Lister
Pro.

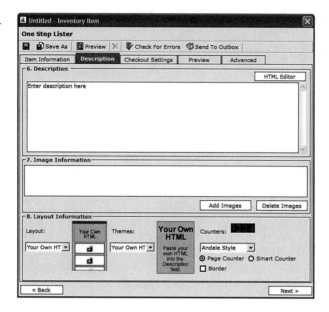

Uploading Your Listings

Your listing now appears in the inventory list in the main Lister Pro window. To
launch some or all of these items as eBay auctions, you have to upload the listings
to eBay, as follows:

1. Select the listings you want to launch. (Hold down the Ctrl key to select multiple listings.)

2. Click the Send to Outbox button. When the next dialog box appears, select
   Selected Items and click OK.

3. When the Schedule Options dialog box appears, select whether you want to
   launch the auctions immediately or on a delayed launch, then click Send to
   Outbox. (If you select Delayed Launch, you'll be prompted as to when you
   want the auctions to start.)

4. Your auctions are now ready to be uploaded to eBay. Click the Send/Receive
   button to connect to the Internet and upload the listings.

Your auctions will now upload to eBay, and start in the manner you selected.

Auctiva Mr. Poster

Auctiva Mr. Poster (www.auctiva.com) enables you to create standard eBay listings (no
fancy templates, sorry) offline, and then upload them in bulk at your convenience.

Unlike some other third-party bulk listers, Mr. Poster is free—although you do have to be an Auctiva member to use it. (Membership is also free.)

Creating a Listing

Since Mr. Poster doesn't have a lot of fancy features, it's probably one of the easiest bulk listing programs to use. You create what Mr. Poster calls a *batch* to hold the listings you want to upload, and then add individual listings to the batch. Then you can upload the entire batch of listings all at once.

note

If you're more interested in fancy-looking listings, check out Auctiva's other listing program, Auctiva Lister, which is available by subscription for $9.95 per month.

To create a new batch and individual item listings, follow these steps:

1. Select File, New Batch to open a new batch window.

2. Click the Add Item button to display the Edit Item form, shown in Figure 11.9.

3. Enter all the information about your new item—title, description, category, price, and so on. Click Preview to view your listing, and Finish when you're done.

FIGURE 11.9

Creating a new item listing with Auctiva Mr. Poster.

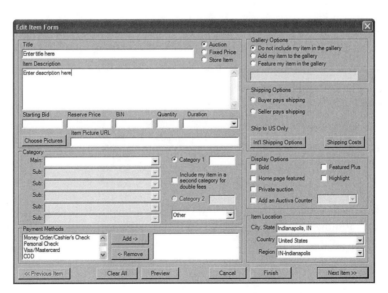

Uploading Your Listings

All your newly created listings are displayed in the current batch window. To upload this batch of listings to eBay, follow these steps:

1. Click the Schedule Batch button. (If you're prompted to save the batch, do so now.)

2. When the Schedule Batch dialog box appears, choose to either post the entire batch now or schedule when the batch should be posted. Click Submit to proceed.

Mr. Poster now uploads the batch of listings and launches the auctions according to your instructions.

Vendio Sales Manager

Vendio Sales Manager (www.vendio.com) is the number-two third-party auction creation service, after Ándale, with more than 100,000 current users. Vendio offers a variety of auction management tools on its site; Sales Manager lets you create sophisticated eBay listings in advance and then upload them in bulk.

Vendio's pricing is a combination of monthly fee, per-item listing fee, and per-item final value fee. It's all a little complicated, especially when you consider that they have both variable rate and flat rate plans. Table 11.2 details Vendio's pricing.

Table 11.2   Vendio Sales Manager Fees

Plan	Monthly Fee	Listing Fee	Final Value Fee
Standard Plan	none	$0.10/$0.05	1%
Variable Rate Premium Plan	$12.95	$0.05	1%
Variable Rate Power Plan	$29.95	none	1.25%
Flat Rate Premium Plan	$12.95	$0.20	none
Flat Rate Power Plan	$39.95	$0.10	none
Listing-Only (Annual)	$250 (yearly)	$0.06	none

These plans (except for the Listing-Only Plan, of course) include all of Vendio's auction management services, of which the bulk lister is only part. And about that listing fee on the Standard Plan—it's 10 cents per item for the first 50 listings each month, and 5 cents per listing thereafter.

Creating a Listing

Like Ándale, Vendio Sales Manager comes in both online and offline versions. The software version is called Sales Manager Pro, and we'll use it for our examples.

Like Auctiva Mr. Poster, Sales Manager Pro works with batches of listings. Follow these steps to create a new batch and new listings:

1. Select File, New Batch, to open a new batch window.

2. Click the New Listing button to display the Select Site for Listing dialog box.

3. Select eBay from the Choose Site list, select Auction from the Select Listing Type list, and then click OK.

4. When the New Batch Listing dialog box appears, select the Basic Information tab (shown in Figure 11.10) and enter the key information about the item.

5. Select the eBay Site Information tab and enter additional information about this item listing. This is also where you choose the look for your listing, by making a selection from the Template list.

> **" Mike Sez "**
>
> Don't ask me which of these plans is the best deal. It all depends on how many listings you intend to make each month and how you like to be charged. My advice is to start with the Standard Plan to see if you like the service, then upgrade to one of the other plans as appropriate.

FIGURE 11.10

Entering information about a new item listing in Vendio Sales Manager Pro.

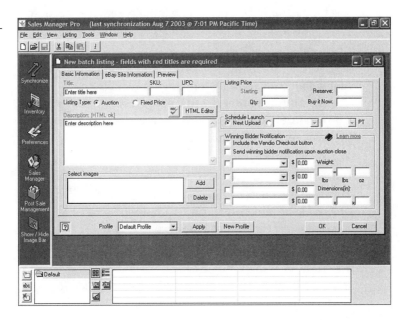

6. Select the Preview tab to see how your listing will look, then click OK.

Uploading Your Listings

Your new listing is now added to the batch. Uploading the listings is as simple as clicking the Upload button.

Other Bulk Listing Options

I've covered the major bulk listing programs and services—but there are more. For your complete edification, here's a list of the other bulk listing options available to you:

- **Auction Hawk** (www.auctionhawk.com). A Web-based listing creator that is part of a larger package of auction management tools. Pricing starts at $12.99 per month.

- **AuctionSubmit** (www.auctionsubmit.com). A freeware bulk lister, without a lot of fancy features.

- **Auction Wizard 2000** (www.auctionwizard2000.com). A software program that includes an image editor, listing creator, report generator, FTP manager, and auction database. Price is $75 for the first year, and $50 per year afterward.

- **Auctionworks ClickLaunch Quick Lister**(www.auctionworks.com). One of several auction tools offered in a bundle. Fees run 2% of the final selling price, with a $0.10 minimum and a $3.00 maximum

- **ChannelAdvisor Pro** (www.channeladvisor.com). A collection of auction listing and management tools, targeted at super-high-volume sellers. (The company also offers **ChannelAdvisor Merchant** and **ChannelAdvisor Enterprise**, for even higher-volume online merchants.) Cost is $29.95 per month.

- **CollectorOnline** (www.collectoronline.com). This Web site offers listing creation and bulk uploading as part of their auction management services, targeted at serious collectors. Pricing starts at $19.95 per month.

- **eBay Seller's Assistant Pro** (pages.ebay.com/sellers_assistant/). A software program offered directly from eBay, although it's being phased out in favor of eBay Turbo Lister. (eBay also offers **eBay**

note

Learn more about the complete range of auction management services offered by these companies in Chapter 20, "Using Professional Auction Tools."

Seller's Assistant Basic, a listing creation program without bulk listing features.) The subscription fee is $15.99 per month.

■ **eLister** (www.blackmagik.com). A Macintosh-only listing creation program. Subscription fee is $9.95 per month.

THE ABSOLUTE MINIMUM

When it comes time to list your items for auction, keep these points in mind:

■ Before you list an item for auction, make sure you're a registered eBay user and that you understand eBay's listing and selling fees.

■ When you're listing a small number of items, use eBay's Sell Your Item page.

■ When you're listing a large number of items—or want to create professional-looking listings—use a bulk listing tool, such as eBay Turbo Lister, Ándale Lister, Auctiva Poster, or Vendio Sales Manager.

MANAGING YOUR AUCTIONS

You might think the hard work would be over once you've listed an item for sale—but you'd be wrong. There's plenty of work to do over the course of an eBay auction, and even more after the auction ends. Not only do you have to keep track of the current bids, but you might also have to answer questions from bidders, update your item listing, cancel bids from questionable bidders, and—on rare occasions—cancel the entire auction. Then, when the auction is over, you need to contact the winning bidder, handle payment, pack and ship the item, leave feedback for the buyer, and add all the auction details to your ongoing records.

That's a lot of work!

You can do all this manually (for free) or enlist the service of an auction management tool (for a fee). Read on to learn more.

Managing Your Auctions Manually

If you only run a few auctions at a time, there's no reason why you can't handle all your auction management manually. It's certainly a lower-cost approach than employing a professional auction management tool, as you'll learn in the "Using Auction Management Tools" section, later in this chapter. Besides, there are a handful of activities that you *have* to do manually—so you might as well learn about them now.

During the Auction

Your chores during the course of an auction chiefly relate to making sure that everything runs smoothly. It's also nice to know how things are going—which auctions are getting a lot of bids, and which aren't. Let's look at what tasks you'll need to deal with.

Monitoring Your Auctions

If you're a high-volume seller, you need some way to consolidate all the information from all your auctions-in-process—the number of bidders, the high bids, and the time left until the auction ends.

One of the most convenient ways to keep track of your in-process auctions is to let eBay do it for you. You can configure eBay to send you an email message every morning, containing key information about all your open auctions—as well as all the auctions in which you're currently bidding. This way you can keep track of your auctions (once a day, anyway) just by reading your email.

You configure eBay to send email messages from your My eBay page. Select the Preferences tab, then click Change My Notification Preferences to select which emails you want to receive.

Another, more timely way to track your auctions is with your My eBay page. When you use My eBay in this fashion, you see the up-to-the-minute status of all your auction activity—at any time of the day.

To use My eBay to track your auctions, select the Selling tab, and scroll down to the Items I'm Selling section. As you can see in Figure 12.1, this displays the item number, title, current price, number of bids, and time left for each of your open auctions. By default, this page sorts your auctions by the time left, with the items ending first shown first in the list. You can change the sort order by clicking any item heading; for example, if you want to sort by current high bid, click the Current Price heading.

FIGURE 12.1

Use My eBay to
keep track of
your current
auctions.

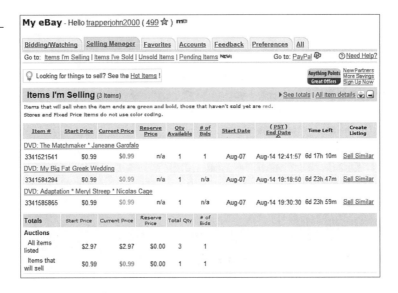

If what you're interested in is how many people are visiting your auctions (which is
different from how many have placed bids), you can do this by placing counters in
all your auction listings. The easiest way to do this is when you first create your auction listing, by checking one of the counter options on the Sell Your Item page. (The
counters are provided, for free, by Ándale.) Once you've added a counter to your listing, you can view the number of hits just by visiting the item listing page. Or you
can view the hits for all your current auctions by going directly to the Ándale site
(www.andale.com).

Updating Your Auction Listing

Sometimes, in the course of an auction, there's a
need to change the contents of a listing. Maybe you
want to include additional information about the
item you're selling. Maybe a bidder has asked a
question and you feel that question (and your
answer) should be included in the listing. Maybe
you flat out made a mistake in your original listing
and need to make a correction.

Fortunately, eBay lets you edit the title, description,
and pictures for any item listing—as long as no
one has yet placed a bid. All you have to do is go
to the item listing page and click the Revise Item
link (located in the Seller Services section). Follow

note

If you've subscribed to
eBay Selling Manager
(described later in this chapter),
My eBay's Selling tab is transformed into a Selling Manager tab.

the onscreen instructions to access the listing editing screen and make the appropriate changes.

What do you do if you need to update your listing and you've already received a bid or two on the item? In this instance, the Revise Item link doesn't appear, so you have to append new information to the end of your current listing. The original listing will display unchanged, but the new information you add will appear underneath the main item description.

To append information in this fashion, you have to go to eBay's Site Map page and click the Add to My Item Description link. When the next page appears, enter the item number of the auction you want to update and click Revise Item. When the Add to Description page appears, enter the text you want to add, then click the Save Changes button.

Deleting Unwelcome Bidders

What do you do if a known deadbeat bidder makes a bid in one of your auctions? You certainly don't want the deadbeat to actually win the auction, since it's likely that he'll end up not paying. (That's why he's a deadbeat!) The best thing to do is dump that bidder immediately, which you can do by canceling that user's bid—and blocking that user from ever bidding in one of your auctions again.

You start by canceling the bid in question. Go to the Site Map page and click the Cancel Bids on My Item link. When the Bid Cancellation page appears, enter the auction number and the ID of the bidder you want to cancel. You should also enter a reason for canceling that bidder. (Saying "poor user feedback" is as good a reason as any.)

Now you want to block the bidder from any future auctions. Go to the Site Map page and click the Blocked Bidder/Buyer List link. When the Bidder/Buyer Management page appears, scroll to the Blocked Bidder/Buyer List section and click Continue. When the Blocked Bidder/Buyer List page appears, add the buyer's user name to the list; separate multiple names with commas. Click the Submit button when done.

Now you don't have to worry about that questionable bid, and the deadbeat bidder won't be able to bother you again.

Canceling an Auction

One last little bit of auction maintenance—what do you do if you need to cancel an auction completely? This happens more often than you'd think—most often when you run out of inventory before all your auctions end.

caution

Frequent early cancellations may cause eBay to cancel your membership.

Fortunately, eBay lets you cancel an in-progress auction, as long as you don't abuse the privilege. Start by going to the Site Map page and clicking the Cancel Bids on My Item link. When the Bid Cancellation page appears, cancel the first bid on your item. Then return to this page as many times as necessary to cancel all the outstanding bids.

After you've cancelled all the bids, go to the Site Map page and click the End My Listing Early link. When the Ending Auction page appears, enter the auction item number. Click the Continue button to proceed, and then click the End Auction button to officially cancel your auction.

> **"Mike Sez"**
>
> I find that it's good form to personally email the bidders in any auction I cancel. Explaining why you're canceling their bids and ending the auction isn't necessary, but it does help to soothe potentially hurt feelings and create always-welcome good will.

After the Auction

What happens after an auction ends is rather cut and dried. Put simply, you contact the winning bidder with a final price; he or she sends payment to you; you pocket the payment; you package and ship the item; the buyer receives the item; and you both leave feedback for each other.

In checklist form, here's what you have to look forward to:

Checklist—After the Auction

- ☐ Receive end-of-auction email from eBay
- ☐ Send email to the high bidder
- ☐ Receive payment from buyer—and wait for payment to clear, if necessary
- ☐ Package the item
- ☐ Ship the item to the high bidder
- ☐ Leave feedback for the buyer
- ☐ Close your books on this auction/item

We'll look at each of these steps in slightly more detail.

Communicating with the Winning Bidder

Minutes after the conclusion of your auction, eBay will notify you via email that your auction has ended. This email message will include the user ID and email address of the item's high bidder.

It is now your responsibility to contact that high bidder to arrange payment and shipping. (See Chapter 15, "Dealing with Customers," for more details.) You can do this manually (by sending an individual email message), or by using an automated end-of-auction tool, such as eBay Selling Manager (which I'll discuss later in this chapter). If you've activated eBay's Checkout feature, the winning bidder can access the Checkout page (from the original item listing page) and provide shipping and payment info there; otherwise, the buyer should respond to your email with this information.

If you haven't heard back from the buyer in a day or two, send another email. If, after three days, you still haven't been able to contact the buyer, you can consider that person a deadbeat bidder and take appropriate action (as detailed in Chapter 16, "Dealing with Problems").

Accepting Payment

Now it's time to get paid. I won't go into all the details here (read ahead to Chapter 13, "Managing Customer Payments," for more); suffice to say that you always wait until you're paid before you ship the sold item.

Many sellers notify the buyer (via email) when they receive payment. (This is also part of most automated end-of-auction tools).) I find this a nice touch; too much communication is better than too little.

Packing and Shipping

After you receive payment—and that payment has cleared—you can pack and ship the item to your seller. (See Chapter 14, "Managing Packing and Shipping," for more details.) Again, it's good form to send the buyer an email notifying him that you've shipped the product—and if you have a shipping confirmation number, include it in the email.

Leaving Feedback—and Closing Your Books

The very last thing you need to do, after you've shipped the item, is to leave feedback for the buyer. Many auction management tools automate this process; otherwise, you need to do it manually, as described in Chapter 2, "Using eBay's Advanced Features."

Once you've done all this, you can close the books on this particular auction. Make sure all the appropriate information is entered into your inventory and customer databases, then you can remove this auction from your current auction list and add it to your archives.

Using Auction Management Tools

If you're a high-volume seller, trying to manage each and every auction individually gets real tedious real fast. Many high-volume sellers choose to outsource their auction management to an outside service or utilize dedicated software programs to do the management for them. These programs and services not only track the progress of in-process auctions, but also manage all manner of post-auction activity.

We'll look at some of the top auction management tools next—including those "official" tools provided by eBay.

eBay Selling Manager

eBay Selling Manager (pages.ebay.com/selling_manager/) is eBay's official auction management tool. When you subscribe to Selling Manager, the Selling tab of your My eBay page is transformed into a Selling Manager tab, where you can manage all your auction and post-auction activity—including sending customer emails and leaving feedback. Cost is $4.99 per month.

As you can see in Figure 12.2, the main Selling Manager page provides an overview of your active and closed auctions. You can click on any link to see a finer cut of your activity—to view only your active listings, for example, or only those listings that are paid and ready to ship.

FIGURE 12.2

Managing your auction activity with eBay Selling Manager.

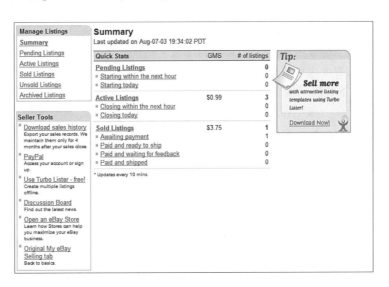

The most useful aspect of Selling Manager comes after the close of an auction. When you display any of the Sold Listings pages (such as the one shown in Figure 12.3), you see a list of closed auctions, with the customer status indicated by a series of icons. You can select an individual auction to mark it paid or shipped, or to send it to your personal archive. Click the Buyer Email link to send a series of post-auction email messages, or click the Record # link to view complete listing details—and enter buyer shipping information and print invoices and shipping labels.

FIGURE 12.3

Use the Sold Listings page to view and manage all post-auction activity.

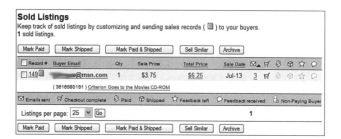

eBay Selling Manager Pro

Selling Manager isn't perfect. One of its biggest problems is that you pretty much have to manage one auction at a time—it lacks features that let you manage multiple auctions in bulk. If you're a high-volume seller, a better solution is eBay's higher-end Selling Manager Pro, which offers bulk management features. For $15.99 per month, Selling Manager Pro does everything the basic Selling Manager does, plus more:

- Sends email messages in bulk
- Leaves feedback in bulk
- Manages individual inventory items, and issues restock alerts
- Generates a monthly profit and loss report, including all eBay fees and cost of goods sold

Selling Manager Pro also incorporates all the bulk listing features of Turbo Lister. As you can see, this is a more complete auction management tool meant to compete directly with the offerings from Ándale, Vendio, and other third parties.

> **"Mike Sez"**
>
> I find eBay Selling Manager an extremely useful tool if I have a moderate number of auctions running simultaneously. Running just a few auctions makes Selling Manager cost-prohibitive on a per-auction basis—and if I'm managing several dozen auctions, I come to curse its lack of batch email features. Still, for many sellers, Selling Manager does a fine job—and is a lot better than trying to manage post-auction activity manually.

Ándale Checkout

Ándale Checkout (www.andale.com) provides a post-sale checkout option similar to eBay's Checkout feature, as well as automated post-auction tools similar to those of Selling Manager Pro. At the close of an auction, Ándale automatically sends the high bidder an email with a link to an Ándale Checkout page. (Buyers can also check out by responding to the end-of-auction email.) You can view the entire post-auction process for all your auctions from Ándale's sales console; you can also use this page to generate invoices and shipping labels.

The charge for Ándale Checkout depends on the number of customers who use the service. Table 12.1 details the various fee plans:

> **" Mike Sez "**
>
> While I like Selling Manager Pro, I do have an issue with its pricing. If you only run a dozen or so auctions a month, that $15.99 monthly fee equates to a dollar or so per auction. You have to be running a hundred or more auctions each month to make Selling Manager Pro a cost-effective auction management tool.

Table 12.1   Ándale Checkout Fees

Monthly Fee	Checkouts Included	Each Additional Checkout
$2.00	10	$0.20
$7.50	40	$0.18
$16.95	110	$0.15
$33.95	275	$0.12
$56.95	550	$0.10
$89.95	1,100	$0.08
$149.95	2,750	$0.05
$224.95	5,600	$0.04

The nice thing about Ándale Checkout is that its fees are scalable based on the number of auctions you run in a given month. If you only run a handful of auctions, you pay a low fee—twenty cents an auction, roughly. You're not forced into a high fixed monthly cost, which can translate into high per-auction costs. It's a good choice for low-volume sellers, or sellers whose volume varies from month to month.

Auctiva eBud

Auctiva eBud (www.auctiva.com) is an interesting auction management tool in that it tracks all your current and closed auctions in a separate software program that looks and works pretty much like an Excel spreadsheet. Each auction is displayed in a row in the spreadsheet; auction details are displayed in columns. You can use eBud not only to track your auctions, but also to send post-auction emails, print invoices and shipping labels, and generate various eBay sales reports. Auctiva charges $11.95 for eBud subscriptions.

Vendio Sales Manager

As you learned in Chapter 11, "Creating Item Listings," Vendio Sales Manager is a powerful set of listing creation and auction management tools. You can use Sales Manager not only to create new item listings, but also to manage all of your current and post-auction activity. Sales Manager will automatically generate end-of-auction emails, print invoices and packing slips, and upload customer feedback to eBay.

If you remember from Chapter 11, the fees for Vendio's services are unnecessarily (in my opinion) complex. The problem with this type of fee schedule is you're never really sure which is the lowest-cost plan. I suppose the Standard Plan makes sense if you're a low-volume seller, or one whose sales volume tends to vary from month to month. If you know you're going to achieve a high sales level, then one of the other plans might be in order—and if you're committed to a really high sales level, the Power plans might be cost-effective. But choosing which plan you'll need in advance is often difficult—especially if you're just starting out.

THE ABSOLUTE MINIMUM

Auction management entails a lot of different activities—keep these points in mind:

- eBay lets you make changes to an auction listing until the first bid is placed; after that, you can append additional text to your listing, if necessary.
- All sales activity can be monitored from your My eBay page—at no charge.
- eBay's Selling Manager tool provides more advanced auction management services, such as sending end-of-auction emails to buyers.
- Other popular auction management tools include Ándale Checkout, Auctiva eBud, and Vendio Sales Manager.

13

MANAGING CUSTOMER PAYMENTS

How do you like to get paid? That's an important question when it comes to eBay auctions, and you have a variety of options.

When you're selling on eBay, you can choose what types of payment you'll accept from your customers. This may seem like an easy decision, but each different type of payment needs to be handled differently on your end.

This chapter, then, evaluates the different types of payment available— so you can select the payment options that work best for your eBay business.

Evaluating Different Payment Options

As any experienced eBay seller will tell you, not all dollars are the same. A dollar paid by one method might actually cost you more (or be more risky) than a dollar by another method. And you definitely want to minimize your costs, especially when they're taken directly from what you're paid.

Fortunately, eBay doesn't force you to use any one payment method. For example, you can limit your payments to credit cards only; there's no law that says you have to accept cash or checks. So you can pick and choose which payment methods you'll accept—just as long as you specify this up front in your item listings.

Of course, the more payment options you offer, the more potential bidders you'll attract. Still, some methods are better than others for different types of sellers. What are the pros and cons of the various types of payment? Take a look at Table 13.1:

TABLE 13.1   Pros and Cons of Common Methods of Payment

Payment Method	Pros	Cons
Cash	Fast payment, no hassles	Unattractive to buyers
C.O.D.	Cash payment	High non-completion rate; lots of paperwork
Personal check	Convenient for buyers	Slow, have to wait to clear
Money order/ cashier's check	Fast payment, almost like cash	Hassle for buyers
Credit cards/ PayPal	Fast payment, buyers like it	Fees involved

Let's look at each of these payment methods separately.

Cash

As a seller, there's nothing better than opening up an envelope and finding a few crisp new bills inside. Unfortunately, sending cash through the mail is not one of the smartest things a buyer can do; cash is too easily ripped off, and virtually untraceable. You can ask for cash payment (not that you should, of course), but unless the selling price is extremely low (under $5), don't expect buyers to comply.

One other thing. Cash is hard to keep track of—even for extremely organized sellers. There's no paper trail, and it's tempting to take any cash you receive and just stuff it in your wallet. If you do receive a cash payment, try your best to treat it like a money order or cashier's check, at least in terms of how you track it.

The bottom line: If it's bad for your customers, it's bad for you too. You should probably discourage payment by cash.

C.O.D.

Cash on delivery (C.O.D.) sounds good on paper. You ship the item, with the stipulation that the deliveryman (or woman) collect payment when the item is delivered.

There are problems with this method, however. What happens if the buyer isn't home when the delivery is made? What if the buyer is at home, but doesn't have the cash? What if the buyer refuses to pay—and rejects the shipment? I've heard stories of up to 25% of all C.O.D. orders being refused, for one reason or another.

Even worse, C.O.D. service often comes with a high fee from the carrier—and it's a fee that you, the seller, have to pay. The additional fee alone rules out C.O.D. for many sellers.

Then there's the fact that you don't get your money until after the item is delivered. The delay in your getting your cash reduces the appeal considerably.

All things considered, it's easy to see why few eBay sellers offer C.O.D. payment. The problems with this payment method tend to outweigh the benefits, and I can't recommend it.

Personal Checks

One of the most common forms of payment is the personal check. Buyers like paying by check because it's convenient, and because checks can be tracked (or even cancelled) if problems arise with the seller.

As a seller, you should like personal checks a little less, because they're not instant money. When you deposit a check in your bank, you're not depositing cash. That $100 check doesn't turn into $100 cash until it tracks back through the financial system, from your bank back to the buyer's bank, and the funds are both verified and transferred. That can take some time, typically 10 business days or so.

Because buyers prefer paying by check, you should be prepared to handle this payment method. (You'd dramatically reduce the number of potential buyers if you refused to take payment by check.) When you receive a check, deposit it as soon as

"Mike Sez"

In all my auctions, I accept personal checks, money orders, cashier's checks, and credit cards (via PayPal). Note, however, that while I like the immediacy of credit card payment (some buyers pay just minutes after the auction ends), the fees charged dampen my enthusiasm somewhat. That said, PayPal accounts for the vast majority of my payments these days, so I just factor in those charges into my overall cost of doing business.

possible—but do *not* ship the merchandise. Wait until the check clears the bank (two weeks if you want to be safe—longer for checks on non-U.S. banks) before you ship the item. If, after that period of time, the check hasn't bounced, it's okay to proceed with shipment.

If you are on the bad end of a bounced check, all hope is not lost. The first thing to do is get in touch with your bank and ask them to resubmit the check in question. Maybe the buyer was just temporarily out of funds. Maybe the bank made a mistake. Whatever. In at least half the cases, bounced checks unbounce when they're resubmitted.

Whether or not you resubmit the check, you should definitely email the buyer and let him know what happened. At the very least, you'll want the buyer to reimburse you for any bad check

> **caution**
>
> If a check bounces, the depositor (you) will likely be assessed a fee from your bank. (Of course, the writer of the bad check will also have a fee to pay—but that's not your problem.) If the buyer who wrote the check offers to make good on the payment, make sure they reimburse you for your bad check fee, over and above the final auction price.

fees your bank charged you. The buyer might also be able to provide another form of payment to get things moving again. (Credit cards are nice—as are money orders.)

Money Orders and Cashier's Checks

Money orders and cashier's checks are, to sellers, almost as good as cash. You can cash a money order immediately, without waiting for funds to clear, and have cash in your hand. When you receive a money order or cashier's check, deposit it and then ship the auction item. There's no need to hold the item.

The only bad thing about money orders and cashier's checks is that you have to wait for them to arrive. Even if the buyer puts payment in the mail the very next day, you'll still wait anywhere from 3 to 5 days after the auction to receive payment. Still, there's not a lot to dislike about this method of payment—it's hard to get burned with either a money order or cashier's check.

There's also the (extremely slight) possibility that you can receive a bad cashier's check. To be precise, a cashier's check or money order isn't *exactly* the same as cash; your bank still needs to be reimbursed by the issuing institution, and if this doesn't happen, the cashier's check/money order will bounce. Be particularly careful of money orders or cashier's checks drawn on foreign banks, or issued by unfamiliar institutions. When in doubt, hold the merchandise and ask your bank to verify that the payment is good.

Credit Cards

Until very recently, if you wanted to accept credit card payment for your auction items, you had to be a big-time retailer, complete with merchant account and bank-supplied charge card terminal. This limited the number of sellers who could accept credit card payment, which probably cut down on potential bidders because many buyers like the convenience and relative safety of paying by credit card.

caution

There's a popular scam going around where a buyer will send you a money order or cashier's check for an amount larger than the purchase price, and ask you to send them funds for the difference. Don't fall for this—accept payment for the amount of the purchase, only!

Today, however, there are several options available that enable you to accept credit card payments for your auction items. First, there are several financial institutions that provide merchant credit card accounts for smaller retailers, as we'll discuss later in this chapter. Second, you have PayPal—an online payment service that lets any auction seller easily accept credit card payments, with little or no setup hassle. PayPal works by accepting credit card payments from your customers, and then sending you a check or depositing funds directly in your bank account for that amount—minus PayPal's fee, of course.

Any time you accept a credit card, with either a merchant account or PayPal, you are charged a fee—typically a couple of percentage points of however much the buyer pays. When you consider that you have to pay eBay's listing fee and final value fee, paying another few points for the convenience of accepting credit cards can really sock it to a small seller—or anyone selling a low-priced item. You should definitely research the payment service's fees before you sign up.

We'll look at credit cards in more detail in the "Accepting Credit Card Payments" section, later in this chapter.

Escrow Services

A final payment option, used primarily in higher-priced auctions, is the use of an escrow service. An escrow service is a company that acts as a neutral third party between you and the buyer, holding the buyer's money until the buyer receives the purchased merchandise. You get paid only when the buyer is satisfied, which is good protection for the buyer—but delays you receiving your money.

Here's how a typical escrow transaction works:

1. At the end of an auction, you and the buyer contact each other and agree to use an escrow service. The escrow service's fees can be split between the two parties, but are more typically paid by the buyer. Fees differ widely from service to service.

2. The buyer sends payment (by check, money order, cashier's check, or credit card) to the escrow service.

3. After the payment is approved, the escrow service notifies you and instructs you to ship the item.

4. The buyer receives the item, verifies its acceptability, and notifies the escrow service that all is hunky-dory.

5. The escrow service pays you.

> **"Mike Sez"**
>
> I admit to never using an escrow service, and not offering escrow in my auctions. It's just too much hassle—and totally unnecessary—in most auctions. (Escrow's value increases when you're dealing with extremely high-priced items.)

eBay recommends that customers use an escrow service when

- The transaction is over $500
- The seller doesn't accept credit card or PayPal payments

So, if you accept credit card payments (via PayPal or otherwise), you shouldn't have to bother with escrow. If you do find yourself in a situation that calls for an escrow service, eBay recommends Escrow.com (www.escrow.com), shown in Figure 13.1. If you choose to use another escrow company, make sure that it's bonded and legitimate; there are some phony escrow companies operating on the Internet that you need to watch out for.

FIGURE 13.1

Accepting escrow payments at Escrow.com.

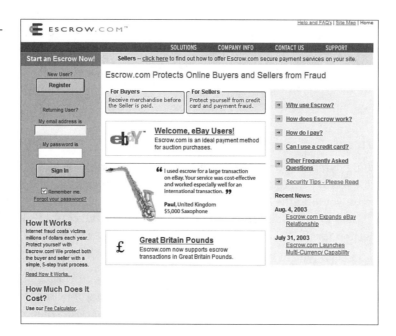

Accepting Credit Card Payments

As you might expect, there's no big preparation necessary to accept payment by cash, check, or money.
Accepting credit cards is another issue. Fortunately,
you have a couple of options available to you—the
most popular is using PayPal to handle all your
credit card transactions.

Setting Up a PayPal Account

PayPal (www.paypal.com), shown in Figure 13.2, serves
as the middleman for your credit card transactions.
The buyer pays PayPal via credit card, PayPal handles all the credit card paperwork, and then PayPal
sends a check to you (or deposits funds in your
checking account). PayPal service accepts payments
by American Express, Discover, MasterCard, and Visa—
and, although it's primarily a U.S.-based service, it also accepts payments to or from
37 other countries.

> **" Mike Sez "**
>
> What do you do
> when a nearby buyer
> wants to come by and pick up the
> item personally, rather than ship-
> ping via normal means? There's
> nothing wrong with this, as long
> as you get a verifiable payment.
> That means asking the buyer to
> bring cash, money order, or
> cashier's check—or to pay via
> PayPal before they arrive. Definitely
> do *not* let someone pick up an
> item and pay via personal check!

FIGURE 13.2

Use PayPal to
accept credit
card payments
from your cus-
tomers.

Signing Up for PayPal

Before you can use PayPal as a seller, you must sign up for PayPal membership. You do this by going to the PayPal Web site and clicking the Sign Up for Your Free PayPal Account link. This displays the Account Sign Up page, shown in Figure 13.3; fill in the blanks and follow the onscreen instructions to complete your registration.

You can choose from three different types of PayPal accounts:

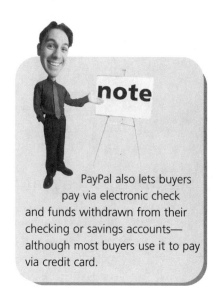

note

PayPal also lets buyers pay via electronic check and funds withdrawn from their checking or savings accounts—although most buyers use it to pay via credit card.

FIGURE 13.3

Signing up for your PayPal account.

Personal Account Sign Up - Just 1-Page!   Personal | **Business** | **Non-U.S. Sign Up**

Your Profile Information - Enter your name as it appears on your credit card or bank account.

First Name:
Last Name:
Address 1:
Address 2: (optional)
City:
State:
Zip: (5 or 9 digits)
Country: U.S.A.
Home Telephone:
Work Telephone: (optional)

Your Email Address and Password - Your email address will be used as your PayPal login. Your password must be at least **8 characters** and is case sensitive.

Email Address:
Re-enter Email Address:
Password:
Re-enter Password:

- A **Personal** account is great for eBay buyers, but not quite enough for sellers. While you can send money for free (to pay for auctions in which you're a buyer), as a seller you can only receive non-credit card payments. (For no charge, though.)

- A **Premier** account is a type of personal account that works better for small business sellers. With a Premier account, you can accept both credit card and non-credit card payments (for a fee). You sign up for Premier status by checking the appropriate option on the Personal Account Sign Up page.

■ A **Business** account is necessary if you're receiving a high volume of payments. With this type of account you can do business under a corporate or group name, and use multiple logins.

"Mike Sez "

I recommend you sign up initially for a Premier account. If your sales volume gets too high, PayPal will automatically switch you to a Business membership.

There is no charge for becoming a PayPal member—although there are fees for actually using the service.(The exception being the Personal account, which charges no fees for anything—but doesn't let you accept credit card payments.)

Paying for PayPal

Even though PayPal is owned by eBay, the fee you pay to PayPal is separate from the fees you pay to eBay. PayPal doesn't charge the buyer any fees; instead, it charges you, the seller, a fee based on the *amount of money transferred.*

This last point is important. PayPal charges fees based on the total amount of money paid, *not* on the selling price of the item. That means if a $10 item has a $5 shipping/handling cost, the buyer pays PayPal a total of $15—and PayPal bases its fee on that $15 payment.

PayPal's fee (as of Summer 2003) is either 2.2% (the Merchant rate for Business sellers with an average of $1,000 per month of sales over the past three months) or 2.9% (the Standard rate for lower-volume Premier sellers) of the transaction amount, plus an additional $0.30 per transaction. These fees are deducted from your account with every transaction.

Activating PayPal in Your Auction Listings

The easiest way to accept PayPal payments in your eBay auctions is to choose the PayPal option when you're creating an item listing. This is as simple as checking the PayPal box and entering your PayPal ID on the Sell Your Item page.

When you choose this option, a PayPal payments section is added to your item listing. PayPal will also appear as a payment option in your eBay Checkout, on your post-auction item listing page (as shown in Figure 13.4), and in eBay's end-of-auction email to the winning bidder. Most third-party checkout tools will also recognize and accept PayPal payments.

Collecting PayPal Payments

A buyer can make a PayPal payment in a number of ways. They can

- Respond to the PayPal link embedded in the end-of-auction email they receive from eBay.
- Click the PayPal button in your item listing.
- Select the PayPal option when accessing the eBay Checkout page.
- Pay directly from the PayPal Web site.

When a buyer makes a PayPal payment, those funds are immediately transferred to your PayPal account, and you receive an email notification of the payment. In most cases, this email will include all the information you need to link it to a specific auction and ship the item to the seller.

In most cases, the buyers' payments come into your account free and clear, ready to be withdrawn from your checking account. There are two primary exceptions to this, however:

- eCheck payments, where a buyer pays PayPal from his or her personal checking account. Because PayPal has to wait until the "electronic check" clears to receive its funds, you can't be paid until then, either. PayPal will send you an email when an electronic payment clears.

- Buyers with unconfirmed addresses. Every PayPal member is encouraged to enter his or her street address. This address is then confirmed by PayPal. If you receive a payment from a buyer who has not entered an address (or whose address has not yet been confirmed), PayPal won't automatically authorize the transaction. Instead, you'll be

note

You can also use PayPal to send end-of-auction notices to your high bidders, and to function as a checkout site for all your eBay auctions. As nice as this feature is, it assumes that all your customers will pay via PayPal, which they won't—which means you probably don't want to use PayPal as your primary auction management tool.

asked whether you want to accept the payment, unconfirmed address and all. Only after you manually accept the payment will the funds be transferred to your PayPal account.

Withdrawing PayPal Funds

You have to manually withdraw the funds due to you from PayPal; there's no automatic payment option available. You can let your funds build up in your PayPal account, or you can choose (at any time) to withdraw all or part of your funds.

You have the option of okaying an electronic withdrawal directly to your checking account (no charge; takes 3–4 business days) or requesting a check for the requested amount ($1.50 charge; takes 1–2 weeks). Just click the Withdraw tab (from the Overview tab) and click the appropriate text link.

> **" Mike Sez "**
>
> I prefer to empty my PayPal account at the end of each day, via an electronic transfer to my checking account. I find this a fast, no-hassle way to receive PayPal funds due.

Setting Up a Traditional Merchant Credit Card Account

There's little downside to using PayPal for your credit card transactions—except for the cost. If you're a real high-volume seller, you may be able to get a lower per-transaction rate by signing up for a merchant credit card account with a separate banking or financial institution.

However, there are a few downsides to establishing a traditional merchant credit card account. First, it's more hassle than signing up for PayPal; you may have to submit various business documentation and possibly have your own credit checked. Second, getting everything up and running may also be more involved than simply plugging into the PayPal system. And finally, there may be upfront or monthly fees involved.

That said, if you can save half a point or more on every credit card transaction, it may be worth it—if your credit card volume is high enough. A quick search of services available in August of 2003 revealed rates in the 2% to 2.5% range, which beats PayPal's 2.9% Standard rate. (Although it's no better than PayPal's Merchant rate, which you can qualify for if your volume is high enough.) Still, many eBay sellers prefer to handle their credit card processing directly, without having to rely on the PayPal service.

> **caution**
>
> Setup fees for a merchant account can range from $25 to $400 or more. Some services also make you purchase expensive software or credit card terminals. Since these fees vary so much, make sure you shop around before you commit.

If you're interested in establishing a merchant credit card account, here are some services that specialize in providing credit card services to online merchants:

- 2CheckOut.com (www.2checkout.com)
- Cardservice International (www.expandyourbusiness.com)
- Charge.com (www.charge.com)
- CreditCardProcessor.com (www.creditcardprocessor.com)
- Fast Merchant Account (www.fast-merchant-account.com)
- Merchant Account Inc. (www.creditcard-acceptance.com)
- Merchant Accounts Express (www.merchantexpress.com)
- Monster Merchant Account (www.monstermerchantaccount.com)
- Total Merchant Services (www.merchant-account-4u.com)

> **caution**
>
> Know that using a traditional merchant account places you, the seller, at risk in the case of credit card fraud. If you accept payment from a buyer using a stolen credit card, the credit card company will charge back your account for the bad funds. That's one advantage to using PayPal to accept credit card payments; PayPal assumes this risk when you accept payments from one of its approved users.

And here's another place to check out—Costco. That's right, the Costco wholesale club offers merchant credit card processing to its Executive members, through Nova Information Systems. Costco waives the $25 setup fee, and offers a discount rate just over 2%. (Of course, the Executive membership itself costs $100, so you'll need to factor that in, as well.) See the Costco Web site (www.costco.com) or call 888-474-0500 for more details.

THE ABSOLUTE MINIMUM

There are many different ways your customers can pay for the merchandise they buy; when deciding what types of payment to accept, keep these facts in mind:

- Cash isn't as attractive as you might think, and C.O.D. is darned unappealing.
- Cashier's checks and money orders spend just like cash, with fewer hassles.
- Personal checks take up to two weeks to clear, but are preferred by many buyers.
- Accepting credit card payments is a must for all serious sellers; you can do this by establishing a merchant credit card account, or by signing up for the PayPal service.

14

Managing Packing and Shipping

One of the most labor-intensive parts of the entire eBay auction process is packing the merchandise you've sold and getting it ready to ship. This is where smart eBay businesspeople really shine, by learning how to streamline their packing/shipping operations.

We discussed packing supplies back in Chapter 7, "Step Five: Set Up Your Back Office"; you should review the advice in that chapter about setting up your in-home packing center. Assuming you have your packing center set up and ready to go, this chapter focuses on the mechanics of packing and shipping—and how you can become as efficient as possible at both.

Choosing a Shipping Method

You have a number of choices when it comes to shipping your package. You can use the various services offered by the U.S. Postal Service (regular mail, Priority Mail, Express Mail, Media Mail, and so on) or any of the services offered by competing carriers, such as UPS or Federal Express. You can deal directly with any shipping service or you can use a local shipping store to handle the shipping—and even the packing—for you. (Know, however, that having another company do your work for you will cost you—which means it's preferable to deal directly with your shipping service of choice.)

Which service should you use? That's a good question, but not always an easy one to answer. Ultimately, you have to strike a compromise between cost, convenience, and speed. Pick the cheapest method possible, and customers will gripe when they don't receive their merchandise in a timely manner. Pick the fastest method possible, and customers will gripe that they're paying too much for shipping/handling. (You also may turn away potential buyers with your high shipping/handling fees.) Like I said, you need to strike a balance—and also choose a shipper that is easy for you to deal with.

And here's what makes the decision particularly difficult. Once you start checking around, you'll find that shipping rates vary wildly from one service to another—and I mean *wildly*. For example, the costs for shipping a 2 pound box from New York to Los Angeles range from under $2.00 (USPS Media Mail) to around $30 (UPS Next Day Air and FedEx Priority Overnight). That's a *big* difference.

You definitely want to check out shipping costs before you specify a shipper in your auction listings. To compare shipping costs for a variety of services on a single Web page, check out iShip (www.iship.com). This site not only lets you compare shipping costs, but also provides tracking services for all major carriers.

This variation in shipping costs is yet another good reason to standardize the type of merchandise you sell in your eBay auctions. If you only sell one or two types of items, you can easily calculate your shipping fees ahead of time—and know that they'll stay constant from auction to auction. If you're selling a wide variety of items, calculating shipping for all those different items becomes extremely time-consuming. (Standardizing the merchandise you sell also helps when buying your packing boxes—you only have to buy one or two types of boxes, instead of having to keep a wide variety of packaging on hand.)

Of course, cost isn't the only factor you want to consider. You also want to compare how long it takes the package to arrive, what kind of track record the shipping service has, and how convenient it is for you to use. If you have to drive 20 miles to get to a UPS office but you have a post office just down the street, that might offset a slightly higher cost for Priority Mail.

The main thing to keep in mind is that you want to, as much as possible, settle on a single shipper and method of shipping for your eBay auctions. The last thing you want to do is to make trips to multiple shipping stations each day, and deal with a myriad number of packing boxes and shipping instructions. Standardize on a single shipper and method, and you'll make your shipping "department" much more efficient. Don't, and you'll waste a lot of time unnecessarily.

We'll look at each of the major shipping services separately, but with a decided emphasis on the U.S. Postal Service—which is the shipper of choice for a majority of eBay businesses.

> **tip**
>
> You may need to factor weather conditions into which type of shipping you choose. If it's summertime and you're shipping something that might melt in extreme heat (like an old vinyl LP), pick the fastest shipping method possible.

U.S. Postal Service

The United States Postal Service (USPS) is used by almost all eBay sellers, for at least some of their shipping needs. Dealing with the Postal Service is convenient, as most sellers have a post office within a short driving distance, and they're set up to easily handle the shipping of small items from individuals.

The Postal Service offers several different shipping options:

- **Priority Mail**. This is the preferred shipping method for a majority of eBay sellers, big and small. Pricing is generally quite reasonable, and if you're shipping out a small item under two pounds, you can quote a flat rate ($3.85, as of summer 2003). Service is typically in the one-to-three day range, and—as you learned in Chapter 7—the postal service has lots of free Priority Mail shipping boxes you can use. You can also print out your own Priority Mail shipping labels and postage, direct from the USPS Web site—which we'll discuss in the "Automating Postage" section, later in this chapter.

> **" Mike Sez "**
>
> Which shipping services do I use? For small items, I typically default to USPS Priority Mail; it's inexpensive and relatively fast, plus I get free packing materials from my local post office. For CDs, DVDs, and books, I use USPS Media Mail, which is cheaper and almost as fast. For really big items (over 10 pounds or so), I go with UPS. But I find that, 9 times out of 10, Priority Mail or Media Mail does the job for me.

- **Express Mail**. This is a less-used option, primarily because of its high cost—considerably more expensive than Priority Mail. Express Mail is the Postal Service's fastest service, offering guaranteed next-day delivery 365 days a year, including weekends and holidays. Merchandise is automatically insured up to $100.

- **First Class Mail**. This is an option if your item fits into a standard-sized envelope or small box. It also provides the benefit of shipping directly from your mailbox, without necessitating a trip to the post office—assuming you can figure out the correct postage yourself. Delivery is similar to Priority Mail: typically three days or less. If your item is relatively small, First Class can cost somewhat less than Priority Mail.

> **caution**
>
> You can't use Media Mail to ship every type of printed material. The service is reserved for publications without advertising—so you can't use it to ship magazines, newspapers, or comic books.

- **Parcel Post**. This used to be known as the "slow" USPS service for larger packages, but it's gotten faster of late—and it's priced much lower than Priority Mail. Still, it might take seven to nine days to ship something Parcel Post from coast to coast, as opposed to Priority Mail's two (or three) days.

- **Media Mail**. This is a hidden treasure. Media Mail is what USPS used to call "book rate," and can be used to ship books, DVDs, videotapes, compact discs, and other printed and prerecorded "media." The rates are much cheaper than Priority Mail, especially when you're shipping heavy items, and delivery times are somewhere between First Class and Parcel Post—typically less than a week. This is a good, low-cost way to ship many popular items; the cost for shipping a CD or DVD across country is less than two bucks, compared to $3.85 for Priority Mail.

You can find out more about USPS shipping at the USPS Web site, located at www.usps.com. You can also access the USPS Domestic Calculator (postcalc.usps.gov), shown in Figure 14.1, to calculate postage for all levels of service.

UPS

While UPS is a little pricey for small, lightweight items, it's a good option for shipping larger or heavier packages. UPS offers a variety of shipping options, including standard UPS Ground, Next Day Air, Next Day Air Saver, and 2nd Day Air.

You can find out more about UPS shipping—and access a rate calculator—at the UPS Web site, located at www.ups.com.

FIGURE 14.1

Go to the U.S.
Postal Service
Domestic
Calculator to
calculate
postage for your
merchandise.

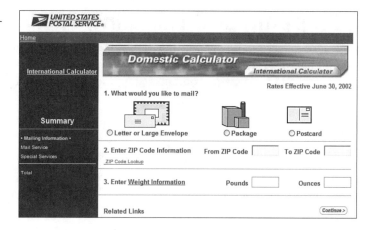

FedEx

FedEx is probably the fastest shipping service, but it's also the most costly. FedEx tends to target the business market (which can afford its higher rates), so it isn't widely used for auction or retail shipping.

FedEx's most popular shipping options are Priority Overnight, Standard Overnight, and 2Day. You can find out more about FedEx shipping at its Web site, located at www.fedex.com. You can access its rate finder directly at www.fedex.com/us/rates/.

Other Shipping Companies

USPS, UPS, and FedEx are the three most popular shipping services in the U.S.; they're not the only services available, however. Among the other services available are

- Airborne Express (www.airborne.com)
- DHL Worldwide Express (www.dhl.com), great for international shipments
- Purolator Courier (www.purolator.com)

That said, you'll probably find that the U.S. Postal Service or UPS offers all the shipping options you need for your new eBay business.

note

Less-experienced or occasional sellers might choose to do their packing and shipping through a professional shipping store, such as Mail Boxes Etc./The UPS Store (www.mbe.com). Because of the high fees these stores charge, this really isn't a good option for high-volume sellers. Still, you might want to go this route if you have the occasional large or overly fragile item to ship. You can check out shipping stores in your area at AuctionSHIP (www.auctionship.com), a national network of retail stores that provide packing and shipping services.

Calculating Shipping and Handling Fees

One of my earlier pieces of advice was that you should include all the details about shipping and handling (how much and who pays) up front in your item listing. While this is a good idea, how do you figure shipping costs before you know where the item is going?

Working with Flat Fees

The solution is easy if you're shipping something that weighs (packaging included) less than a pound. For these lightweight items, you can use USPS Priority Mail, which ships one-pound packages anywhere in the U.S. for a single price ($3.85 at the time I write this). Because you can also use free boxes (provided by the postal service), you know your cost to package and ship a one-pound item will be $3.85. Easy.

If you're shipping books, CDs, or videos, you also have it easy—if you choose to ship via USPS Media Mail. These rates are so cheap that you can do some creative rounding of numbers and say that any item weighing two pounds or less can ship anywhere in the for $2.00. The actual Media Mail rate might be $1.42 or $1.84 or whatever, but $2.00 makes a convenient number to state up front; the gap between actual and projected shipping can go toward the purchase of an appropriate box or envelope.

Working with Variable Fees

When you're shipping items that weigh more than a pound, the calculation gets much more complex. The fact is that if you're selling an item that weighs, let's say, four pounds, the actual shipping costs (via Priority Mail) can range from $5.30 to $10.35, depending on where you are and where the buyer is. That's because Priority Mail rates—most shipping rates, actually—vary by distance. So there's no way to quote an exact shipping cost until the auction is over and you get the buyer's ZIP code.

That said, there are three ways you can deal with this situation in your auction listings.

First, you can calculate an *average* shipping cost for your item, figuring a cost halfway between the minimum and the maximum possible costs. Using our four-pound example, the minimum cost for Priority Mail shipping is $5.30 and the maximum is $10.35, so you would charge the buyer the average of these two numbers, or $7.83. (Maybe you round up to $8.00.) The theory here is that you lose money on some shipments and make it back on others, so over the long term it's a wash. Of course, nearby buyers might complain that they're paying too much (which they are, because they're in fact subsidizing sellers who live further away). You'll have to decide if you can live with the occasional complaint—or refund the difference if it's too large.

Next, you can simply state that buyers will pay actual shipping cost based on location, which will be calculated at the conclusion of the auction, and not include a flat shipping/handling charge in your listing. If you take this approach, you have to request the buyer's ZIP code at the end of the auction, refer to various rate charts to figure the shipping cost, and then relay that cost to your buyer. It's a bit of work, but it gets the job done. (It's also made easier by the fact that eBay now includes the buyer's ZIP code—when available—in its end-of-auction notification emails.)

Using eBay's Shipping Calculator

Finally, and this is my new preferred method, you can choose to include eBay's Shipping Calculator in your item listings. The Shipping Calculator, shown in Figure 14.2, is a great tool; it lets buyers enter their ZIP code on the auction listing page, and then calculates the actual shipping cost, based on the shipping service you selected. (You can also choose to have the Shipping Calculator add a predetermined *handling charge* for each shipment, which we'll discuss in a minute.) When a buyer uses eBay Checkout at the end of the auction, or chooses to pay via PayPal, they can also use the Shipping Calculator to automatically add shipping/handling fees to their total.

FIGURE 14.2
Add eBay's Shipping Calculator to your item listings so buyers can automatically determine shipping and handling fees.

You can activate the Shipping Calculator when you're creating a new item listing on the Sell Your Item page. Just follow these steps:

1. Click Calculated Shipping Rates to open the Shipping Calculator section, shown in Figure 14.3.

2. Enter the package weight, in pounds and ounces.

3. Select a package size from the pull-down list.

4. Select which shipping service you plan to use, from the pull-down list.

5. Enter your ZIP code.

6. Enter any handling fee you want to charge (over and above the actual shipping rate) into the Packaging & Handling Fee box.

7. Select whether you want to offer shipping insurance.

8. Select whether you charge sales tax, and the sales tax rate.

FIGURE 14.3

Activating eBay's Shipping Calculator from the Sell Your Item page.

Flat shipping rates Same rate for all buyers	Calculated shipping rates Based on buyer address **NEW!**

To have shipping rates calculated automatically for your buyers based on their address, enter the information below. See how it works.

Package weight ___ lbs. ___ oz.

Package size [Package/Thick Envelope ▾]
☐ The packaging is irregular or unusual.
Learn more about weight and package size.

Shipping service [Select One ▾]

Seller zip code ___ (US only)

Packaging & handling fee $ [0.00]
This will **not** be shown to buyers, but will be included in your shipping total.

Shipping insurance [Not offered ▾]
Calculated based on the final item price.
UPS includes free insurance up to $100.

Sales tax [hide] [No Sales Tax ▾] [0.0] %
☐ Apply sales tax to the total which includes shipping & handling.

Since the Shipping Calculator can be added to your item listings free of charge, there's no reason not to use it—especially as it greatly simplifies the task of calculating exact shipping charges to your customers.

Determining the Handling Charge

Aside from the pure shipping costs, you should consider adding a handling charge to your shipping fees your customers pay. After all, you need to be sure that you're compensated for any special materials you have to purchase to package the item. That doesn't mean you charge one buyer for an entire roll of tape, but maybe you add a few pennies to your shipping charge for these sorts of packaging consumables. And if you have to purchase a special box or envelope to ship an item, you should

"Mike Sez"

When I'm supplying quality packaging for a shipment, I find that a handling charge of $1.00 meets with little or no objection from my customers. If I'm using free Priority Mail packaging, I charge less.

definitely include that cost in your shipping charge. (This argues for planning your shipping before placing your item listing—which is always a good idea.)

So you should have no compunction against "padding" your shipping fees with an additional handling charge. In fact, eBay's Shipping Calculator lets you add a separate handling charge to its calculations. It's an accepted part of doing business online.

Combining Items for Shipping

If you have multiple items for sale, there is every possibility that a single buyer will purchase more than one item. If that happens, you don't need to pack two or more separate boxes for that buyer; you can easily pack all the item purchased in a single box, which will reduce shipping costs. You should pass on that savings to your customer, in the form of a combined shipping/handling fee for all items purchased. If you're inflexible in adjusting your shipping/handling for multiple purchases, you're ripping people off—and will lose customers for it.

Packing Your Items

Packing your merchandise is a lot of work. Let's look at what's involved in packing an item so that it arrives at its destination intact—but doesn't cost you an arm and a leg to get there.

Picking the Right Shipping Container

It's important to choose the right type of shipping container for a particular item. First, you have to decide whether to use a box or an envelope. If you have a very large item to ship, the choice is easy. But what if you have something smaller and flatter, such as a baseball card or a coin? Your choice should be determined by the fragility of your item. If the item can bend or break, choose a box; if not, an envelope is probably a safe choice.

Whichever you choose, pick a container that's large enough to hold your item without the need to force it in or bend it in an inappropriate fashion. Also, make sure that the box has enough extra room to insert cushioning material.

On the other hand, the container shouldn't be so big as to leave room for the item to bounce around. Also, you pay for size and for weight; you don't want to pay to ship anything bigger or heavier than it needs to be.

If you're shipping a breakable or bendable item in an envelope, consider using a bubble-pack envelope or reinforcing the envelope with pieces of cardboard. This is especially vital if your item shouldn't be bent or folded.

If you're shipping in a box, make sure it's made of heavy, corrugated cardboard and has its flaps intact. Thinner boxes—such as shoe boxes or gift boxes—simply aren't strong enough for shipping. When packing a box, never exceed the maximum gross weight for the box, which is usually printed on the bottom flap.

caution

Use the combination box technique judiciously, as it can significantly increase the weight of the package—and thus your shipping costs.

Although there are a bunch of different-sized boxes available, sometimes you need something somewhere in between this size and that size box. When you face this situation, you have two choices.

First, you can take a larger box and cut it down. That means cutting through each corner of the box to make it shorter, and then cutting off the ends of the flaps accordingly. Sometimes it's difficult to fold unscored flaps, so you may want to make your own scores by slicing a knife (shallowly) where you want to bend the box closed. (Also, many mailing centers have their own folding machines that you can use to create custom-sized boxes—at a cost.)

Second, you can combine two smaller boxes. If your box is 16" long and your item is 20", just take two boxes and insert the open end of one inside the open end of the other. You'll need to use sufficient packing tape to keep the boxes from sliding apart, but you'll have created a box custom-sized for the item you're shipping.

How to Pack

How do you pack your box?

Don't just drop your item in an empty box; you need to position the item toward the center of the box, away from the bottom, sides, and top, and surround it with cushioning material. Professional shippers use Styrofoam peanuts, and lots of them; another option is to use crumpled up old newspapers. Know, however, that peanuts are *much* lighter than newspaper. Since weight is a factor in how much you'll pay for shipping, so anything you can do to lighten the weight of your package is important. Because peanuts cost… well, *peanuts*, they're the cushioning material of choice.

If you're shipping several items in the same box, be sure to wrap each one separately (in separate smaller boxes, if you can) and provide enough cushioning to prevent movement and to keep the items from rubbing against each other. Not only should items be separated from each other in the box, but they should also be separated from the corners and sides of the box to prevent damage if the box is bumped or dropped.

The previous point argues for another technique—double boxing especially fragile items such as glass or ceramic items. That means packing the item tightly in a smaller, form-fitting box, and then placing that box inside a slightly larger, shock-absorbing box—with at least 3" of cushioning material between the boxes.

caution

Make sure you include the weight of the box *and the cushioning material* when you weigh your item for shipment. A big box with lots of crumpled paper can easily add a half-pound or more to your item's weight—excess weight you'll have to pay for.

If your item has any protruding parts, cover them with extra padding or cardboard. And be careful with the bubble wrap. Although it's great to wrap around objects with flat sides, it can actually damage more fragile figurines or items with lots of little pieces and parts sticking out. If the bubble wrap is too tight, it can snap off any appendages during rough handling.

When you're packing an item, watch the weight. Have a postal scale at your packing counter, and weigh the item—shipping container and all—during the packing process. With Priority Mail, the difference between shipping a one-pound package and a one-pound, one-ounce package is as much as $1.90, depending on where it's going. Finding some way to cut that extra ounce of packing material can save almost two bucks in shipping costs!

After you think you're done packing, gently shake the box. If nothing moves, it's ready to be sealed. If you can hear or feel things rattling around inside, however, it's time to add more cushioning material. (If you can shake it, they can break it!)

One Size Doesn't Fit All

As you might expect, packing needs vary for different types of items. Table 14.1 provides some item-specific packing tips you might find useful:

Table 14.1 Packing Tips

Merchandise	Tips
Books	Books are heavy to ship; use USPS Media Mail to reduce shipping rate. Wrap the book in bubble wrap or cardboard to cushion the corners against damage. Enclose in a plastic bag or shrink wrap to protect against water damage. Padded envelopes work well for single books; use traditional boxes for multiple-book shipments.
CDs	Use padded or bubble wrap envelopes sized for CDs. Can ship via Media Mail, although First Class is often just as cheap for single units.
Clothing	Standard Priority Mail boxes work great for most items. For single or smaller items, Tyvek envelopes are ideal.
Coins	Avoid the temptation to ship in a standard envelope. Use a larger box that will travel easily.
Computer parts	When shipping circuit boards, video cards, memory chips, and so on, pad the item well and pack it in an Electro Static Discharge (ESD) bag to prevent damaging static buildup. *Don't* use peanuts for filler—all that Styrofoam can carry a damaging static charge.
Consumer electronics	Remove the batteries before you ship; wrap and place the batteries next to the items in the shipping container.
DVDs	Use padded or bubble wrap envelopes sized for DVDs. Can ship via Media Mail, although First Class is sometimes just as cheap. If shipping via Priority Mail, use free box number O-1096L.
Framed artwork/pictures	Take the glass out of the frame and wrap it separately. Do not let artwork come in direct contact with paper or cardboard. Enclose photographs in plastic bag to protect against wetness.
Glassware and vases	Stuff hollow items with newspaper, tissue paper, or other packing material; this provides an extra level of cushioning in case of rough handling. Wrap items in tissue paper, bubble wrap, or foam padding. Use masking tape to affix cut-off paper towel rolls to spouts and handles. Allow at least 3" of cushioning around the item in the box; consider double boxing.
Jars and items with lids	Either separate the lid from the base with several layers of bubble wrap or tissue paper or (better still) pack the lid in a separate small box.
Jewelry	Use a standard size box that won't draw attention to itself. Do not label the box as to its contents. Insure the package appropriately.
Magazines and comics	Wrap in some sort of plastic bag or wrap to protect against wetness in shipment. Ship magazines First Class or Priority Mail—*not* Media Rate.
Stamps	Avoid the temptation to ship in a standard envelope. Use a larger box that will travel easily.

Merchandise	Tips
Videotapes	Can ship via Media Mail. If you choose to ship Priority Mail, use free box number O-1096S (for single tape) or O-1096L (for multiple tapes).

How to Seal the Package

After your box is packed, it's time to seal it. A strong seal is essential, so always use tape that is designed for shipping. Make sure you securely seal the center seams at both the top and the bottom of the box. Cover all other seams with tape, and be sure not to leave any loose tape or open areas that could snag on machinery.

caution

Don't use wrapping paper, string, masking tape, or cellophane tape to seal your package.

You should use sealing tape designed for shipping, such as pressure-sensitive tape, nylon-reinforced Kraft paper tape, glass-reinforced pressure-sensitive tape, or water-activated paper tape. Whichever tape you use, the wider and heavier, the better. Reinforced is always better than non-reinforced.

One last thing: If you plan to insure your package, leave an untaped area on the cardboard where your postal clerk can stamp "Insured." (Ink doesn't adhere well to tape.)

How to Create the Perfect Label

You've packed the box. You've sealed the box. Now it's time for the label.

Addressing the Label

The best-packed box won't go anywhere if you get the label wrong. For fast and efficient delivery, you need to create a label that can be both clearly read and clearly understood. And it goes without saying that the address information needs to be accurate and complete—partial addresses just don't cut it.

tip

Don't know the ZIP code for the address you're shipping to? Then, look it up at the U.S. Postal Service's ZIP Code Finder at www.usps.com/zip4/.

To create the perfect label, you need to write, type, or use your computer to print the address as neatly as possible. You should also use complete address information, including all street suffixes—Dr., Ave., St., Blvd., and so on. And make sure to include the recipient's apartment or suite number (if applicable). Naturally, you should use the proper two-letter state abbreviation, and the correct ZIP code—and, when possible, the four-digit ZIP+4 add-on.

Now for some things you might not know.

When you're shipping to a P.O. Box or rural route destination, it helps to include the recipient's telephone number on the label; sometimes the carrier has to call to notify the recipient of a delivery. Including a telephone number is also useful when shipping outside the U.S.—and don't forget to include the country name as part of the address, either.

After you've created the delivery label, place it on the top (not the side) of the box. To avoid confusion, place only one address label on the box. If using a packing slip, place it on the same surface of the box as the address label. Do not place the label over a seam or closure or on top of sealing tape.

To avoid ink smudges and rain smears, place a strip of clear packing tape over the address label. And if you're reusing a box for shipping, remove or cross out all old address labels or markings on the box.

And here's one last tip. Make a duplicate of your shipping label and stick it *inside* the box, before you seal it. This way if the original shipping label gets torn off or destroyed, anyone opening the box can read the duplicate label and figure out where the box is supposed to go.

Choosing the Right Label

For most purposes, you can't beat the standard 4"×6" blank white label. There's a reason it's such a great workhorse; anything smaller is tough to work with, and anything larger just leaves a lot of wasted space. You can purchase these labels at any office supply store, or even get free versions (for Priority Mail shipping) at your local post office. And if you want to

note
You can also purchase or create your own return address labels, to use in conjunction with your main shipping labels. It's easy enough to print out a full page of smallish labels in Microsoft Word; most printing firms (such as Kinkos) can also do up a roll of addresses labels for a nominal charge. If you don't use a preprinted label, you'll want to hand-print your return address on the shipping container or use some sort of return address label.

tip
If you're unsure what label to use, go with Avery; just about every software program out there supports Avery labels.

splurge, you can have labels preprinted with
your business name and return address.

If you use computer-generated labels, you can
program your label-making program (or
Microsoft Word) to include your return address
when it prints the label. This is a good (and
lower-cost) alternative to using preprinted labels.
There are several dedicated label-printing programs on the market. These programs work with
just about any standard-issue major-manufac-
turer blank labels.

tip

Some auction manage-
ment tools also have label
printing functions—although
many of these services print
extremely generic labels that
might not suit your tastes.

The most popular label-making programs include

- Avery Wizard and DesignPro (www.avery.com)
- NiceLabel Express, Pro, and Suite (www.nicelabel.com)
- PrimaSoft Label Printer (www.primasoft.com/lb.htm)
- Visual Labels (www.rkssoftware.com/visuallabels/overview.html)

Printing Priority Mail Labels

If you're shipping via Priority Mail, you can print labels on your home printer
directly from the USPS Web site. To use the Click-N-Ship service (www.usps.com/
shipping/label.htm), all you have to do is pre-register (no charge) and fill in the
shipping information. As you can see in Figure 14.4, you can print either plain
labels or labels with prepaid postage—as discussed next.

FIGURE 14.4

Printing Priority
Mail labels with
the Postal
Service's
Click-N-Save
service.

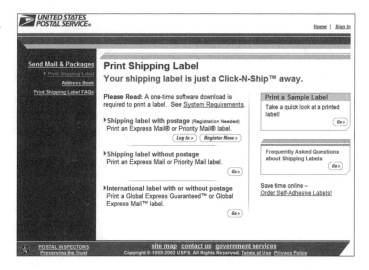

Automating Postage

If you do a lot of shipping with the U.S. Postal Service, you'll pay a lot of postage—and stand in a lot of lines waiting to pay. Fortunately, you can cut out all this line-waiting by purchasing your postage electronically and printing out your "stamps" on your printer, without ever leaving home. (If you put your own postage on your packages, your mail carrier can pick up your packages along with your regular mail.)

tip

One plus to printing your own Priority Mail labels is you get Delivery Confirmation included, at no charge. A minus is that you can't add insurance with this method.

The Postal Service's Click-N-Save service, in addition to printing labels, also lets you purchase and print your own Priority Mail postage. After you've registered, entered the address information, and advanced to the Service Options page, choose the type of service you want, then select the Purchase and Print Label with Postage option at the bottom of the page. Your account will be charged for the amount of the postage, and the label your print out will include necessary postage information. Just affix the label to your package and drop it in the mail; no need to visit the post office!

If you want to purchase other types of postage online, you can use Stamps.com (www.stamps.com). Using Stamps.com is fairly simple. Just install the site's e-postage software on your computer and prepay for specified amount of postage. Enter the appropriate information (package size and weight, destination ZIP code, and so on) into the e-postage program, which then uses that information to calculate exact postage and print that postage to an envelope or "stamp," via your printer.

Shipping Insurance

If you're shipping a moderately expensive item (over $50, let's say), it might be worth the trouble to offer insurance to the buyer. It's relatively easy (on the Sell Your Item page) to give the buyer the option of buying insurance—or just do it yourself and include the costs in your normal shipping/handling fee.

The U.S. Postal Service charges $1.30 to insure items up to $50, or $2.20 for items between $50 and $100. UPS includes $100 worth of insurance in its basic rates; additional insurance can be purchased for additional cost.

You can also arrange shipping insurance via a third-party firm. Universal Parcel Insurance Coverage (www.u-pic.com) provides insurance for packages shipped via the USPS, UPS, FedEx, and other carriers. There are two advantages to using U-PIC for your shipping insurance—it's cheaper than carrier-provided insurance, and you can do it all from your home computer. (The big disadvantage is that it doesn't integrate into your auction checkout or automated end-of-auction emails.)

As to pricing, U-PIC charges $1 per $100 of insurance for USPS orders, considerably less than what the Postal Service charges. (U-PIC's rates vary by carrier.) If you insure a lot of items, it's worth checking out.

Tracking and Confirmation

If you think the package might be lost in transit, you can always avail yourself of the tracking services provided by UPS, FedEx, and other major carriers. These services typically provide tracking numbers for all packages shipped. In most cases, you can track your package by entering the package's tracking number into the carrier's Web site.

The one major shipping service that doesn't offer tracking (by default) is the U.S. Postal Service. What you can get from the postal service (at a cost of from $0.45 to $0.55) is their Delivery Confirmation service. USPS confirmation, however, does not confirm that an actual person received the package; it only confirms that the mail carrier delivered it. (Stuck it in the mailbox, that is—or in many instances, left it on the porch.)

You can opt for Delivery Confirmation when you ship your item from your local post office, or have it included free if you print your own labels with the Click-N-Save service. You can also purchase USPS delivery confirmation forms in bulk from ShipperTools.com (www.shippertools.com). ShipperTools.com uses the official USPS delivery confirmation system, and lets you print an unlimited number of confirmation forms for just $6.95 a month.

If you want a signature confirmation on a USPS shipment, you need to send your item with the certified mail option. Certified mail requires the recipient to sign on delivery, and costs $2.30. This is a preferred option if you're shipping something extremely valuable.

Streamlining the Packing and Shipping Process

One of the most important things you can do to make your eBay business more efficient is to streamline the entire process of packing and shipping your merchandise. If you find yourself in the routine of schlepping down to the post office every day, loaded down with armfuls of packages, you're not doing it right. Read on to learn how to be a more efficient shipper.

Setting a Packing/Shipping Schedule

The first thing you want to do is get yourself out of the "do everything right now" syndrome. Novice eBay sellers hover over their computer screens or mail boxes, waiting for payments to come in. As soon as that payment arrives, they rush to send out a confirmation email, print an invoice, and pack the merchandise. Then they hop in the car and drive as fast as possible to the post office, stand in line, and ship the thing out.

Wrong, wrong, wrong.

You should not put yourself at the mercy of your customers. Instead, you should work your customer sales into *your* routine.

That means, of course, that you have to establish a routine—a schedule that you follow for all your packing and shipping. If your sales volume is low and your time free, it's okay to pack and ship once a day. But do it at the same time each day, on an appropriate schedule. If your mail arrives around noon, for example, set 2:00 p.m. as your packing/shipping time; that gives you time to process all payments received in that day's mail. When 2:00 p.m. rolls around, gather all the orders that are ready to go and start packing. When you're done—around 3:00 p.m., let's say—you head down the post office with your daily delivery.

You don't have to ship every day, however. Many eBay sellers only ship a few days out of the week, so that they're not wasting time traveling to the post office very day. You may choose to ship all your packages on Monday, Wednesday, and Friday, for example—or maybe just Tuesday and Friday. Whatever days you choose, you let your paid orders build up until your scheduled shipping day, and then get it done all at once.

Creating a Packing Assembly Line

When it comes to packing your items, it pays to have the process down to a science. Have all your boxes and packing material lined up and ready to go, so that you can run each item through the "assembly line." Wrap, pack, cushion, seal, and label— that's the routine. And the more uniform the items you sell, the more automated this procedure can become.

What you don't want is to have your routine interrupted. That means not running out of tape or peanuts or having to rush out and purchase a special box just for that one special item. (Which is yet another reason, of course, to standardize the items you sell.) The smoother the process (and the fewer interruptions), the faster you can get everything packed and ready to ship.

Getting It There

When it comes to shipping your items, be prepared. If you use the U.S. Postal Service for shipping, try to time your visits so that you don't have to stand in long lines. That means avoiding lunch hour and the last half hour or so before closing;

avoiding Mondays and Saturdays; and avoiding peak shipping periods around major holidays, such as Christmas and Valentine's Day. Early morning and mid-afternoon are typically low-volume times at the post office window.

If you have a lot of packages to ship, don't go to the post office by yourself—take a helper. If large shipments are common, invest in a small hand truck to help you cart all those boxes to the counter.

Arranging Regular Pickups

The more items you sell, the more you ship. The larger and more successful your eBay business gets, the more burdensome the whole shipping process gets—and all those trips to the post office become especially time consuming.

As you become a heavy shipper, consider setting up an account with a single shipper and arranging daily pickups from your home. This is easy enough to do if you ship via Priority Mail, as you can use Click-N-Save to print your labels and postage, and have your mail person pick up all your packages when he makes his normal rounds. If you tend to use First Class, Parcel Post, or Media Mail, invest in a Stamps.com account so you can print all that postage at home, as well; your postal carrier can pick up all these pre-postaged items.

If your volume is high enough, you can also arrange regular pickup service from UPS and FedEx. These carriers can also pick up single items if you arrange so in advance—but at a much higher fee.

Shipping Larger Items

Some items are just too big to ship via conventional means. Suppose you just sold an old pinball machine, or a roll-top desk, or a waterbed. How do you deal with items that big?

Assuming that the item is too big even for UPS, you have to turn to traditional trucking services. Some of these services will pack or crate the item for you (for a fee); others require you to do all the crating. In addition, some of these firms require you to deliver the item to their shipping terminal, and for the buyer to pick it up from their dock. (Other firms offer door-to-door service—again, sometimes for a higher fee.) In any case, it helps to make a few calls and ask for specifics before you decide on a shipper.

tip

Another option is to use Greyhound PackageXPRESS (www.shipgreyhound.com), which lets you ship large (and small) packages via Greyhound bus. You and the buyer have to live relatively close to a Greyhound bus station, and the item will have to be delivered to and picked up from the station—but costs are substantially less than with traditional trucking services.

When you have an oversized item to ship, here are some of the trucking services that other eBay sellers have used. Check with each firm individually as to its fees and shipping policies.

- AAA Cooper Transportation
  (www.aaacooper.com)
- Forward Air (www.forwardair.com)
- Vintage Transport Services
  (www.vintagetransport.com)
- Yellow Freight (www.yellowfreight.com)

In addition, eBay itself offers a Freight Resource Center (ebay.freightquote.com) for shipping large items. As you can see in Figure 14.5, you can obtain freight quotes and initiate shipping directly from this page. You can also contact Freightquote.com via phone, at 888-875-7822.

FIGURE 14.5

Use eBay's Freight Resource Center to arrange shipping for large items.

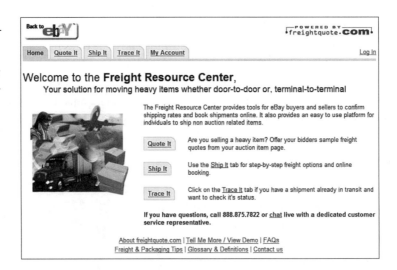

Shipping Internationally

Packing for international customers shouldn't be any different than for domestic customers—as long as you do it right. Foreign shipments are likely to get even rougher treatment than usual, so make sure the package is packed as securely as possible—with more than enough cushioning to survive the trip to Japan or Europe or wherever it happens to be going.

What *is* different about shipping internationally is the paperwork—and the shipping costs.

Chances are your normal method of shipping won't work for your international shipments. For example, you can't use Priority Mail to ship outside the U.S.—not even to Canada or Mexico. This means you'll need to evaluate new shipping methods, and possibly new shipping services.

tip

Given the increased chances of loss or damage when shipping great distances, you should purchase insurance for all items shipping outside North America.

If you want to stick with the U.S. Postal Service, check out Global Express Mail (fast but expensive), Airmail (almost as fast, not quite as expensive), or Surface/Parcel Post (slow but less expensive). In addition, UPS offers its Worldwide Express service, FedEx offers FedEx Express service internationally, and DHL is always a good option for shipping outside the U.S. Make sure you check out your options beforehand, and charge the buyer the actual costs incurred.

You'll also have to deal with a bit of paperwork while you're preparing your shipment. All packages shipping outside U.S. borders must clear customs to enter the destination country—and require the completion of specific customs forms to make the trip. Depending on the type of item you're shipping and the weight of your package, you'll need either Form 2976 (green) or Form 2976-A (white). Both of these forms should be available at your local post office.

tip

eBay offers several pages of advice for international trading at `pages.ebay.com/internationaltrading/`.

In addition, there are certain items you can't ship to foreign countries—firearms, live animals and animal products, and so on. (There are also some technology items you can't ship, for security reasons.) You need to check the government's list of import and export restrictions to see what items you're prohibited from shipping outside U.S. borders. (Go to `www.export.gov` for more information.)

THE ABSOLUTE MINIMUM

Packing and shipping are time consuming. The better you can manage this process, the more efficient your eBay business will be. Keep these points in mind:

- When you standardize the items you sell, you make packing and handling much simpler.

- Most eBay sellers use the U.S. Postal Service for the majority of their shipping—primarily Priority Mail, Media Mail, and First Class mail.

- You should state your shipping and handling fees up front in your item listings; include eBay's Shipping Calculator in your listings so buyers can figure out fees on their own.

- Work your packing and shipping process into an efficient assembly line—and set a schedule for when you pack and ship your merchandise.

- Avoid trips to the post office by printing your own postage and labels, so your mail carrier can pick up your packages as part of his regular route.

IN THIS CHAPTER

- Answering bidder questions
- Managing end-of-auction correspondence
- Mining your customer lists
- Handling buyer complaints

15

DEALING WITH CUSTOMERS

Customers. They're either one of the joys or one of the major annoyances of running your own business. That's because when you're running a business with your eBay auctions, you have customers to deal with. Lots of them. So you'd better get used to it.

When you sell items via auction on eBay, there are plenty of opportunities for you to reach out and touch the people who bid on your items. Some customers will actually reach out and touch you, by asking questions in the middle of the auction. Other customers you have to reach out to yourself, when the auction is over, so that they'll know who and how much to pay. And then you have the kind of customer no one likes—the one with problems.

How do you deal with all these customers? Read on and find out.

Answering Bidder Questions

The more auctions you run, the more likely it is that you'll run into potential bidders who have questions about what you're selling. eBay lets bidders email sellers during the course of an auction, so don't be surprised if you get a few emails from strangers asking unusual questions. And, as a responsible eBay seller, you need to answer these queries.

It's relatively easy for a potential bidder to ask you a question. All they have to do is click the Ask Seller a Question link on the item listing page. This generates an email message, which is sent to the email account you specified when you became an eBay member.

When you receive a question from a potential bidder, you should answer the question promptly, courteously, and accurately. It's in your best interest to make the questioner happy; after all, that person could turn out to be your high bidder. Remember, you are running a business, and all good businesses go to great lengths to respond appropriately to customer queries.

What happens if you get a *lot* of questions from potential bidders? I have no great advice for you here. There is no secret auction tool that can respond automatically to specific customer questions; you have to craft each response individually, answering the questions as posed. You may want to batch all the query emails into a bunch, however, and answer them once a day. (Although this might not be prompt enough for bidders asking questions in the waning minutes of a live auction.) But you shouldn't worry too much about this; for most sellers, the volume of customer queries will be small and easily manageable.

Managing End-of-Auction Correspondence

The bigger challenge comes in managing all the customer correspondence that happens after the auction is over. In order, here are the emails that (ideally) will flow between you and the winning bidder—after you both receive your end-of-auction confirmations from eBay:

- From you to the winning bidder: Notification of winning bid, request for street address so you can finalize shipping/handling costs.
- From winning bidder to you: Full shipping information, including street address and ZIP code.
- From you to the winning bidder: Total amount due, including shipping and handling.

- From you to the winning bidder (after payment is made): Notification that payment was received.
- From you to the winning bidder (after item is shipped): Notification that item was shipped.

That's three, possibly four outgoing emails on your part, and at least one incoming email from the buyer. (And you may have to repeat any of these messages as a reminder if the customer doesn't reply promptly.) Multiply this by the total number of auctions you're running, and you can see that email management is a major issue for high-volume sellers.

Communicating Manually

If your sales volume is low, there's no reason you can't handle all this correspondence manually, using your normal email program. Just fire up Outlook or Outlook Express, type in the text of your message, and click the Send button.

You can automate this process, to some degree, by creating your own form letters. That means creating boilerplate text you use for each of your different customer emails, loading that text into a new message, and then customizing the message with the details of that particular auction. This is a better option than starting from scratch with every sale you make.

Communicating with eBay Selling Manager

Even better is to let somebody else handle your correspondence—and by "somebody else," I mean using an auction management tool that has customer email features.

For many sellers, the customer email features of eBay Selling Manager make it the program of choice for end-of-auction communication. While Selling Manager isn't quite as automated as other programs, you can't beat the low $4.99 per month price.

We first talked about eBay Selling Manager (pages.ebay.com/selling_manager/) back in Chapter 12, "Managing Your Auctions." Well, in addition to keeping track of all your open and closed auctions, Selling Manager also lets you send prewritten email end-of-auction messages to all your winning bidders. Selling Manager includes six different boilerplate messages, all of which you can customize. These messages are

- Winning buyer notification
- Payment reminder
- Request shipping address
- Payment received

■ Item shipped

■ Feedback reminder

You can also use Selling Manager to send custom emails to customers.

Sending a Customer Email

As you recall, you can access Selling Manager from your My eBay page. To send an email to a customer, follow these steps:

1. Go to any of Selling Manager's Sold Listings pages.

2. Click a specific Buyer Email link.

3. When the Email Buyer page (shown in Figure 15.1) appears, select the type of message you want to send from the Template list.

note

You can edit your email address by clicking the Edit link. Edit the customer's email address by accessing the Sales Record page and clicking the Edit the Buyer's Email Address link.

FIGURE 15.1

Using eBay Selling Manager to send a post-auction email.

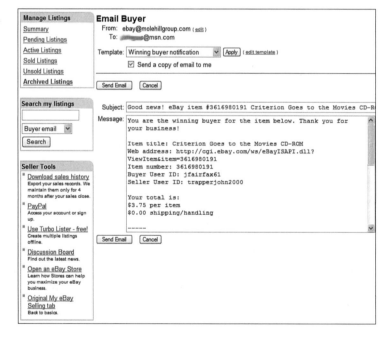

4. If you want, edit the subject of the message in the Subject box.

5. If you want, edit the text of the message in the Message box.

6. If you want to receive a copy of this message, select the Send a Copy of Email to Me option.

7. Click Send to send the message.

Editing a Template

Don't like Selling Manager's prepared email templates? Then customize them! Here's how:

1. From the Email Buyer page, click Edit Template.

2. When the Edit Email Templates page (shown in Figure 15.2) appears, select the template you want to edit from the Template list.

FIGURE 15.2

Customizing a Selling Manager email template.

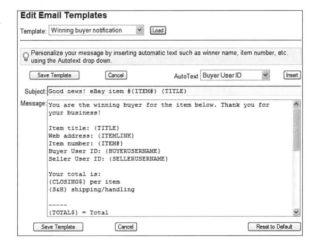

3. Edit the text in the Subject and Message boxes, as desired.

4. Insert automated text (such as buyer name, buyer item number, and so on) into the message by selecting text from the Autotext list, then clicking the Insert button. The automated text (surrounded by curly brackets) now appears at the bottom of your message; cut and paste this text into it's correct position within the message.

5. Click the Save Template button when done.

note

You can revert to the original template at any time by clicking the Reset to Default button.

Emailing in Bulk with Selling Manager Pro

There are two major drawbacks to eBay Selling Manager's email management tool. First, you have to manually send email messages; the messages are not sent automatically at the end of an auction. Second, you have to send one message at a time; there's no provision for sending bulk messages to multiple customers.

If you want your messages sent automatically, you'll need to switch to another auction management tool, such as those discussed in the next section. If you want to send messages in bulk, however, all you have to do is upgrade from eBay Selling Manager to eBay Selling Manager Pro.

That's right, one of the big differences between Selling Manager and Selling Manager Pro is the capability of sending bulk email messages. You'll pay more for this feature, of course—$15.99 per month versus regular Selling Manager's $4.99 per month. But for many high-volume sellers, it's worth the expense.

Sending a batch of emails in Selling Manager Pro is relatively simple. Just follow these steps:

1. Go to any Sold Listings page.
2. Check the boxes next to those customers to whom you wish to send emails.
3. Click the Email button.
4. When the Preview Email page appears, select the template you wish to send, from the Template list.
5. Click the Send Emails to send the selected message to the selected customers.

Communicating with Other Auction Management Tools

Other auction management tools also offer email features. Some of these tools totally automate the end-of-auction communication process, automatically sending the proper emails when your auction ends (and when the customer pays via PayPal). In most cases, the email management features are included as part of the overall price of the tool.

Ándale Checkout

Ándale's (www.andale.com) end-of-auction emails are integrated into their Ándale Checkout tool. Ándale Checkout is similar to eBay's Checkout feature, in that it provides a Web page that customers use to enter their shipping and payment information. When you activate Ándale Checkout for a particular auction, Ándale will automatically send a winning buyer notification e-mail at the end of the auction. Other emails included with Ándale Checkout include checkout reminder, shipping address request, invoice, payment request, payment receipt, item shipped notice, and feedback notice.

The costs for Ándale Checkout are based on volume, and start at $2.00 per month (for 10 checkouts). For more detailed information on pricing and features, see Chapter 12.

Auctiva eBud

Auctiva (www.auctiva.com) includes email management as part of its eBud software. As you recall from Chapter 12, eBud is a software program that you license for $11.95 per month.

eBud manages a variety of customer correspondence, linking into your normal email program to send the messages you select. It includes a variety of prewritten form letters, which you can edit to your liking. The program is also smart enough to let you combine information about multiple auctions won by a single user into one email.

The big drawback to eBud is that you have to manually send all your emails, even though it does operate in bulk. It doesn't automatically send a message to the winning bidder at the close of an auction.

HammerTap Manager

HammerTap Manager (www.hammertap.com) is an auction management tool that includes easy-to-use customer email features. HammerTap Manager can be configured to automatically send end-of-auction emails to all your customers, and also consolidates multiple sales onto a single invoice. HammerTap Manager costs $29.95 per month.

Vendio Sales Manager

As you learned in Chapter 12, Vendio Sales Manager includes a variety of customer correspondence features as part of its advanced auction management services. You can configure Vendio Sales Manager to automatically send winning bidder notifications at the end of your auctions, and use it to send payment and shipping notifications. Vendio's fees, unfortunately, are rather complex; see Table 12.2 for more details.

Mining Your Customer Lists

All of the tools mentioned so far perform similar functions, primarily the automation of end-of-auction customer communication. But you don't have to limit your communication with customers to that short period right after an auction ends; smart eBay sellers mine their customer lists to generate repeat sales from their auction customers.

Have similar items to sell? Have a new product available? Having a big sale? Then email your previous customers and let them know—it's a cheap and easy way to increase your revenues. After all, the customer names you have on hand are known buyers; it's cheaper to sell more merchandise to an existing customer than it is to find a new one.

Several companies have entered into the advanced customer management business. We'll look at three of these tools next.

Ándale Email Manager

Ándale Email Manager (www.andale.com) is a new tool that helps you manage all your incoming customer emails, store important customer information, and then use that customer information to generate future mailings. Email Manager is an email plug-in that is compatible with Microsoft Outlook; it automatically sorts your eBay-related correspondence into Outlook folders, and extracts and stores customer history information. It also includes reusable templates you can use to respond to buyers, or to generate future correspondence. Cost is $5.95 per month.

Vendio Customer Manager

Vendio Customer Manager (www.vendio.com) is similar to Ándale Email Manager in that it filters and sorts all your incoming eBay-related emails. It also includes templates you can use to create bulk customer mailings. In addition, Customer Manager stores and tracks your customers' transaction history, including a generated "customer rating." It integrates with Vendio Sales Manager to better manage all your auction-related correspondence.

Vendio Customer Manager is Web-based, so you can access it from any computer, at any time. Pricing plans are typically complex, starting at $3.95 per month for 200 outbound emails and going up to $39.95 per month for 10,000 messages.

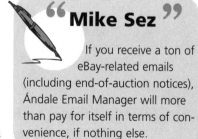

" Mike Sez "

If you receive a ton of eBay-related emails (including end-of-auction notices), Ándale Email Manager will more than pay for itself in terms of convenience, if nothing else.

HammerTap BayMail Pro

HammerTap BayMail Pro (www.hammertap.com/baymailpro/) is a unique program that lets you send email to any eBay user or group of users, even if you don't know their email address. It's a good program to check out if you intend to mass market your merchandise to other eBay users.

As you can see in Figure 15.3, all you have to know to send an email with BayMail Pro is the user's eBay user ID. BayMail Pro automatically retrieves lists of user IDs directly from eBay. You can use BayMail Pro to create mailing lists of users, or to bulk email all the bidders in your current auctions. The program costs $14.99.

FIGURE 15.3

Use BayMail Pro to send bulk email to other eBay members.

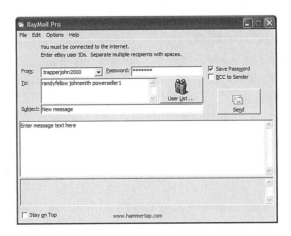

Handling Buyer Complaints

Not all auctions go smoothly. Maybe the item arrived damaged. Maybe it didn't arrive at all. Maybe it wasn't exactly what the buyer thought he was getting. Maybe the buyer is a loud, complaining, major-league son of a rutabaga.

In any case, if you have a complaining customer, you need to do something about it. Unfortunately, there are really no hard and fast rules for handling post-auction problems. You have to play it by ear and resolve each complaint to the best of your ability.

On the plus side, most eBay users are easy to deal with and just want to be treated fairly. Others won't be satisfied no matter what you offer them. You have to use your own best judgment on how to handle each individual situation.

What are you options when you have a complaining customer? Well, you could just ignore them—not that I recommend this. If you specified that the merchandise was sold "as-is" or that "all sales are final," you're technically in the clear and don't have to respond to customer complaints. That's not a good way to run a business, however, as dissatisfied customers don't generate good word of mouth—and are prone to leave negative feedback on eBay.

Better to try to work something out. If the item never arrived, you can contact the shipping service to put a trace on the shipment. If the item was insured, you can initiate a claim for the lost or damaged item. And if the item doesn't work or isn't what the customer thought he was buying, you can work out some sort of refund. Even if you're not disposed to offer a full refund, you can perhaps negotiate a lower price or discount with the customer, and then refund the difference—which may be preferable to taking the thing back and losing the entire sale.

Guaranteeing Your Merchandise

You can head off some customer complaints by guaranteeing the merchandise you sell. (Alternately, you can sell all items "as-is"—as long as you clearly indicate this in your item listings.)

Some novice eBay sellers might worry that the costs of guaranteeing their merchandise might be prohibitive. This is not the case—simply because the vast majority of merchandise arrives intact and in good working condition. The number of customers who will actually take you up on a "money back guarantee" will likely be extremely small.

When a customer is dissatisfied with their purchase and takes you up on your guarantee, you have a couple of options. First, you can offer to refund the purchase price if the item is returned to you. This approach prevents unsavory customers from taking advantage of you, either by claiming something is bad when it's not or by doing the old switcheroo and shipping you a defective unit while they keep the good unit you sent them; you get to inspect the returned merchandise before you send the refund.

Second, you can offer a full refund on the item, no questions asked, no further action necessary. With this option, the buyer doesn't have to bother with shipping it back to you; this is the way high-class merchants handle their returns. The upside of this method is the extra measure of customer satisfaction; the downside is that you could get taken advantage of, if the customer is so inclined.

You also have to determine just *what* it is that you're guaranteeing. Do you guarantee that the item is in good working condition? Or that it is completely free of defects? Or simply that it's as

note

You can choose to refund (1) just the purchase price; (2) both the purchase price and the original shipping/handling charge; or (3) the purchase price, the shipping/handling charge, and the customer's costs to ship the item back to you. Make it clear which it is before you ask the customer to return the item.

described in your item listing? Whatever your guarantee, you're likely to come across the occasional buyer who feels that the item he received is not as it was described. (Which is another good reason to include a detailed description of the item—and a photograph—in all your item listings.) This situation can quickly deteriorate into an exercise in who said what; it might be best to defuse the situation early by offering some sort of compensatory partial refund, whatever your policy states.

How long your guarantee lasts is another question. Certainly, most retailers guarantee their merchandise to arrive intact and in good working condition—or at least as described in the auction listing. Should you respond to customer complaints if the item stops working after 30 days, or 90 days, or even a year after the auction? While a manufacturer might offer an unconditional one-year guarantee, you probably don't have the same obligation. I'd say that any problems that crop up after the first 30 days shouldn't be your obligation. Most customers will understand and agree.

Whatever guarantee you offer, state it up front in your item listing. You can include your guarantee as part of the boilerplate text you include at the end of all your listings.

Resolving Complaints with a Mediation Service

Of course, you still might run into that rare customer who just can't be satisfied. They want a full refund, and you don't see that it's justified. When a transaction devolves into a shouting match, it's time to bring in a mediator—a neutral third party who will look at all the facts and then make a (supposedly) fair and balanced judgment.

eBay offers mediation services through SquareTrade (www.squaretrade.com). This site, shown in Figure 15.4, settles disputes through a possible two-part process. You start out with what SquareTrade calls Online Dispute Resolution. This free service uses an automated negotiation tool to try to get you and your customer to neutral ground. Communication is via email; the process helps to cool down both parties and let you work out a solution between the two of you.

If the two of you can't work it out in this manner, you have the option of engaging a SquareTrade mediator to examine the case and come to an

> **note**
>
> Of course, some problem customers are real problems—especially if they don't pay, or send you rubber checks. Learn more about dealing with deadbeat bidders and other frauds in Chapter 16, "Dealing with Problems."

impartial decision. This will cost the party who filed the case $20. Both parties agree to abide with the results. If the SquareTrade mediator says you owe the customer a refund, you have to arrange the refund. If the representative says you're in the clear, the customer has to stop complaining. (At least to you.)

Given the low costs, there's no reason *not* to use SquareTrade in a disputed transaction—especially if the customer files the claim and pays the cost.

FIGURE 15.4

Use SquareTrade to resolve disputes between you and disgruntled customers.

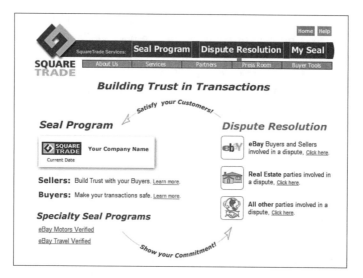

THE ABSOLUTE MINIMUM

Running an eBay business creates lots of opportunities to communicate with your customers, including

- During the course of the auction, when potential bidders can contact you with questions about the item you have for sale

- After the auction, when you have to notify the winning bidder that they've won (which is the type of communication you can automate with eBay Selling Manager or other auction management tools)

- After the customer has paid, when you should notify them that you've received payment and shipped the item

- When you have other merchandise to sell to your established customer base

- When you have a dissatisfied customer—in which case you need to work something out or refund their money

16

DEALING WITH PROBLEMS

When you're doing volume business on eBay, not all transactions go smoothly. At the very least, not every item you list sells. Some high bidders don't pay. Others send you bad checks, or try to pay with a stolen credit card.

In other words, when you run an eBay business, you have to be prepared to deal with a few problems.

Contacting eBay for Help

Your first recourse when you run into problems with one of your auctions is to contact eBay. It's unlikely that you're the very first eBay member who has experienced that particular problem (whatever it may be), so there's no point reinventing the wheel; let eBay try to handle it, if they can.

The easiest way to contact eBay is through their Web form support system. Start at the Contact Customer Support page (shown in Figure 16.1), located at `http://pages.ebay.com/help/contact_inline/`. Select a topic, subtopic, and specific issue, and then click Continue. The following "instant help" page includes links that answer the most common questions. To continue through to contact eBay, click the Continue button to display the Submit Email form. Enter your email address and message, then click the Submit button.

FIGURE 16.1

Contact eBay by using the form on the Contact Customer Support page.

Support: Select a Topic

Please select the topic and issue that most closely fits what you'd like to say to Customer Support. When we know at a glance what kind of issue you have, we can give you help more quickly.

For questionable items, transaction problems, or eBay user violations, Contact Rules & Safety. To learn more about the Webform and how to use it, please click here.

1. Select a topic:
Registration and Account Information ->
Sign In ->
Finding Items ->
Bidding/Buying ->
Selling ->
Billing ->
Feedback ->
Buying and Selling Tools ->
Technical Issues ->
Rules and Safety ->

2. Select a subtopic:
My Seller Account ->
Auction Types ->
Listing ->
Listing Tools ->
During the Auction ->
After the Auction ->
Bidder Issues After the Auction ->
PayPal Questions ->
eBay Stores ->

3. Select an issue:
How do I set up a seller account?
Are there fees for selling on eBay?
What are the fees for Store listings?
Why are credit cards required in order to sell?
How do I post a credit card to my seller's account?
How can I change the credit card information on my seller's account?

Continue ->

You can also contact eBay by phone (800-322-9266 or 408-369-4830) or by snail mail, at

eBay Inc.

2145 Hamilton Avenue

San Jose, CA 95125

Relisting Unsold Items

As you'll soon find out, not every item up for auction on eBay sells. In fact, the success rate is close to 50%—which means that it's possible that half your auctions will end with no buyers. If you reach the end of an auction and you haven't received any bids—or you haven't received high-enough bids in a reserve auction—you can easily relist the item in a follow-up auction. In fact, you can relist items with no additional insertion fee, if the following conditions are met:

- You didn't receive any bids on a regular (no-reserve) auction.
- For a reserve price auction, you didn't receive any bids that met or exceeded your reserve price.
- You are relisting an item within 30 days of the closing date of the first auction.
- If you're relisting a reserve price auction, the new reserve price is the same or lower than the original reserve price.

eBay likes to have your repeat business, so it makes it easy to relist unsold items. All you have to do is go the item listing page for your completed auction and click the Re-list This Item link. As you proceed through the normal listing creation procedure, you'll see that all the information from your previous listing will already be entered, saving you the trouble of re-entering it. You can, however, make any changes you want for this new listing.

eBay won't charge you a listing fee for this item the second time, although you will be charged a final value fee if it sells. If your item *doesn't* sell the second time around, there's no third chance—you'll have to create a completely new item listing, and all normal fees will apply.

Checking Up on Questionable Bidders

What do you do if you're suspicious about someone bidding on one of your items—or if you can't contact a winning bidder via traditional email methods? eBay can provide you with more complete contact information about any user bidding on (or having won) one of your auctions. All you have to do is ask.

note

You can't request user info for just *any* eBay member. You can only request user info for those users bidding in a current auction—or for sellers of auctions in which you're currently bidding.

Just click the Search button on the eBay Navigation Bar; when the Search page appears, click the Find Members button on the sub-bar. This opens the Find Members page; scroll down to the Contact Info section, then enter the user's ID and the item number of the auction in question. Click the Submit button when you're done. eBay will now display the user's ID history (shifty users sometimes change IDs frequently) and contact info.

Dealing with Deadbeat Bidders

To an eBay seller, the worst thing in the world is a high bidder who disappears from the face of the earth—a *deadbeat bidder* who bids but never pays. If this happens to you, you're stuck holding the now-unsold merchandise. (Which is also the good news—you might not have gotten paid, but at least you still have the merchandise to re-sell in another auction.)

If you find yourself a victim of a deadbeat bidder, you can report the bum to eBay, ask for a refund of your final value fee, and maybe offer the item in question to other (unsuccessful) bidders. But you have to initiate all of these activities yourself—eBay doesn't know that you've been shafted until you tell them. You'll want to follow the procedure outlined in the following checklist:

Deadbeat Bidder Checklist

- ☐ Contact the bidder (again)
- ☐ File a Non-Paying Bidder Alert
- ☐ Request a final value fee credit
- ☐ Leave negative feedback to the deadbeat bidder
- ☐ Block bidder from future sales
- ☐ Offer the item in question to the second-highest bidder

    or

- ☐ Relist the item

Let's walk through these steps, one by one.

Step One: Contact the Unresponsive Bidder

It's on your shoulders to go to whatever lengths possible to contact the high bidder in your eBay auctions. This should start with the standard post-auction email, of course. If the buyer hasn't responded within three days, resend your original email with an "URGENT" added to the subject line. You should also amend the message to give the buyer a deadline (two days is good) for his response.

If another two days go by without a response, send a new message informing the buyer that if you don't receive a response within two days, you'll be forced to cancel his high bid and report him to eBay as a deadbeat bidder.

If a full week goes by and you still haven't heard from the buyer, you can assume the worst—and proceed to Step Two.

tip

If your email bounces or if the buyer doesn't respond, see the "Checking Up on Questionable Bidders" section, previously in this chapter, to learn how to obtain additional contact information.

Step Two: File a Non-Paying Bidder Alert

The way you notify eBay about a deadbeat bidder is to file a Non-Paying Bidder Alert. You have to fill out this form between 7 and 45 days after your auction ends; you can't file earlier, even if you know you have a deadbeat on your hands.

You file a Non-Paying Bidder Alert by going to the Site Map page and clicking the Request Final Value Fee Credit link—or going directly to `pages.ebay.com/help/community/npb.html`. This page tells you all about how to deal with bad bidders; follow the instructions here to file the Alert.

Now what happens? When eBay receives a Non-Paying Bidder Alert, the service automatically sends a warning to the user in question—not that this typically does a lot of good. (Although sometimes eBay will scare only slightly deadbeat bidders into walking the straight and narrow—you never know.) If the alleged deadbeat receives three such warnings, he or she will be indefinitely suspended from the eBay service.

If, by some quirk of fate, you end up working things out with the buyer after you've filed a Non-Paying Bidder Alert, you should file a Non-Paying Bidder Warning Removal form. You can find this form on the same page you use to file a Non-Paying Bidder Alert.

note

If the item in question was sold in a Dutch auction, this process gets a little trickier. You can only file one Non-Paying Bidder Alert form per auction—which means you have to include all the deadbeat bidders in that auction in a single form; you can't file additional alerts after the initial form has been filed.

Step Three: Ask eBay to Refund Your Fees

After a Non-Paying Bidder Alert is filed, you have to wait another 10 days before you can request a refund of your final value fee. (A lot of waiting, I know!) This refund request must be made no later than 60 days after the end of your auction, and your claim has to meet one of the following criteria:

- The high bidder did not respond to your emails or backed out and did not buy the item.
- The high bidder's check bounced or a stop payment was placed on it.
- The high bidder returned the item and you issued a refund.
- The high bidder backed out, but you sold the item to another bidder at a lower price.
- One or more of the bidders in a Dutch auction backed out of the sale.

If your situation fits, you're entitled to a full refund of eBay's final value fee—if you request it. To request a refund, go to eBay's Site Map page and click the Final Value Fee Request link (in the Seller Services section). Follow the instructions there to receive your credit; eBay generally issues a credit to your account within 48 hours.

Step Four: Leave Negative Feedback

Naturally, you want to alert other eBay members to the weasel among them. You do this by leaving negative feedback, along with a description of just what went wrong (no contact, no payment, whatever).

To leave negative feedback, go to the item listing page, click the Leave Feedback to Bidder link, and when the Leave Feedback About an eBay User page appears, check Negative and enter your comments. Click the Leave Comment button when done.

Step Five: Block Bidder from Future Sales

Next, you want to make sure that this deadbeat doesn't bid in any of your future auctions. You do this by adding the bum to your blocked bidders list, which you learned about back in Chapter 12, "Managing Your Auctions."

Basically, you go to the Site Map page and click the Blocked Bidder/Buyer List link. When the Bidder/Buyer Management page appears, scroll to the Blocked Bidder/Buyer List section and click Continue. When the Blocked Bidder/Buyer List page appears, add the buyer's user name to the list; separate multiple names with commas. Click the Submit button when done.

Step Six: Give Other Bidders a Second Chance

Now all that's left to do is deal with the merchandise that you thought you had sold. Assuming you still want to sell the item, what do you do?

You can, of course, relist the item for sale—which we'll go into in step seven. However, you may be able to save yourself this hassle by offering the item to other bidders in your failed auction. eBay's Second Chance Offer feature lets you try to sell your item to someone else who was definitely interested in what you had to sell.

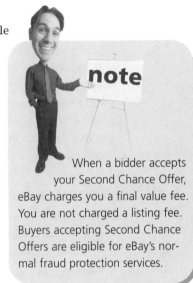

You can make a Second Chance Offer to any of the under-bidders in your original auction. The offer can be made immediately on the end of the auction, and up to 60 days afterward.

To make a Second Chance Offer, return to your original item listing page and click the Make a Second Chance Offer link. When the Second Chance Offer page appears, follow the onscreen instructions to fill out the form and make the offer.

When a bidder accepts your Second Chance Offer, eBay charges you a final value fee. You are not charged a listing fee. Buyers accepting Second Chance Offers are eligible for eBay's normal fraud protection services.

Step Seven: Relist Your Item

If you don't have any takers on your Second Chance Offer, you can always try to sell the item again by relisting the item. See the "Relisting Unsold Items" section, earlier in this chapter, for specific instructions.

Coping with Complaints About *You*

Of course, it's always possible that a disgruntled customer will accuse you of various types of wrongdoing. What do you do when you've been (presumably unjustly) accused?

Responding to Negative Feedback

Probably the most common form of customer complaint on eBay takes the form of negative feedback. Since maintaining a high feedback rating is important to the long-term success of your eBay business, you need to respond appropriately to any negative feedback you receive.

Unfortunately, there's not much you can do if you receive negative feedback; feedback comments cannot be retracted, except in the most

Second Chance Offers can also be used, in a successful auction, to offer duplicate items to non-winning bidders.

extreme instances. What you can do is respond to the negative comments, thus providing some sort of balance to the original negativity.

Start by going to the Feedback Forum page (pages.ebay.com/services/forum/ feedback.html) and clicking the Review and Respond to Feedback Comments Left to You link. When the next page appears, click the View Feedback button. When the next page appears, click the Respond link next to the comment in question. Then, when the next page appears, enter your response in the text box, then click the Leave Response button. Your new comment is now listed below the original feedback comment on the Feedback Profile page.

Getting Negative Feedback Removed

If you feel that negative feedback has been left maliciously, you can petition eBay to remove the feedback. They won't often do so, except in extreme cases—but there's no harm in asking.

You can learn more about feedback removal at pages.ebay.com/help/index_popup. html?policies=feedback-removal.html#. (That's a long URL, I know; eBay doesn't like to publicize this particular service.) Scroll through the text until you find the Contact Us link; click this link to display the Web form for feedback removal. Enter the appropriate information and click the Submit button. If eBay agrees with your arguments, you'll be notified that the feedback in question has been removed. If not, you won't.

Your Best Resource—Other eBay Sellers

There's another source for advice and help with eBay-related problems: other eBay sellers. Having trouble with a deadbeat bidder? Ask other members for advice. Not sure how to ship an odd-sized package? No need to reinvent the wheel; chances are some other member has shipped something similar, and can tell you what to do. Got a gripe with eBay itself? You're not alone—as you'll soon find out if you voice your complaint on one of the many online forums devoted to online auctions in general and eBay in particular.

Using eBay's Community Forums

When you want to talk with other eBay users, the first place to look is on the eBay site itself. eBay hosts a variety of discussion boards and chat rooms where you can ask questions, offer comments, or just hang out and socialize with other eBay members. Some of these boards are even frequented by eBay personnel, so you can use them as a kind of real-life help system when you encounter difficulties.

eBay's discussion boards and chat rooms are found on the eBay Community page (pages.ebay.com/community/). You can also access this page by clicking the Community button on the eBay Navigation Bar.

eBay offers a variety of discussion boards, which are like giant electronic bulletin boards where you can read and respond to short messages about specific topics. For example, the Seller Central board is a great place for advice from high-volume sellers.

eBay also posts official information on several of these boards. For example, information about the status of the eBay site itself (when maintenance is scheduled, when a technical outage might be repaired, and so on) is found on the System Status Announcement board (www2.ebay.com/aw/announce.shtml). More formal eBay announcements are posted on the General Announcement board (www2.ebay.com/aw/marketing.shtml).

Communicating via Third-Party Forums

You don't have to log on to eBay to talk about eBay. Some of the most popular message boards exist outside the eBay service, hosted by third-party Web sites and organizations. The most popular of these message boards include

- Ándale's Online Traders Web Alliance (OTWA) Community (community.otwa.com)
- AuctionBytes Forums (www.auctionbytes.com/forum/phpBB/)
- Vendio Community (www.vendio.com/mesg/)
- Online Auction Users Association (OAUA) Discussion Board (www.auctionusers.org/forums/www.auctionusers.org/forums/)

Another good source of online auction community and information is the TAGnotes email mailing list, hosted by the Auction Guild at Yahoo! Groups. Go to groups.yahoo.com/group/TheAuctionGuildnotes/ to subscribe.

Also worthwhile is the Online Auction Users Association (OAUA), located at www.auctionusers.org. The OAUA is an association formed to provide a collective voice for small buyers and sellers in the online auction community by identifying shared issues, providing training, education, and support services, and lobbying to promote laws and regulations that benefit the online auction users. It's a worthwhile organization for all eBay members—and membership is free.

THE ABSOLUTE MINIMUM

When you face an eBay-related problem, keep these facts in mind:

- Your first recourse should be to contact eBay directly, using the appropriate Web form.

- If you have an item that didn't sell, you can relist the item without being charged a second listing fee.

- If a buyer doesn't pay, you can petition eBay for a refund of the final value fee—and then make a Second Chance Offer to non-winning bidders.

- If an irate customer leaves negative feedback about you, feel free to respond—or to ask eBay to retract the feedback, if it's wholly unwarranted.

PART IV

MOVING FROM SELLER TO POWERSELLER

17

BECOMING AN EBAY POWERSELLER

One of the steps to running your own eBay business—although not a requirement, by any means—is to become an eBay PowerSeller. eBay's 90,000-some PowerSellers generate enough business to warrant special attention from eBay, in the form of dedicated customer support, premier tools, and the occasional special offer. Plus they get to display that cool PowerSeller logo in all their auction listings.

Should you be aiming for PowerSeller status? Read on and find out what's involved—and whether it's worth it.

What Is a PowerSeller?

PowerSellers are the most profitable sellers on the eBay site—that is, they generate the most profits *for eBay*. They don't necessarily sell the most merchandise; instead, they generate the most revenue, which is how eBay generates its fees. Still, an eBay PowerSeller does a fair amount of business, however you measure it.

You can't choose to be a PowerSeller—eBay chooses you, based on your past sales performance. If you're chosen, you don't have to pay for the privilege; membership in the PowerSellers program is free.

When you become a PowerSeller, a special logo (shown in Figure 17.1) is displayed next to your user ID in all your eBay auctions, and you automatically qualify for the rewards appropriate to your level.

Just because you qualify as a PowerSeller doesn't mean you have to display the logo in your item listings. Some PowerSellers prefer to forgo the logo in an attempt to seem more like normal folks and less like ruthless business types.

FIGURE 17.1

The sign of an eBay PowerSeller.

Do You Qualify?

To become a PowerSeller, you must meet the following requirements:

- Maintain a consistently high level of eBay sales, as described in Table 17.1
- Maintain a minimum of four average monthly total item listings for three straight months
- Have been an active eBay seller for at least 90 days
- Achieve and maintain a minimum feedback rating of 100, 98% positive
- Deliver post-auction messages to successful bidders within three business days
- Be an eBay member in good standing, and uphold eBay's "community values"—including honesty, timeliness, and mutual respect

The most important point is the first, because it's the most quantifiable. There are five levels in the PowerSeller program; qualification for each level is based on average gross monthly sales, calculated over the past three months of selling activity. Table 17.1 shows the qualifying requirements for each level.

TABLE 17.1   PowerSeller Requirements, by Level

Level	Requirement (Average Monthly Sales)
Bronze	$1,000
Silver	$3,000
Gold	$10,000
Platinum	$25,000
Titanium	$150,000

caution

To keep your PowerSeller status, you have to *maintain* this sales rate. If your sales drop below these levels, eBay will give you 30 days to bring your account back into compliance; if you don't, your membership in the program will be revoked. (You're free to requalify at a later date, however.)

That's right, there are some eBay sellers who average $150,000 or more a month. That's almost two million dollars a year in revenues from eBay auctions—no slight accomplishment!

Should you become a PowerSeller? As you'll soon see, the choice isn't yours to make; you'll either qualify for the program (based on your current eBay sales rate) or you won't.

PowerSeller Benefits

Each level in the PowerSeller program comes with its own collection of rewards. We'll look at these benefits next.

Priority Customer Support

Chief among the benefits of PowerSeller status is priority customer support, as detailed in Table 17.2. It's great to have the extra handholding from eBay, if you need it.

TABLE 17.2   PowerSeller Priority Customer Support

Level	Fast 24/7 Email Support	Phone Support	Dedicated Account Manager
Bronze	Yes	No	No
Silver	Yes	Business Hours	No
Gold	Yes	24/7	Yes
Platinum	Yes	24/7	Yes
Titanium	Yes	24/7	Yes

Other Official Benefits

Other benefits offered to members of the PowerSeller program include

- Healthcare Solutions, a medical insurance plan provided by Marsh Advantage America
- Rebates for use of eBay's Direct Pay billing
- Use of the PowerSeller Entrepreneur Resource Center, a one-stop site for third-party business services
- Access to the PowerSeller discussion board
- Monthly PowerSeller eNewsflash and *Pillars* newsletter
- Invitations to special eBay events, including the yearly eBay Live convention
- Ability to display the PowerSeller logo in all item listings and About Me pages

note

In the past, eBay offered a special PowerSeller Recognition and Reward Program to its PowerSellers. It also offered a variety of PowerSeller merchandise for sale. However, the site discontinued both these programs at the end of 2002, so being a PowerSeller today isn't quite as rewarding as it used to be.

Psychological Benefits

As you can see, the concrete benefits that accrue from PowerSeller status are less than awe-inspiring. (Fast responses to your emails—boy, is that impressive or what?) No, the real benefits of being a PowerSeller are psychological.

Some buyers see a listing that features the PowerSeller logo and assume that they're dealing with a trustworthy and presumably savvy seller. If, to potential buyers, the PowerSeller logo inspires a greater degree of confidence, then membership in the program is beneficial. On the other hand, some users view the PowerSeller logo as the sign of a big business; if these users prefer dealing with individuals, displaying the PowerSeller logo can actually be detrimental.

Bottom line, it's probably a wash. If you qualify, great. If not, no big deal—although a lot of users really like the status that goes with the qualification.

Unofficial Benefits

Then you have the "unofficial" benefits of achieving PowerSeller status. Chief among these is access to the advice and camaraderie of the PowerSeller community.

In addition to eBay's PowerSeller discussion board, there are several Web sites that cater to PowerSellers. These sites offer news and information, discussion forums, and (in some cases) discounts on purchases from other PowerSellers. These independent sites include e-Powersellers.com (`www.e-powersellers.com`), shown in Figure 17.2, and The Powerseller Report (`www.tprweb.com`).

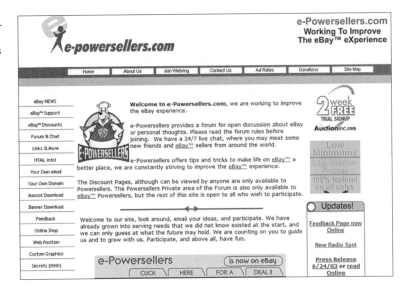

How to Become a PowerSeller

The eBay PowerSellers page (`pages.ebay.com/services/buyandsell/welcome.html`), shown in Figure 17.3, offers more information about the PowerSellers program. This is also where you go if want to become a PowerSeller.

But the thing is, you can't become a PowerSeller just by asking. In fact, there's really no way to request membership at all; the program operates by invitation only. Each month eBay sends out invitations to sellers who meet the PowerSeller criteria. You become a member by (1) meeting the criteria; (2) receiving an invitation; and (3) responding positively to the invitation.

You can, however, see if you qualify for the program. Just go to the main PowerSeller's page and click the Qualified Yet? link. eBay will calculate your recent sales and tell you whether you qualify.

> **"Mike Sez"**
>
> Don't sweat it if you don't qualify for PowerSeller status. The benefits offered aren't all that great, and I've been unable to quantify any sales increases that accrue from displaying the PowerSeller logo. Better to concentrate on improving the profitability of your eBay business than on reaching some artificial PowerSeller level!

FIGURE 17.3

Learning more
about the eBay
PowerSeller pro-
gram.

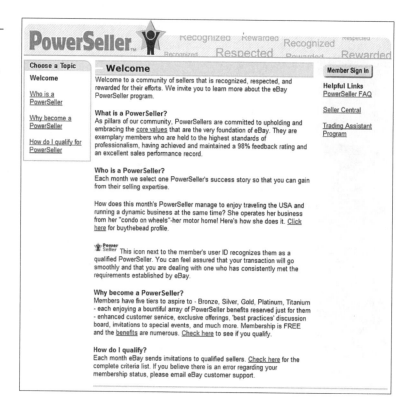

Ten Tips for Achieving PowerSeller Status

The key to becoming a PowerSeller is to increase the number of auctions you close—
and to increase your final selling prices. To that end, anything you can do to make
your auctions more effective will improve your chances of achieving PowerSeller
status.

What can you do to improve the success of your eBay auctions? Here are 10 tips that
will benefit *any* eBay seller, PowerSeller or not:

1. **Tip #1: Focus your sales activity**. Occasional sellers can get by selling
   onesies and twosies that they pick up here and there. High-volume sellers
   focus on a specific type of merchandise—and sell lots of it. By focusing your
   activities, you can be much more efficient in your packing and shipping, as
   well as have a better feel for the category you're working with.

2. **Tip #2: Buy low, sell high**. It goes without saying—you want to make as
   much money as possible on each item you sell. That means obtaining your
   inventory at the lowest possible prices. Some sellers try to double or triple
   their cost when they sell an item. You may not be able to achieve this type of

profit margin, but you should definitely be aiming to reduce your product costs however possible.

3. **Tip #3: List in volume**. You won't become a PowerSeller by selling one or two items a week. You need to list in volume to sell in volume. That means running multiple listings simultaneously, having listings close daily, and utilizing the Dutch auction feature when you have multiple quantities to sell.

4. **Tip #4: Be organized**. When you're closing a large number of auctions every week, you have to get the process down to a science. That means being more efficient every step of the way—from creating your listings to shipping out the merchandise. Wasted time and energy costs you money.

5. **Tip #5: Create professional-looking listings**. The better-looking your item listings, the more auctions you'll close—at higher prices. For best results, invest in a good-quality digital camera (for crisp product photos) and utilize a professional auction creation and listing service.

6. **Tip #6: Write powerful headlines and descriptive listings**. Pack as much useful information as you can into the item list's headline; avoid fluff words and focus on words and phrases that are "search-friendly." In the body of your listing, be as descriptive as possible. Include all the information a buyer might need to make an intelligent purchasing decision.

7. **Tip #7: Use auction management tools**. Running dozens—or hundreds—of auctions a week can task even the best-organized sellers. Utilize one of the many auction management programs or services to help you track every step of your auction activity—including the crucial post-auction communication and shipping processes.

8. **Tip #8: Accept credit-card payments**. A large number of your potential customers want the convenience of paying via credit card. Don't turn away business; at the very least, sign up as a PayPal merchant so you can accept payment by plastic. Make it as easy as possible for your customers to pay.

9. **Tip #9: Provide stellar customer service—and fast shipping.** Remember, the customer is king. Bend over backward to satisfy your auction customers—which includes shipping your merchandise promptly and securely.

10. **Tip #10: Take it seriously**. To run a successful eBay business, you have to be serious about it. For most PowerSellers, it's a full-time activity. Treat it like a business—*not* a hobby or occasional pastime. Be professional in everything you do, and you'll reap the rewards.

In fact, this entire section of the book is focused on increasing your eBay sales—which can help you achieve PowerSeller status. Read on to learn even more ways to become a more effective and efficient eBay seller!

THE ABSOLUTE MINIMUM

eBay's PowerSeller program recognizes those sellers that generate the most revenues in their eBay auctions. Remember these key points:

- Membership in the PowerSeller program is free—but by invitation only.
- You qualify for the PowerSeller program by being an eBay member in good standing, and by averaging at least $1,000 in sales for the past three months.
- All PowerSellers have the option of displaying the PowerSeller logo in their auction listings.
- The rewards of PowerSeller status are chiefly psychological—although you do get improved customer support and access to a healthcare plan.

18

MAKING YOUR AUCTIONS MORE EFFECTIVE

In the last chapter we talked about eBay's PowerSellers—the cream of the crop of eBay's high-volume sellers. If you want to achieve PowerSeller status, you have to generate a large amount of revenue from your eBay auctions—which you can do by running more auctions and by making the auctions you run more effective.

This chapter is full of tips and advice for making you more successful as an eBay seller. You'll learn everything from the best days and times to list items for sale to how to make your listings more attractive. Read on—and learn!

Determining the Best Days and Times to List

We'll start with the simple issue of when you want to start—and end—your eBay auctions. As you'll soon find out, some days and times are more effective than others.

Best Time of Day to List

When you start your auction is important—because that affects when your auction *ends*. If you start a seven-day auction at 6:00 p.m. on a Saturday, it will end exactly seven days later, at 6:00 p.m. the following Saturday.

Why is when your auction ends important? Because some of the most intense bidding takes place in the final few minutes of your auction, from snipers trying to steal the high bid at the last possible moment. To take advantage of last-minute bidders, your auction needs to end when the most possible bidders are online.

For example, if you end your auction at 3:00 in the morning, most of your potential bidders will be asleep and you'll lose out on any last-minute bids. End your auction in the middle of the day, and you'll miss those bidders who are stuck at work or in school.

Better, then, to end your auction during early evening hours. That's when the most number of users are online, and when you're likely to receive the most number of last-minute bids.

Remember, though, that you're dealing with a three-hour time-zone gap between the east and the west coasts. So if you time your auction to end at 7:00 p.m. EST, you're ending at 4:00 p.m. PST—when many potential bidders are still at work. Conversely, if you choose to end at 9:00 p.m. PST, you just hit midnight in New York—and many potential bidders are already fast asleep.

The best times to end—and thus to *start*—your auction are between 9:00 p.m. and 11:00 p.m. EST, or between 6:00 p.m. and 8:00 p.m. PST. That way you'll catch the most potential bidders online—on both coasts—for the final minutes of your auction.

Note, however, that the best time to end an auction can be influenced by the type of item you're selling. For example, if you're selling an item that appeals to grade school or high school kids, try ending your auction in the late afternoon, after the kids get home from school and before they head off for

note

eBay operates on Pacific (West Coast) time. If you're in another time zone, be sure to do the math to determine the proper time for your area.

dinner. Items with appeal to housewives do well with a late morning or early after-noon end time. And business items sell best when they end during normal business hours.

Best—and Worst—Days to List

Just as the time of day your auction ends affects your results, so does the day of the week. While different types of items perform better on different days, the general consensus is that Sunday is the default "best day" to end most auction items.

Here's why.

When you end your auction on a Sunday, you get one full Saturday and *two* Sundays (the starting Sunday and the ending one) for a 7-day item listing. Sunday is a great day to end auctions because almost everybody's home—no one's out party-ing, or stuck at work or in school. End your auction on a Sunday evening, and you're likely to get more bids—and higher prices.

There are exceptions, however.

As with the time you end your auction, your ending day might also be influenced by the type of item you're selling. If you're selling an item of interest to college students, for example, you might be better ending on a night during the week, as a lot of stu-dents travel home for the weekend; you're more likely to catch them in the dorms on a Wednesday or Thursday night. Items targeted at churchgoers might also be better ending during the week, so you don't catch bidders when they're at Sunday evening church services. (Which makes this one big exception to the Sunday evening rule!)

So if Sunday is normally the best night of the week to end your auction, what's the worst night?

Friday and Saturday are probably the worst nights to end most auctions, because a lot of eBay users are out partying on these non-school nights. End an auction for any item (especially youth-oriented items) on a Friday or Saturday night, and you eliminate a large number of potential buyers.

You should also try not to end your auction right in the middle of a hit television series or major sporting event—some potential bidders might find it difficult to tear themselves away from the old boob tube. That means avoiding "Must See TV" Thursdays, and any blockbuster sporting events or award shows.

> **tip**
>
> Get more specific informa-tion on the best days and times for specific auction items at Ándale Research (www.andale.com). See Chapter 9, "Step Seven: Research Other eBay Auctions—and Set a Pricing Strategy," for more details.

Seasonal Variations

When you're planning your projected eBay sales and revenue, you need to take into effect the fact that sales rates vary throughout the year. It's no surprise that sales go up in November and December, due to the Christmas buying season. But did you know that sales go down—way down—in the summertime? That's right, eBay traffic in general drops significantly during June, July ,and August; lots of potential buyers are on vacation, and even more are outside enjoying the sunshine.

Keep these seasonal trends in mind when planning your business. That might mean putting fewer items up for auction during the summer months, or holding your highest-potential items for the fall or winter. Just don't assume you'll keep a steady sales rate throughout all 12 months of the year—because you won't.

Selecting the Right Auction Length

eBay lets you choose from four different lengths for your auctions: 3, 5, 7, and 10 days. The first three options come at the standard listing price; 10-day auctions cost you an additional 10 cents.

The default—and most common—length is 7 days. Choose anything shorter, and you miss any potential buyers who only check in one day a week. Choose the longer option, and it's probably overkill. (Plus you have to wait an extra three days to collect your money.)

Know, however, that some sellers like a 10-day auction that starts on a Friday or Saturday, so that they get two weekends in their bidding schedule. Others prefer a shorter auction (as long as it runs over a weekend), recognizing that most bidding happens during the last few hours, anyway.

If you really need your money quickly, go with a 3- or 5-day auction, but try to time the listing so that you get in a bidding weekend. Also know that some buyers expect and plan on 7-day auctions, so you might not get as much last-minute sniping if you opt for the shorter length.

" Mike Sez "

I recommend you go for the standard 7-day auction, which is what I use for all my items. It's what users expect, and it allows for bidding on each day of the week—without taking *too* long to get the process over with.

Picking the Right Category

This one sounds simple. You have an item, you find the category that best describes the item, and you're done with it. To be fair, sometimes it is that simple.

If you have *Singin' in the Rain* on DVD, you put it in the **Entertainment: DVDs & Movies: DVD: Music & Concert: Musicals** category, no questions asked.

But not every product fits neatly within a single category. Maybe you're selling a model of an American Airlines jet airplane. Does it fit better in **Collectibles: Transportation: Aviation: Airlines: American**, or in **Toys & Hobbies: Models: Air**?

Where you put your item should be dictated by where the highest number of potential bidders will look for it. In the model airplane example, if there are more bidders traipsing through the Collectibles category, put it there; if there are more potential buyers who think of this as a toy or model kit, put it in the Toys & Hobbies category. Think like your potential buyers, and put it where you would look for it if you were them.

You can also use the Ándale Research service (www. andale.com) to provide data on where other sellers placed similar items. Ándale will even tell you which category provided the best results, in terms of success rate and highest selling price.

If you determine that you can improve your results by listing your item in more than one category, take advantage of eBay's offer to list your item in two separate categories. It costs a whole 10 cents more, but it potentially doubles your exposure. (You make this choice on the Sell Your Item page, in the Choose a Second Category section.)

Choosing Listing Enhancements

When you're creating an item listing, eBay provides all sorts of listing "enhancements" you can use to make your listing stand out from the millions of others currently running. All of these listing options cost extra, above and beyond the normal listing fee, whether or not they actually improve your success rate. Let's look at each option in more detail.

Gallery

The Gallery is a section of eBay that displays listing pictures, along with titles, as shown in Figure 18.1. Shoppers can browse through the listings in the Gallery by clicking the Gallery link on the Site Map page, selecting Gallery View in the Show section on any search results or category page, or going directly to pages.ebay.com/buy/gallery.html. Items listed with the Gallery option are also displayed (with photo) on all browsing category pages.

FIGURE 18.1

Browsing items for auction in the Gallery.

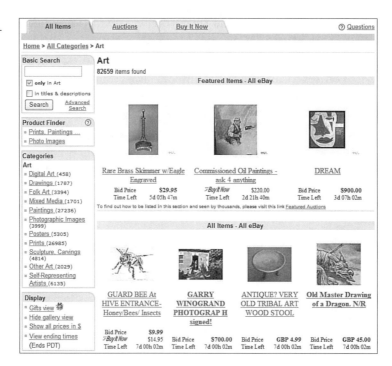

eBay also offers a second Gallery option, called Gallery Featured. When you pay for this option, your item will periodically show up in the special Featured section above the general Gallery.

Pricing for the standard Gallery listing is just 25 cents. Pricing for the Gallery Featured option is $19.95.

The problem with both Gallery options is that most users never access the Gallery. While you might think the Gallery provides additional exposure for your item, most buyers either search for specific items or browse through the normal category pages. (That might be due to the fact that the Gallery is kind of hidden on eBay's site.) Bottom line: the Gallery is simply not an effective listing option.

Bold

How do you make your item stand out on a page full of listings? How about displaying the listing title in boldface? This option, which costs $2.00, displays your item title in bold in any category or search results listings. A boldfaced item listing is shown in Figure 18.2.

" Mike Sez "

Save your money. Even though a basic Gallery listing is cheap (just a quarter!), few users actually venture to the Gallery, which makes this a good-sounding option that seldom pays for itself.

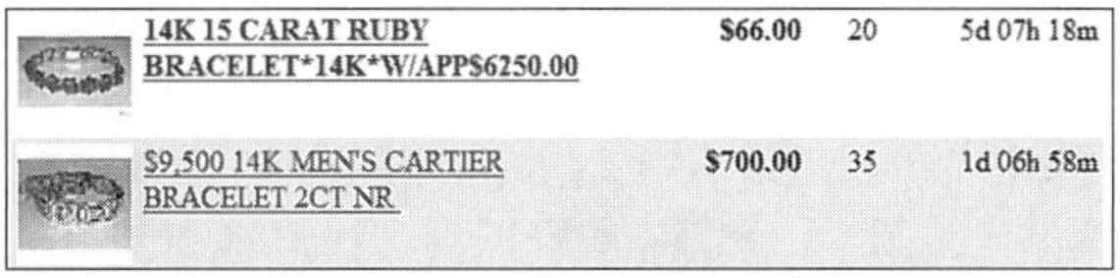

FIGURE 18.2

Two item list-
ings—the first
one in bold.

| | 14K 15 CARAT RUBY BRACELET*14K*W/APP$6250.00 | $66.00 | 20 | 5d 07h 18m |
| | $9,500 14K MEN'S CARTIER BRACELET 2CT NR | $700.00 | 35 | 1d 06h 58m |

Highlight

What's more attention-getting than a bold title? How about a *shaded* item listing?

When you select the Highlight option, your listing (on any category or search results page) is displayed with a colored shade, as shown in Figure 18.3. This little bit of color will cost you $5.00.

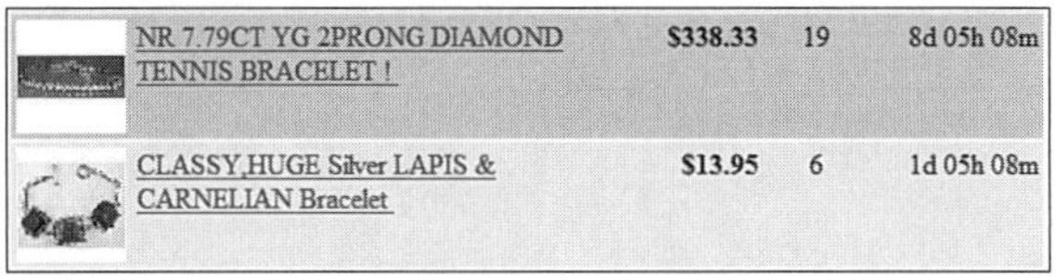

FIGURE 18.3

Two item list-
ings—the first
one enhanced
with the
Highlight option.

| | NR 7.79CT YG 2PRONG DIAMOND TENNIS BRACELET ! | $338.33 | 19 | 8d 05h 08m |
| | CLASSY,HUGE Silver LAPIS & CARNELIAN Bracelet | $13.95 | 6 | 1d 05h 08m |

Featured Plus!

The Featured Plus! option displays your item in the Featured Items section at the top of the appropriate category page and in the Featured Items section at the top of any search results page. This option will set you back a whopping $19.95.

Home Page Featured

Ever wonder how much it costs to have your item featured on the main eBay home page? Here's the answer: $99.95. (And it doesn't even guarantee how often your item will pop up. What a deal—*not*.) All you have to do is select the Home Page Featured option, and your item will *periodically* be displayed on the home page. (And for the same low price, your item also gets displayed in the Featured Items section of normal category and search results pages.)

Gift Icon

Think your item would make a great gift for a specific occasion? Then pony up $0.25 to add a Gift icon beside your item's listing. Figure 18.4 shows an listing enhanced with one of these icons.

> **" Mike Sez "**
>
> In general, I find that spending money on boldface, highlight, or other listing updates isn't much different from just throwing your money away. Whether you're spending a buck or a hundred, these options just don't increase traffic that much—so I try to avoid them.

FIGURE 18.4

An item enhanced with a Gift icon.

	BARBIE Odette Swan Lake princess NEW mint	$15.99 $19.99 Buy It Now	-	6d 21h 54m

Counter

The final listing option available is the free page counter. When you opt to put a counter at the bottom of your item listing (like the one in Figure 18.5), you and (in most cases) potential bidders can see how many other users have visited the page. The more page visitors, the more likely it is that you'll receive a substantial number of bids.

FIGURE 18.5

An Ándale counter at the bottom of an eBay listing page.

You can choose from three different types of counters, all supplied (free of charge) by Ándale. The Andale Style counter is a black-and-white "odometer"-type counter; the Green LED Counter is a little more colorful, displaying bright green "digital" numbers against a black background; and the Hidden counter is hidden to bidders but visible to you, the seller. Choose one of these three, or the Do Not Add a Counter option—no payment necessary!

Writing a Powerful Item Listing

Here's a tip that's fairly self-evident. The better written and more effective your listing title and description, the more successful your auction will be. It's just like advertising copy: Great copy produces the best results.

Write a Title That SELLS!

Let's start right at the top, with the title of your item listing. You can use up to 45 letters, numbers, characters, and spaces, and you need to accomplish two things:

> **"Mike Sez"**
>
> If you think you're going to get a lot of traffic to your item listing page, by all means display a counter. (It's free, after all.) If, on the other hand, you don't want to tip your hand as to how many potential bidders you might have, go with the hidden counter.

- You have to include the appropriate information so that anyone searching for a similar item will find your item in his search results.
- You have to make your title stand out from all the other titles on those long listing pages.

tip

If you're unsure how best to word the title for your item listing, research a few auctions for similar items and "borrow" their wording.

Let's tackle the first point first. You have to think like the people who will be looking for your item. Most users will be using eBay's search feature to look for specific items, so you want to put the right keywords into your item title to make your item pop up on as many search results pages as possible. And you have to do this while using the absolute minimum number of words.

If your item has a model number or series name, that's definitely something to include. As an example, you might be selling a **1956 Gibson ES-175 Red Jazz Guitar**. This title gets in the year (1956), the manufacturer (Gibson), the model number (ES-175), the color (Red), and a brief description of what it is (a jazz guitar)—which pretty much covers all the bases.

Beyond including as many relevant facts as possible in your title, how do you make your title POP off the page and STAND OUT from all the other boring listings? Obviously, one technique is to employ the judicious use of CAPITAL LETTERS. The operative word here is *judicious*; titles with ALL capital letters step over the line into overkill.

It also pays to think like an advertising copywriter. What words almost always stop consumers in their tracks? Use attention-getting words such as **FREE** and **NEW** and **BONUS** and **EXTRA** and **DELUXE** and **RARE**—as long as these words truly describe the item you're selling and don't mislead the potential bidder.

In short, use your title to both inform and attract attention—and include as many potential search keywords as possible.

Write the Right Description

If the listing title is the headline of your ad, the listing description is your ad's body copy. Which means it's time to put on your copywriter's hat, and get down to the nitty-gritty details.

What makes for good copy? Remember, you have all the space you need, so say as much as you need to say. So, unlike the title description, you don't have to scrimp on words or leave anything out. If you can describe your item adequately in a sentence, great; if it takes three paragraphs, that's okay, too.

When you're writing the description for your ad, make sure you mention anything and everything that a potential bidder might need to know. There are certain key data points that users expect to see in your item description. Refer to the following checklist for the key points you should definitely include in your item listings:

Item Description Checklist

- ☐ Name (or title)
- ☐ Condition (new, used, mint, and so on)
- ☐ Age (if it's a used item)
- ☐ Original use (if it's a used item)
- ☐ Value (if you know it)
- ☐ Any included accessories
- ☐ Any known defects or damage
- ☐ Warranty or guarantee (if you offer one)

When you're writing the item description, you need to put the most important and motivating information in your initial paragraph, since a lot of folks won't read any further than that. Think of your first paragraph like a lead paragraph in a newspaper story; grab 'em with something catchy, give them the gist of the story, and lead them into reading the next paragraph and the one after that.

And, although you need to be descriptive (and in some collectibles categories, you need to be *obsessively* so), it doesn't hurt to employ a little marketing savvy and salesmanship. Yes, you should talk about the features of your item, but it's even better if you can talk about your product's *benefits* to the potential buyer.

Let's say you're selling a used cordless phone, and the phone has a 50-number memory. Saying "50-number memory" is stating a feature; saying instead that the phone "lets you recall your 50 most-called phone numbers at the press of a button" is describing a benefit. Remember, a feature is something your item has; a benefit is something your item does for the user.

Use the Right Abbreviations

When dealing with some types of items, collectibles especially, you can use abbreviations and acronyms to describe the product's condition. This helps to conserve valuable space, especially in the listing's title.

Table 18.1 presents some of the most popular abbreviations that you might want to incorporate in your item listings.

TABLE 18.1   Listing Abbreviations

Abbreviation	Description	Meaning
ARC	Advanced readers copy	A pre-publication version of a book manuscript, typically released to reviewers and bookstores for publicity purposes
BU	Built up	For models and other to-be-assembled items; indicates that the item has already been assembled
CC	Cut corner	Some closeout items are marked by a notch on the corner of the package
CO	Cut out	Closeout item
COA	Certificate of authenticity	Document that vouches for the authenticity of the item; often found with autographed or rare collectible items
COC	Cutout corner	Same as CC (cut corner)
COH	Cut out hole	Some closeout items are marked by a small hole punched somewhere on the package
FS	Factory sealed	Still in the original manufacturer's packaging
GP	Gold plate	Item is gold plated
HC	Hard cover	Used to indicate hardcover (as opposed to softcover, or paperback) books
HE	Heavy gold electroplated	Item has heavy gold plating
HTF	Hard to find	Item isn't in widespread circulation
LE	Limited edition	Item was produced in limited quantities
LSW	Label shows wear	Item's label shows normal usage for its age
MCU	Might clean up	Might show a higher grade if cleaned or otherwise restored
MIB	Mint in box	Item in perfect condition, still in the original box
MIMB	Mint in mint box	Item in perfect condition, still in the original box—which itself is in perfect condition
MIP	Mint in package	Item in perfect condition, still in the original package
MISB	Mint in sealed box	Item in perfect condition, still in the original box with the original seal
MNB	Mint, no box	Mint-condition item but without the original package
MOC	Mint on card	For action figures and similar items, an item in perfect condition still in its original carded package
MOMC	Mint on mint card	Item in perfect condition, still on its original carded package—which is also in mint condition
MONMC	Mint on near-mint card	Same as MOMC, but with the card in less-than-perfect condition

TABLE 18.1   (continued)

Abbreviation	Description	Meaning
MWBMT	Mint with both mint tags	For stuffed animals which typically have both a hang tag and a tush (sewn-on) tag, indicates both tags are in perfect condition
MWBT	Mint with both tags	Same as MWBMT, but with the tags in less-than-mint condition
MWMT	Mint with mint tag	Mint-condition item with its original tag, in mint condition
NIB	New in box	Brand-new item, still in its original box
NOS	New old stock	Old, discontinued parts in original, unused condition
NR	No reserve	Indicates that you're selling an item with no reserve price
NRFB	Never removed from box	An item bought but never used or played with
NWOT	New without tags	Item, unused, but without its original tags
NWT	New with tags	Item, unused, that still has its original hanging tags
OOP	Out of print	Item is no longer being manufactured
P/O	Punched out	Same as CC (cut corner)
RR	Re-release	Not the original issue, but rather a reissue (typically done for the collector's market)
SC	Soft cover	A paperback (non-hardcover) book
SS	Still sealed	As it says, still in the original sealed package
SW	Slight wear	Only minor wear commensurate with age
VHTF	Very hard to find	Self-descriptive
WOC	Writing on cover	Item has markings on front surface

Don't Reinvent the Wheel—Reuse Item Listings That Work

Here's another good reason to standardize the type of items you sell on eBay. Once you create the perfect item title and description, *reuse it*. That's right, there's no reason to write a new listing every time you put another item up for auction. Use the old cut and paste to recycle your winning title and description text. That's not to say you shouldn't tweak your copy over time, but once you come up with a winner, why change it? High-volume

tip

The single most effective way to improve your item listings is to include a photograph of the item for sale. This is such an important step that I've devoted an entire chapter to the process. Turn to Chapter 19, "Working with Photographs," to learn more.

sellers use the same copy over and over—just as real-world advertisers do—for a simple reason. It works!

Creating Better-Looking Item Listings

Now it's time for the fun stuff—making your item listings look more attractive. Yes, we're talking style over substance, but style draws the eyeballs. So let's look at the various ways you can make your listings stand out from eBay's standard plain-text listings.

eBay's Listing Designer

We'll start with the listing templates that are available with eBay's Listing Designer. As you can see in Figure 18.6, Listing Designer is available to all users from the Sell Your Item page—providing you pay the extra 10 cents per listing to use it.

Listing Designer provides more than two dozen predesigned templates, which eBay calls *themes*. You choose a theme from the Select a Theme list, and then choose a layout for your pictures from the Select a Layout list. Listing Designer is easy to use, and requires no additional software or ongoing subscription.

eBay Turbo Lister

The same themes that are available in Listing Designer are also available in eBay's Turbo Lister bulk listing software (`pages.ebay.com/turbo_lister/`). You choose your template on the Design Your Listing screen, shown in Figure 18.7. As you learned in Chapter 11, Turbo Lister is available free of charge—making it the listing creation software of choice for cost-conscious sellers.

FIGURE 18.6

Any seller can use eBay's Listing Designer to choose a template for their item listing.

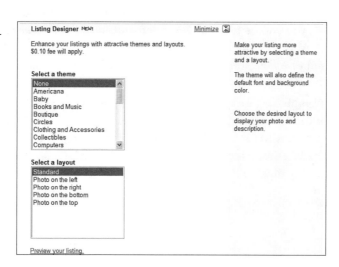

FIGURE 18.7

Apply a theme to all your bulk listings with eBay Turbo Lister.

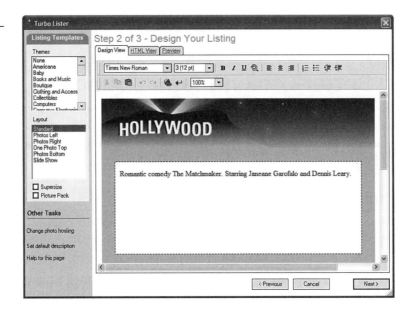

Third-Party Listing Tools

When it comes to creating great-looking item listings, you're not limited to eBay's "official" listing creation tools. There are a plethora of listing creation programs and services available, all of which provide a variety of predesigned templates you can use for your item listings.

Most of these tools work in a similar fashion. You go to a particular Web page or program screen, select a template from a list, choose available layout options, and then enter your normal listing title and description.

For example, the Design Center section of the Web-based Ándale Lister (www.andale.com) lets you choose from dozens of templates (which Ándale calls themes), in five general categories: Category Specific, Gallery/Store, Holiday/Seasonal, Basic, and Other. Vendio Sales Manager (www.vendio.com) offers a Template Workshop, that lets you customize an equally large selection of category-specific templates.

Ándale and Vendio are just two of the many companies offering listing creation tools. Most of the major auction management sites (described in Chapter 20, "Using Professional Auction Tools") include template-driven listing creation tools as part of their overall services. In addition, the following standalone tools let you create sophisticated eBay auction listings:

- Adomatic Professional (www.slconsultancy.co.uk/adomatic/)
- Auction Lizard (www.auction-lizard.com)
- Auctiva Poster (www.auctiva.com)
- Dominant Ad Creator (dac.volcanicsoft.com)
- EZAd (www.etusa.com/auction/atrix.htm)

Comparing Listing Templates

Let's compare of some of the different templates available with these listing tools. Admittedly, template choice and design is somewhat subjective, so you'll have to trust my decisions here. What I've done is chosen templates appropriate to an item listing for a DVD movie, to give you an idea of what you might expect from the major listing creation tools. Figure 18.8 shows the Entertainment template available with eBay Listing Designer and Turbo Lister, Figure 18.9 shows the Movies template from Ándale Lister, and Figure 18.10 shows The Show template from Vendio Sales Manager. As you can see, the listings vary wildly in look and feel, even though they all present similar information. Of course, other templates are available, and (with some) you can do a degree of tweaking to personalize the final listing. In any case, it behooves you to test drive a particular listing creation tool before you commit; it's definitely a matter of personal taste!

FIGURE 18.8

eBay's Entertainment template.

FIGURE 18.9
Ándale's Movies
template.

FIGURE 18.10
Vendio's The
Show template.

Using HTML in Your Listings

Here's a secret known to successful sellers: eBay lets you use HTML to spruce up your item listings. All you have to do is know which HTML codes to enter in the Description box when you're creating your item listing.

eBay's HTML Text Editor

The easiest way to add HTML to your item description is to use the HTML Text Editor that eBay includes as part of the Sell Your Item page. When you click the HTML Text Editor link next to the Description box, you open the editor (shown in Figure 18.11), which lets you add HTML effects in a WYSIWYG environment, much the same way you add boldface and italic in your word processor. Just highlight the text you want to format then click the appropriate formatting button. No manual coding necessary.

caution

eBay lets you insert HTML code into your item's description, but forbids the use of HTML in the item's title.

FIGURE 18.11

Add text formatting to your item description with eBay's HTML Text Editor.

Other HTML Editors

Many other item listing tools include similar easy-to-use HTML editors. For example, eBay's Turbo Lister includes a Design View tab that has a built-in HTML editor. Format your text in Design View—or switch to the HTML View tab (shown in Figure 18.12) to see the raw HTML coding.

Inserting Your Own HTML Codes

You also have the option of inserting your own raw HTML codes into your item listings. While this isn't a task for the faint of heart, writing your own code lets you create highly individualized item listings—much fancier than you can do with a standard HTML editor.

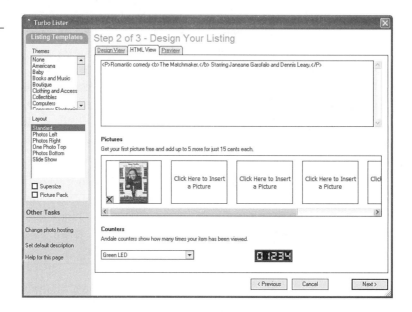

HTML coding might sound difficult, but it's really pretty easy. HTML is really nothing more than a series of hidden codes that tell Web browsers how to display different types of text and graphics. The codes are embedded in a document, so you can't see them; they're only visible to your Web browser.

These codes are distinguished from normal text by the fact that they're enclosed within angle brackets. Each particular code turns on or off a particular attribute, such as boldface or italic text. Most codes are in sets of "on/off" pairs; you turn "on" the code before the text you want to affect and then turn "off" the code after the text.

For example, the code <h1> turns specified type into a level-one headline; the code </h1> turns off the headline type. The code <i> is used to italicize text; </i> turns off the italic. (As you can see, an "off" code is merely the "on" code with a slash before it.)

tip

Many experienced sellers create HTML templates that they can cut and paste into multiple item listings. When you get a boilerplate listing you like, save the text—HTML codes and all—into a text file, using Microsoft Notepad or a similar program. You can then paste that boilerplate text file into a new item description, and edit it as appropriate.

Codes to Format Your Text

We'll start off with some of the most common HTML codes—those used to format your text. Table 18.2 shows some of these text-formatting codes you can use in your item description.

Table 18.2   HTML Codes to Format Text

Effect	On Code	Off Code
Bold	`<b>`	`</b>`
Italic	`<i>`	`</i>`
Underline	`<u>`	`</u>`
Center	`<c>`	`</c>`
First-level headline	`<h1>`	`</h1>`
Second-level headline	`<h2>`	`</h2>`
Third-level headline	`<h3>`	`</h3>`
Monospaced "typewriter" text	`<tt>`	`</tt>`

Just surround the text you want to format with the appropriate on and off codes, and you're ready to go. For example, to format a piece of text as bold, you'd write something that looks like this:

`<b>this text is bold</b>`

Codes for Font Type, Size, and Color

You can also use HTML to specify a particular font type or size, using the `<font>` code.

To specify a font type for selected text, use the `<font>` code with the `face` attribute, like this:

`<font face="xxxx">text</font>`

Replace the *xxxx* with the specific font, such as Arial or Times Roman—in quotation marks.

Another common use of the `<font>` code is to specify type size. You use the `size` attribute, and the code looks like this:

`<font size="xx">text</font>`

Replace the *xx* with the size you want, from –6 to +6, with –6 being the smallest, +6 being the biggest, and 0 (or no size specified) being "normal" size type.

You can also use the `<font>` code to designate a specific text color. In this instance, you use the `color` attribute, like this:

`<font color="#xxxxxx">text</font>`

Replace the *xxxxxx* with the code for a specific color. Table 18.3 lists some basic color codes.

TABLE 18.3   Common HTML Color Codes

Color	Code
White	FFFFFF
Red	FF0000
Green	00FF00
Blue	0000FF
Magenta	FF00FF
Cyan	00FFFF
Yellow	FFFF00
Black	000000
Light gray	DDDDDD

Codes for Paragraphs, Line Breaks, and Rules

Some of the simplest HTML codes let you break your text into separate lines and paragraphs—and add horizontal rules between paragraphs. These codes are inserted into your text just once; there are no matching ending codes.

Table 18.4 lists these "on-only" codes.

TABLE 18.4   HTML Codes for Lines and Paragraphs

Action	Code
Line break	
New paragraph	<p>
Horizontal rule (line)	<hr>

Codes for Graphics

Adding pictures to your item listings really brings some excitement to the normally plain-text world of eBay. While you can add pictures the eBay way (via the Sell Your Item page), you can also add pictures in the middle of your item description, using HTML.

tip

For a complete list of the literally hundreds of different HTML color codes, go to the Webmonkey Color Codes Reference (hotwired.lycos.com/webmonkey/reference/color_codes/).

Before you can insert a graphic into your listing, you need to know the address of that graphic (in the form of a Web page URL). Then you use the following code:

```
<img src="URL">
```

No off code is required for inserted graphics. Note that the location is enclosed in quotation marks—and that you have to insert the `http://` part of the URL.

Codes for Links

You can use HTML to add links to your own personal Web pages (a great idea if you have additional images of this specific item) or to related sites. Many sellers also like to provide a direct email link in case potential bidders have questions they need answered.

To insert a link to another Web page in your item listing, you use the following HTML code:

```
<a href="URL">this is the link</a>
```

The text between the on and off codes will appear onscreen as a typical underlined hyperlink; when users click that text, they'll be linked to the URL you specified in the code. Note that the URL is enclosed in quotation marks and that you have to include the `http://` part of the address.

You can also create a "mail-to" link in your listing; users would be able to send email to you by simply clicking the link. Here's the code for a mail-to link:

```
<a href="mailto:yourname@domain.com">click
here to email me</a>
```

note

eBay allows links to pages that provide additional information about the item listed, additional photos of the item, and your other eBay auctions. eBay prohibits links to pages that attempt to sell merchandise outside of eBay. Link at your own risk.

note

To learn more about these and other HTML codes, go to the HTML Goodies (www.htmlgoodies.com/tutors/) or WebMonkey (hotwired.lycos.com/webmonkey/authoring/html_basics/) Web sites. You can also pick up a copy of Todd Stauffer's *Absolute Beginner's Guide to Creating Web Pages, 2nd Edition* (Que, 2002), available wherever good books are sold.

THE ABSOLUTE MINIMUM

There are lots of ways you can improve the effectiveness of your eBay auctions. Here are some of the main ones:

- Start (and end) your auctions on a Sunday evening.

- Choose the standard 7-day auction.

- Be cautious about opting for eBay's paid listing enhancements, such as bold and highlight; most aren't worth the extra cost.

- Craft your item title and description to attract the most number of shoppers—and supply enough information to make them comfortable about bidding.

- Use predesigned templates to create sophisticated auction listings; some of the most popular listing creation tools include eBay's Listing Designer and Turbo Lister, Ándale Lister, and Vendio Selling Manager.

- Format the text in your listing description with HTML codes; use eBay's HTML Text Editor, or insert your own codes by hand.

WORKING WITH PHOTOGRAPHS

Showing a picture of your product in your item listing greatly increases your chances of success. It also helps to increase the average selling price of your item.

Managing product photos is an important part of any successful eBay business. You need to learn how to take good photos of your products and how to insert those photos into your item listings. It isn't hard, once you get it figured out—but it does require some small degree of photographic skill and mastery of a photo editing software program. So clean off your camera lens and get ready to shoot—it's time to learn all about photography for eBay!

Pictures Work—Here's Why

It's a simple fact. Item listings with product photos are more successful than those without. As all successful direct mail retailers know, customers like to see what they're buying before they purchase an item. That's why all those direct mail catalogs are chock full of big, four-color photographs. Seeing a product photo increases the customer's sense of security; not being able to see the product causes a lot of customers to just walk away.

The power of pictures is even greater when all your competitors include product photos and you don't. Photos with listings are the norm these days, and those listings that don't have photos look exceedingly unprofessional. Do *you* want to bid on an auction where the seller hasn't taken the time and effort to include a photo of the item for sale? Probably not. Given the choice of bidding on an auction that includes a nice, clean product photo and one that doesn't, most users choose the auction with the photo, no questions asked. Don't put yourself at a disadvantage; include photographs with all your eBay auctions.

You should even—and especially—include a photo if the item you're selling is damaged or otherwise flawed. You might think that you shouldn't show an unflattering photo, but just the opposite is true. You want bidders to know what they're getting into, regarding damage and flaws, and showing a picture is the best way to do this.

Is there any time when you *don't* want to include a picture of an item? The only situation I can think of is when the item you're selling is nothing more than a black box or a blank book cover. Otherwise, including a product photo should be standard operating procedure.

Taking Effective Photos

Taking an effective product photo takes a bit of effort; it's not quite as easy as snapping off a quick Polaroid. To take quality photos of the items you intend to sell, you'll need a decent digital camera and a variety of photographic accessories, as detailed in the following checklist:

Product Photograph Checklist

- ☐ Digital camera
- ☐ Tripod
- ☐ Lighting
- ☐ Clean space with plain black or white background
- ☐ Graphics or photo editing software

Let's take a detailed look at what's involved.

Shopping for a Digital Camera

Although you can take pictures with a normal film camera, develop the film, and have a film processing lab transfer your photos to graphics files on a photo CD, that's a lot of work. Much better to start with digital photos at the source by using a digital camera to take all your product photos. You can pick up a low-end digital camera for well under $200 these days, and going direct from camera to computer to eBay is a lot easier than any other method.

What type of digital camera should you buy? The good news is that you don't need a really high-end model. In fact, if you buy a super-expensive camera with multi-megapixel resolution, you'll just be wasting a lot of the camera's picture-taking power. When it comes to putting pictures on eBay, you actually need to take relatively low-resolution pictures—so all those megapixels are pretty much photographic overkill.

That doesn't mean you can get by with the cheapest camera available, however. To take good product photos, you want a camera with a quality lens, preferably with some type of optical zoom capability, and with a macro mode. (You use the macro mode to take close-up photos of those very small items you have for sale.) Make sure you can easily configure the camera for low-resolution mode, and that there's a quick and simple way to get your photographs from your camera to your computer's hard disk.

Don't Forget the Accessories

When you're spending $200 or more for a decent digital camera, keep a few bucks back for those accessories that will help you take better photos every time. In particular, you'll want to invest in a tripod and auxiliary lighting.

A tripod is invaluable for steadying your camera when you're taking photographs. A tripod will help you avoid camera shake, and corresponding blurry pictures. It's also useful in low-light situations, where you need to hold your camera especially still for long exposures. And it's not expensive; you can pick up a decent tripod for less than $20.

Of course, you can avoid the low-light problem by using auxiliary lighting. While you might think you have enough natural light to take good photos, you probably don't. A set of low-cost photo floodlights will provide the lighting necessary to take the ultra-sharp photos your customers expect. You can find two-piece lighting kits for under $150.

While we're talking about lights, consider investing a few more bucks for diffuser screens. You get better results when your subject is lit by diffused lighting; direct lighting is a little harsh and can cause glare. Look for a diffuser you can attach directly to your light reflectors.

Finally, think about where you'll be taking your photos. You'll need some sort of flat surface, and some sort of simple background—either flat black or white. That might necessitate buying a small table and an appropriate expanse of colored cardboard or cloth.

Mike Sez

A good lighting kit to consider is the KT500 from Smith-Victor (www.smithvictor.com). It includes two 250-watt lamps with 10-inch reflectors and stands, for about $135—good enough for most eBay product photography.

How to Take a Good Photograph

Once you have the proper equipment, taking a good product photo is as simple as following these steps:

1. Prepare the photo area. Clear off a good-sized flat surface, and cover the surface and background with a plain white or black material. (Use a white background for dark objects, and a black background for lighter objects.)

2. Position the product in the middle of the photo area, at an angle that best shows off the product's visual attributes.

3. Position your floodlights to the sides and slightly in front of the item, as shown in Figure 19.1. (If you have a third light, position it to the back and below the object, to provide a slight amount of backlighting.)

FIGURE 19.1

Position auxiliary lighting to best effect.

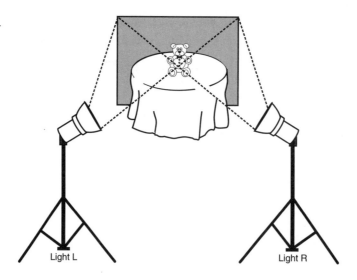

Light L   Light R

4. Mount your camera to the tripod and position it directly in front of the object to be photographed.

5. Start shooting!

The result should be a focused, well-lit, centered photograph, like the one in Figure 19.2.

tip

Depending on the item you're selling, you might want to jazz up your photos with a few props. For example, you might want to display clothing on a mannequin, or jewelry on a display stand.

It's important that you don't just snap off a quick picture and move on. You need to shoot your item from several different angles and distances—and remember to get a close-up of any important area of the item, such as a serial number or a damaged area. You may want to include multiple photos in your listing, or just have a good selection of photos to choose from for that one best picture. Remember, it's always good to have a backup photo, just in case you messed up the first one!

FIGURE 19.2

A good product photo—it's easy to see what you're selling.

Five Types of Pictures *Not* to Take

Okay, you're saying. You know how to take a good picture. Let's just get on with it!

Not so fast, pal. I've seen enough eBay listings to realize that most people who say they know how to take good photos don't. Let's look at five cardinal sins of product photography, and how you can avoid them.

Blurry Picture

See the photo in Figure 19.3? See how blurry it is? That's because the picture was taken *without a tripod*. The camera wasn't held steady, and it moved slightly while the photograph was being taken. The result is a blurry photograph where it's hard to see what the product is—let alone make out fine details.

FIGURE 19.3

A blurry picture—the result of moving the camera when shooting.

A better approach is to mount your camera to a tripod. The results will be clear and crisp—just what you want for your item listing.

Picture Too Dark

Another common mistake amateur photographers make is to shoot the picture without enough light. Figure 19.4 shows the result of inadequate lighting; see how the picture is just too dark, with the details almost completely obscured?

How can you ensure that you have enough light for your picture? Here are your options:

caution

Blurry photos can also result from not focusing the camera lens properly. If your camera has autofocus, make sure that its aimed at the product, and not at the background or another object. If you're focusing manually, do a better job!

- Buy a set of auxiliary lights. One light helps, but can still result in unwanted shadows. Two lights are better, as they'll fill out any unlit areas.

- Shoot outdoors. This is the poor man's lighting solution, but it works. Try to shoot in early morning or late afternoon, when you get a softer, less severe light; avoid shooting in the harsh overhead light of midday.

FIGURE 19.4

The picture's too dark—you didn't use enough lighting!

- Use a flash. Most cameras include a built-in flash, which can shine a ton of light directly onto the front surface of the item being photographed. Watch out for glare and washout, however—as discussed in the next section.

Too Much Flash

Casual photographers are tempted to use the flash whenever they shoot indoors. Used properly, flash can be a good thing. Too much flash, however, can cause the object to wash out. Flash is also bad when you're shooting a glossy object or a product that's encased in plastic or shrink wrap. Figure 19.5 shows the type of glare you can get from a flash photo.

note

Inadequate lighting—or shooting under fluorescent lights—can also affect the color of your photos. More light generally results in more accurate colors.

FIGURE 19.5

Flash photography can produce glare on shrink-wrapped products.

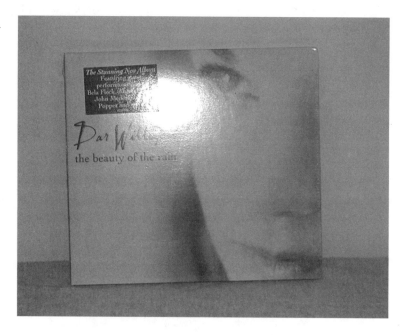

Subject Too Small

Look at the object in Figure 19.6. It's so far away it seems as if the photographer was afraid to get any closer! You need to get that product up front and center, close enough to the camera so that your customers can see what you're selling. You want the object to fill up the entire picture. That means getting close with your camera— or cropping the photo in the editing process.

FIGURE 19.6

Bad composition— the object's way too small!

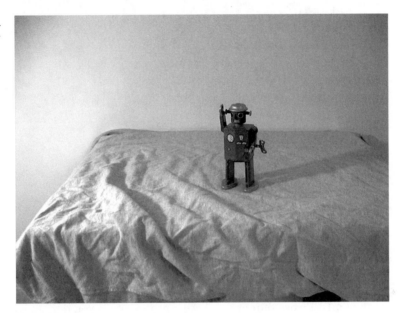

Subject Doesn't Stand Out

You'd think you'd know better. If you shoot your object against a busy background, as shown in Figure 19.7, it detracts from the main point of the photograph. The background competes with the object you're trying to sell, which is less than ideal.

It's far better to remove all competing objects from the picture and hang a white or black sheet (or t-shirt) behind the item. This makes the main object stand out a lot better—and increases the sex appeal of your product.

FIGURE 19.7
There's too much happening here—what are you trying to sell?

Scanning Instead of Shooting

You don't always have to photograph the items you want to sell. If you're selling relatively flat items (books, comics, CDs, DVDs, and so on), you might be better off with a scanner than a camera. Just lay the object on a flatbed scanner and scan the item into a digital file on your computer. It's actually easier to scan something like a book or a DVD case than it is to take a picture of it—you don't have to worry about lighting or focus or any of that.

Here's something else—since your scanner operates just like a camera, you can scan practically anything you can fit on the glass. The item at hand doesn't even have to be perfectly flat. Just about any item in a box can be easily scanned, as can many other small objects. When it doubt, test it.

Editing Your Photos—Digitally

When you're taking a digital photo or making a scan, you want to save your images in the JPG file format. This is the default file format for most digital cameras and scanners, although some devices give you a choice of other formats (GIF, TIF, and so on). The JPG format is de facto

tip

When you're scanning compact discs, take the CD booklet out of the jewel case to scan, instead of scanning the jewel case itself.

standard for Web images, and what eBay expects for your item listings; given the choice, choose JPG.

With your photos in JPG format, it's easy to touch them up with digital photo editing software. What kind of touch up are we talking about? Here's a list of the most common photo editing operations:

- Lighten up photos shot in low light
- Correct the color in poorly shot photos
- Crop the picture to focus only on the subject at hand
- Resize the image to fit better in your eBay listings
- Decrease the resolution or color count to produce a smaller-sized file

If you're a perfect photographer, you may never need to touch up the pictures you take. But since most of us are far from perfect, it's great to be able to "punch up" the photos we take—and make them as perfect as possible for our eBay listings.

Choosing Image Editing Software

To edit your photos, you need a software program designed to edit digital photographs. There are a lot of programs out there, some free and some tremendously expensive. (Adobe Photoshop, used by many professional photographers, falls into the latter category.) You want something in the middle—a low-cost program that's easy to use and includes all the image-editing features you need to create quality product photos.

There are a number of easy-to-use, low-cost programs out there. Those that are the most popular among eBay users include

- Adobe Photoshop Elements (www.adobe.com)
- CorelDRAW Essentials (www.corel.com)
- PaintShop Pro (www.jasc.com)
- Microsoft Picture It! Photo (www.microsoft.com/products/imaging/)
- Roxio PhotoSuite (www.roxio.com)

Most of these programs cost around $50, and have similar features. In the next section I'll focus on Photoshop Elements, probably the most popular of these programs.

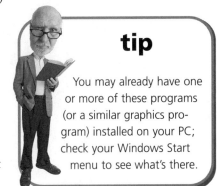

tip

You may already have one or more of these programs (or a similar graphics program) installed on your PC; check your Windows Start menu to see what's there.

Basic Image Editing with Photoshop Elements

Photoshop Elements is both relatively low-cost and relatively easy to use. It's not to be confused with the much more expensive (and much harder to use) Adobe Photoshop; Photoshop Elements is pretty much a consumer-friendly subset of the larger program.

Editing a photograph with Photoshop Elements is as easy as clicking a few buttons. Just follow these steps:

1. To load a photo for editing, select Window, File Browser to open the File Browser. Navigate to the appropriate folder in the folder tree, then double-click the photo you want to edit.

2. Do a quick fix on the image's brightness, contrast, and color levels by selecting Enhance, Auto Levels.

3. If the picture needs further adjustment, select Enhance and then choose Auto Lighting, Auto Color, or Auto Brightness/Contrast. Make the appropriate adjustments.

4. To crop the photograph, click the Crop Tool button in the Toolbox, then drag the cursor across the picture to select the area to be cropped, as shown in Figure 19.8. Double-click the selected area to complete the crop.

FIGURE 19.8

Cropping a photograph in Photoshop Elements.

5. To reduce the image and file size, select File, Save for Web. When the Save for Web window appears, pull down the Settings list and select JPEG Low. Move your cursor to the Width box (in the New Settings area) and enter an appropriate pixel width. (I recommend something in the 300 to 400 pixel range.) Make sure the Constrain Proportions option is checked. Click OK, and when the Save Optimized As dialog box appears, enter a new filename and click Save.

note

When editing a photo, make sure the Toolbox is open by selecting Window, Tools.

Obviously, there's a lot more editing you can do, but these steps cover the basics that work for the majority of eBay product photos. If you're using another photo editing program, you should find similar operations.

Resizing Your Pictures for Best Effect

While you're editing, you'll probably need to resize your photographs to best fit within your eBay listings. Most pictures you take with a digital camera will come out too big to fit on a Web page without scrolling—even the smallest digital photos are typically sized at 640×480—that's 640 pixels wide, which is too wide to fit comfortably on most computer screens.

eBay recommends that you size your image to no more than 300×300 pixels. Personally, I find 300 pixels a little on the narrow side. I aim for 400 pixels wide, but will sometimes go up to 500 or even 600 pixels wide, depending on the item photographed and the importance of viewing item detail. I won't go over 600 pixels, however.

note

Most photo editing programs will have some sort of file info command that lets you see the size of the file you're editing. You can also view the file size from within Windows's My Documents or My Pictures folder, by right-clicking the file and selecting Properties from the pop-up menu.

While you're considering the physical size of the photograph, you should also consider the size of the file that holds the photograph. The bigger the file, the longer it takes to download from the Internet. Create too big a file, and users won't want to wait to view your item listing.

The right file size is something less than 50KB—and less is better. Holding the files under the 50KB level keeps the loading time for each photo down to a reasonable level.

Your photo editing software should include settings that let you reduce both the physical size and the file size for your photographs. And, of course, the two go hand in hand; reduce the physical size and you'll also reduce the file size.

Adding Photos to Your Item Listings

When you have your photos properly edited, it's time to add photos to your item listings. The easiest way to add a photo to an item listing is by using eBay's picture management services and choosing the appropriate options when you're creating your item listings. You also have the option of using third-party image management services; we'll look at both options.

Using eBay Picture Services

When you have eBay host your photos, you have some choices to make. If you only want to show one picture, eBay's built-in picture management is a good choice. It's free (for a single picture), and you can use the Listing Designer (discussed in Chapter 18, "Making Your Auctions More Effective") to choose the right position for your photo.

If you want to include more than one photo in your ad, you'll have to pay for it. Here's how eBay's fee structure works:

- First photo: free.
- Each additional picture (up to six, total): 15 cents each.
- Slide show (multiple pictures in a flip format): 75 cents.
- Supersize pictures (allow users to click a photo to display at a larger size): 75 cents
- Picture pack (up to six pictures, supersized, with Gallery display): $1.00

You can see how the costs start to add up. Let's say you have two pictures of your item (front and back, perhaps) that you want to display large. You'll pay 90 cents for this privilege (15 cents for the second picture, plus 75 cents for supersizing). As you can see, if you have more than one photo in your listing, it might be cheaper for you to find another site to host your pictures, which we'll talk about in the next section.

note

Why would you want to include more than one photo of your product? Maybe to show both the front and the back, or the top and the bottom, or the front and one or both sides. Maybe your product consists of multiple pieces, and you have a separate photo of each. Or maybe you just want to show off your product at multiple angles. Whatever the reason, sometimes one photo just isn't enough.

If you choose to use eBay to manage your photos, here's how you insert a photo into your item listing

1. Start the process to create a new item listing, and work your way to the Pictures & Details page.

2. Scroll down to the Add Pictures section and select the eBay Picture Services tab, shown in Figure 19.9.

tip

One plus to using eBay Picture Services is that you get a free picture of your item in the title bar of your item listing page.

FIGURE 19.9

Using eBay Picture Services to insert photos in your item listing.

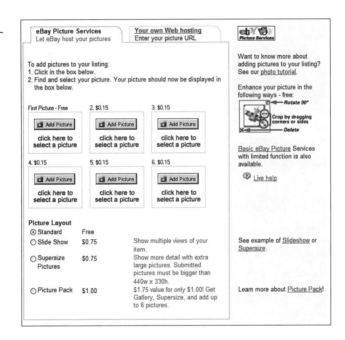

3. Click the Add Picture button in the First Picture   Free box. An Open dialog box now appears on your computer desktop; use this dialog box to locate and select the photo you want to use. Click the Open button when done—the photo you selected now appears on the Pictures & Details page.

4. To insert an additional picture (for 15 cents extra), click the second box and follow the instructions in step 3.

5. To insert even more pictures, click the next box(es) and follow the instructions in step 3.

6. In the Picture Layout section, select what options you want—Standard (single picture), Slide Show, Supersize Pictures, or Picture Pack.

7. If you choose to use eBay's Listing Designer, scroll to the Listing Designer section and select a position for your photo from the Select a Layout list.

That's it. eBay will automatically upload the pictures from your hard disk to their picture hosting server, and automatically insert those pictures into your item listing.

Using Third-Party Image Management Services

Many experienced sellers choose not to use eBay's picture hosting service. They find this service somewhat expensive (if you want to show a lot of pictures) and somewhat limited.

If you don't want to let eBay manage your pictures, you can use another Web hosting service to host your image files, and then manually insert these pictures into your item listings.

There are a large number of Web sites that will host picture files for your eBay auctions. Most of these sites charge some sort of fee, either on a monthly basis for a certain amount of storage space, or on a per-picture basis. You'll want to compare the fees at these sites with what you'll pay at eBay, and then make the smart choice.

The most popular of these services include

- Ándale Images (www.andale.com)
- Auction Pix Image Hosting (www.auctionpix.com)
- ImageHosting.com (www.imagehosting.com)
- MyItem.com (www.myitem.com)
- Picturetrail (www.picturetrail.com)
- PixHost (www.pixhost.com)
- Vendio Image Hosting (www.vendio.com)

Your Internet service provider might also provide image hosting services, often for free. Many ISPs give their users a few megabytes of file storage space as part of their monthly service; you may be able to upload your photos to your ISP's server and then link to that server in your eBay item listings.

Inserting a Single Photo—the Easy Way

After you have your pictures uploaded, you can then add them to your new item listing. If you're adding a single photo, you can do so when you're creating your item listing. Just follow these steps:

1. Start the process to create a new item listing, and work your way to the Pictures & Details page.

2. Scroll down to the Add Pictures section and select the Your Own Web Hosting tab, as shown in Figure 19.10.

3. Enter the full URL (including the `http://`) for the picture into the Picture URL box.

4. If you choose to use eBay's Listing Designer, scroll to the Listing Designer section and select a position for your photo from the Select a Layout list.

That's it. Continue creating your listing as normal, and the completed listing will include the photograph you linked to. Simple as that.

> ## caution
>
> Resist the temptation to simply copy a picture file from someone else's auction to use in your listing. Not only is this unethical, but it misrepresents the exact item you're selling—and you could find yourself on the wrong side of a copyright lawsuit if the owner of the photo takes offense.

FIGURE 19.10

Pointing to a picture file uploaded to another hosting service.

Inserting Photos via HTML

As you learned in Chapter 18, you can include HTML code in your item descriptions—and you can use this code to link to pictures you've already uploaded to an image hosting service. This process isn't as hard as it sounds, assuming you've already found a hosting service, uploaded your picture file, and obtained the full URL for the uploaded picture. All you have to do is insert the following HTML code into your item description, where you want the picture to appear:

```
<img src="http://www.webserver.com/
picture.jpg">
```

> ## "Mike Sez"
>
> If you sell the same product in multiple auctions, you don't have to upload multiple copies of the same photo. You can upload a single image file, and then refer to that file's URL in multiple item listings—thus saving yourself some image hosting fees!

Just replace *www.webserver.com/picture.jpg* with the correct URL for your picture.

If you opt for this method, you'll need to tell eBay that your description includes a picture, so that the picture icon will still display beside your item listing. You do this on the Pictures & Details page in the Add Pictures section. Just check the following option: The Description Already Contains a Picture URL for My Item.

The Absolute Minimum

Including a photograph of what you're selling in your item listing greatly increases your chances of actually selling that item—and for a higher price. When you want to add a photograph to a listing, keep these key points in mind:

- A basic photo setup for eBay auction purposes should include a digital camera, tripod, and floodlights.

- After you've taken the picture, use photo editing software (such as Adobe Photoshop Elements) to touch it up, crop it, and resize it.

- Product photos should be between 300 and 400 pixels wide; image files should be no larger than 50KB in size.

- When it comes to storing your photos online, you can use eBay's picture services or any number of third-party image hosting services.

- You can add photos to your listing by completing the steps on eBay's Sell Your Item page or by inserting URLs into your item description with HTML code.

IN THIS CHAPTER

- Should you be using auction tools?
- Evaluating third-party auction services
- Another option: software tools

20

USING PROFESSIONAL AUCTION TOOLS

Successful eBay sellers make money by listing—and selling—in volume. The more items you list, the more work there is—managing inventory, creating listings, sending post-auction emails, leaving feedback, and packing and shipping the merchandise. Anything you can do to minimize the effort involved helps to make your life easier, and your business more profitable.

The most profitable and professional eBay businesspeople know that they can't handle all this work on their own. These high-volume sellers employ a variety of third-party tools to help them automate much of the auction process. Just as traditional businesses invest in computerized inventory and point-of-sale systems, eBay businesses need to invest in similar systems that help them minimize the amount of work involved in listing and selling their merchandise.

We've discussed some of these auction tools in other parts of this book. This chapter, however, takes a look at the entire suite of services offered by the major third-party auction management sites, and helps you determine which of these sites offer the best tools for your specific needs.

Should You Be Using Auction Tools?

Here's the thing. Auction tools cost money to use. (You can't get good help for free!) So when you decide to utilize a particular auction management service, you automatically increase your business's costs.

Before you decide to use a third-party auction tool, you have to ask yourself if it's worth the cost. Can you afford to spend another 25 or 50 cents per item, just to make your life a little easier? That might sound like peanuts—until you start adding up all your other selling costs. Remember, you have to pay eBay to list each item, then pay another fee when the item is sold. If you accept credit card payment via PayPal, you'll pay another fee when a customer pays via that method. Add all these fees together, and you can easily be out a buck or more on each item you sell—and that comes right out of your profit.

On the other hand, if you're doing a large volume of eBay business, can you afford *not* to use an auction management tool? Add up all the time you spend creating item listings, sending emails, and handling end-of-auction transactions. Is it worth 25 or 50 cents per transaction to cut that workload in half?

An important factor, obviously, is just what operations you can automate with these auction tools. While each site offers a different selection of tools, here are some of the tools you can expect to find at the major third-party auction sites:

- **Auction research**. Search for other auctions in a particular category, and analyze sales data—success rate, average sales price, and so on.

- **Inventory sourcing**. Find wholesale sources for particular types of merchandise.

- **Inventory management**. Enter and track all the items in your inventory and automatically delete items from inventory as they're sold at auction.

- **Image hosting**. Host photos for your auctions on the service's Web site and manage those photos in your item listings.

" Mike Sez "

I wouldn't dream of managing my eBay auctions without the use of these auction management tools. If you run a dozen or more auctions a week, you need to subscribe to one of these services—they're designed to make your auction business easier to run.

- **Gallery**. Create a separate photo page of all the items you have for sale, so potential buyers can link to your item listings and browse through all the merchandise you offer.

- **Bulk listing creation**. Create attractive item listings with predesigned templates, and then list multiple items in bulk.

- **End-of-auction email**. Automatically send notifications to winning bidders and notify customers when payment is received and items are shipped.

- **End-of-auction checkout**. Provide a dedicated page that customers can use to verify their purchases and provide shipping and payment information.

- **Bulk feedback posting**. Automatically post customer feedback in bulk.

- **Storefront**. Provide other non-auction items for sale on the Web.

Not all sites offer all these services. In addition, the level of services offered will also vary—some sites are more automated than others. Read on to learn more about what's available.

Evaluating Third-Party Auction Services

When it comes to third-party tools, there's a lot to choose from. And, while it might be tempting to mix and match different tools from different providers (use this site's lister and that site's checkout), the better bet is to settle on a single service for all your auction needs. While it's not impossible to mix tools and providers, at best it's awkward and at worst it's extremely impractical. For example, while you could use Ándale Lister to create your listings and Vendio Sales Manager for your post-auction management, these tools don't work well together. A much tighter integration is possible when you use tools from the same service—using both Ándale Lister and Ándale Checkout, for example, or employing Vendio Sales for the entire process.

Comparing these different services is a little like comparing apples and jelly beans. That's because some services offer their tools in a single package at a single price, while others offer a menu of different choices, with a la carte pricing. In addition, some services offer a flat monthly price, while others offer different tiers of pricing—and still others offer variable rate pricing based on the number of transactions you make or the final selling price.

"Mike Sez"

My recommendation is to identify a single auction management service and use it for all your auction needs, from creating listings to posting feedback. Don't mix and match; find a single service and commit to it.

That said, let's give this comparison thing a crack. Table 20.1 lists the different tools offered by some of the major auction services, and offers a glance at representative fees.

TABLE 20.1   Major Auction Management Services

Service	Inventory Management	Image Hosting	Gallery	Bulk Listing Creation	End-of-Auction Email	Checkout	Bulk Feedback Posting	Storefront	Pricing
Ándale	X	X	X	X	X	X	X	X	"Quick Packs" from $10.95/month (40 listings); individual services priced separately
Auction Hawk	X	X	X	X	X	X	X		From $12.99/month
AuctionHelper	X	X		X	X	X	X		1.95% of sales (min. $0.15, max. $1.25), plus $0.02 per transaction; $10 min. monthly fee
Auctionworks	X	X	X	X	X	X	X	X	2% of sales (min $0.10 max. $3.00); $14.95 min. monthly fee
Auctiva		X	X	X	X	X	X		From $9.95/month
ChannelAdvisor	X	X	X	X	X	X	X	X	From $29.95/month
HammerTap	X	X	X	X	X	X	X		A la carte pricing for individual tools
SpareDollar	X	X	X	X	X	X	X		$4.95/month
Vendio	X	X		X	X	X	X	X	Various plans from $12.95/month plus combination of listing and final value fees
Zoovy	X	X	X	X	X	X	X	X	Various plans from $25 per month plus per-transaction fees

Let's try a head-to-head pricing comparison. Table 20.2 compares plans from each service for sellers doing 50, 100, and 250 transactions per month. For purposes of this comparison, we'll say that each transaction averages $10, and we want a package that includes image hosting, listing creation, checkout, end-of-auction emails, and automatic feedback posting. Note that I've tried to manually piece together the best possible deal at each site, which sometimes means choosing a combination of different services and other times means going with a prepared package. Your mileage may vary.

TABLE 20.2   Auction Service Pricing Comparison

Service	50 Auctions/Month	100 Auctions/Month	250 Auctions/Month
Ándale	$38.95	$41.85	$80.95
Auction Hawk	$12.95	$21.99	$29.99
AuctionHelper	$15.70	$25.45	$68.70
Auctionworks	$14.95	$20.00	$50.00
Auctiva	$9.95	$25.95	$42.95
ChannelAdvisor	$29.95	$29.95	$29.95
HammerTap	$29.95	$29.95	$29.95
SpareDollar	$4.95	$4.95	$4.95 (might not be appropriate for this volume)
Vendio	$22.95	$32.95	$62.95
Zoovy	$37.50	$60.00	$75.00

As you can see, the price you pay varies wildly from one site to another. In general, a flat-fee site such as ChannelAdvisor or HammerTap is best if you have a high volume of sales, while a variable-rate site like AuctionHelper or Vendio is best if you have a lower sales volume or if your sales tend to vary from month to month. Watch out for those sites, such as Ándale, that price each of their tools separately; a few dollars here and a few dollars there add up fast.

Of course, you don't necessarily get the same level of service at each site, even if pricing is similar. Some sites are simply better than others, especially when it comes to handling large volumes of transactions. For example, while SpareDollar is attractively priced (a flat $4.95 per month), its level of service is somewhat Spartan when compared to a ChannelAdvisor or Vendio; it may not be up for the task if you pump through a lot of transactions.

For that reason alone, it pays to look at each service in depth—and to use any free trial provided to get a feel for how each site works. I'll do my bit by detailing 10 of the top auction service sites separately, in the following sections.

Ándale

Ándale (www.andale.com) probably offers the most variety when it comes to auction-related services. As you can see in Figure 20.1, it's the only site that offers the full range of tools from pre-auction research to post-auction management.

Ándale's auction tools are first-rate, and they're extremely easy to use. Here's a short list of what's available:

- Ándale Checkout—Provides one-stop customer checkout, as well as automatic end-of-auction emails

- Ándale Compete—Detailed analysis of your auction transactions

- Ándale Counters—Free traffic counters for your item listings

- Ándale Email Manager—Enables you to mine your customer list for additional sales

- Ándale Feedback—Post automated bulk feedback

- Ándale Gallery—Displays other items you have for sale

- Ándale Images—Image hosting

- Ándale Lister—Bulk listing creation with pre-designed templates

- Ándale Refunds—Automates filing for non-paying bidder refunds

- Ándale Research—Detailed auction analysis

- Ándale Search—Smart search for eBay buyers

- Ándale Sourcing—Identify and contact suppliers for specified types of merchandise

- Ándale Store—Your own branded fixed-price online storefront

" Mike Sez "

You should definitely compare these third-party services to those offered by eBay. The closest thing eBay has to this type of full-service auction management is eBay Selling Manager Pro, which we discussed in Chapter 12, "Managing Your Auctions." While Selling Manager Pro does offer some degree of post-auction management, automated email communication, and bulk feedback listing, it isn't near as fully featured as most of these third-party tools. (For example, Selling Manager Pro doesn't include image hosting—beyond the one photo per listing eBay gives you for free.) So you'd have to tack on the appropriate fees for that. eBay charges a flat $15.99 per month for Selling Manager Pro, which makes it more affordable than some of these services. However, if you have a really heavy auction volume, you may find that SMP doesn't automate enough of the process for you.

You have the option of using—and paying for—each of these tools separately; you're
not locked into the complete toolkit, unless that's what you want. While some of
these tools can be used free of charge, most carry either a per-month or a per-transaction charge. While the individual fees might seem reasonable, they can add up
very quickly. In fact, the thing I like least about Ándale is the cost; depending on
which services you subscribe to, you could end up spending more money here than
at any other site.

As far as pricing plans go, Ándale bundles several of its services into what it calls
"Quick Packs." For example, the 40 Listings Quick Pack includes Ándale Research,
3MB of Ándale Images, 40 listings with Ándale Lister, and Ándale Counters, for
$10.95. Other Quick Packs offer more services and more listings, up to the
$229.95/month 1,110 Listing Quick Pack. And, of
course, you can pick and choose Ándale's individual
services on an a la carte basis.

Auction Hawk

Auction Hawk (www.auctionhawk.com) is an up-and-
coming auction management service with affordable pricing. As shown in Figure 20.2, Auction
Hawk offers a variety of tools in its main service,
including image hosting, bulk listing creation, end-
of-auction checkout with automated winning bidder email, bulk feedback posting, and
profit-and-loss reporting.

note

In case you're wonder-
ing, Ándale is pronounced
on-de-lay, not *an-dale*.

One nice aspect of Auction Hawk's services is that it doesn't charge any per-transaction or final value fees. In addition, all their services are included in a single price, so you're not nickel-and-dimed to death with a la carte pricing. Its full-service monthly plans range in price from $12.99 (for 50 listings) to $44.99 (unlimited listings). At these prices, it's worth checking out.

AuctionHelper

AuctionHelper (www.auctionhelper.com) offers a variety of auction management tools, including image hosting, customer tracking and invoicing, and inventory management. The site, shown in Figure 20.3, also offers a number of auction reporting tools.

AuctionHelper charges no monthly fees. (Although it does have a $10 monthly minimum, which you'll need to plan for.) Instead, the site charges 1.95% of gross merchandise sales, with a minimum $0.15 and a maximum $1.25 charge per auction. It also adds a flat $0.02 fee to each transaction. In addition, you'll pay for image hosting above and beyond your first nine items; the charge for up to 200 items is $4.95 per month.

A little complex, but ultimately not a bad deal, especially if you're not sure what your sales volume will be. You pay for those services used, so if you have a low-volume month, you're not socked with a set fee.

FIGURE 20.3
AuctionHelper charges no monthly fees— pay only for those auctions you run in a given month.

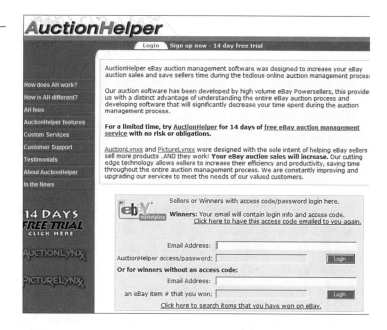

Auctionworks

Auctionworks (www.auctionworks.com) is one of the oldest and most established third-party auction management services. The Auctionworks site, shown in Figure 20.4, offers a variety of professional auction tools, including inventory management, the ClickLaunch Quick Lister bulk listing creator, traffic counters, image hosting, automatic end-of-auction emails, the proprietary Clickout checkout system, reciprocal feedback posting, Web-based storefronts, and customizable reports.

FIGURE 20.4
Auctionworks claims to power more than two million eBay auctions every month.

Auctionworks charges no monthly fees for its service, instead opting for a 2% fee on each successful transaction, with a $0.10 minimum and $3.00 maximum fee per transaction. Image hosting, however, does come with a monthly fee, as low as $14.95 for 100MB of hosting space.

Auctiva

Auctiva (www.auctiva.com), shown in Figure 20.5, offers two different services—Auctiva Basic and Auctiva Pro. Auctiva Basic includes Listing Tracker counters and the Mr. Poster bulk lister; these services are free. Auctiva Pro adds the following features:

- Auctiva FastPix and Auctiva Pictures—Image-hosting services
- Auctiva Manager (eBud)—Tracks and manages all your auction listings, and handles post-auction management and email
- Auctiva Poster—Listing creation with predesigned templates
- Auctiva Showcase Pro—A photo gallery of all your auction listings

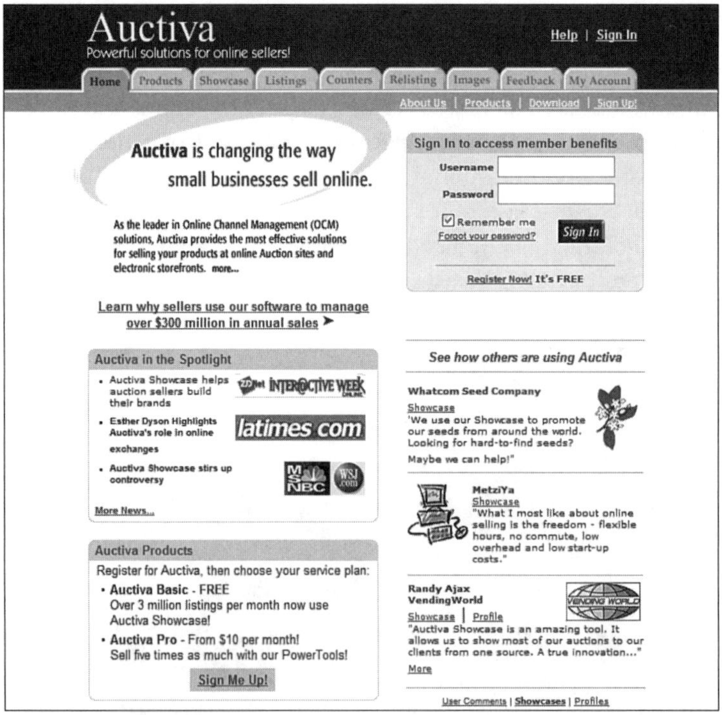

FIGURE 20.5

Auctiva offers a variety of auction management tools.

Auctiva Pro is available in several different pricing plans. The Starter Seller Plan gives you 50 listings for $9.95 per month; the most expensive plan, the Power Seller Plan, offers unlimited listings for $179.95 per month.

ChannelAdvisor

ChannelAdvisor (www.channeladvisor.com) is the latest incarnation of GoTo.com and Auction Rover, two third-party sites from the early days of the online auction business. Today, ChannelAdvisor positions itself as the service for "industry leading companies" who want to "use online marketplaces to acquire customers and maximize inventory yield."

Yikes!

However, if you can get past all that professional positioning, the ChannelAdvisor site (shown in Figure 20.6) offers a fairly affordable suite of auction management tools—as well as services for bigger online merchants. Here are the "solutions" that ChannelAdvisor offers:

FIGURE 20.6

Dig through the slick positioning to find an affordable set of auction management tools from ChannelAdvisor.

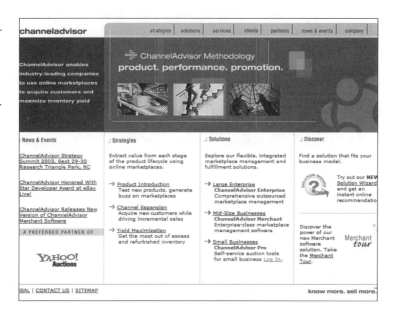

- ChannelAdvisor Pro—Auction management tools for high-volume eBay sellers, including template-based listing creation, image hosting, post-auction management, and fixed-price storefront
- ChannelAdvisor Merchant—Enterprise-level auction management, for mid-sized businesses and "super powersellers"

- ChannelAdvisor Enterprise—Outsourced auction management for Fortune 1000 businesses

The service you want to look at is ChannelAdvisor Pro. Not only is ChannelAdvisor Pro a surprisingly easy-to-use collection of auction management tools, it's also quite reasonably priced, at a flat fee of just $29.95 per month. If you're doing more than 50 auctions a month, it's definitely worth considering—even more so if you're a heavier lister.

> **note**
>
> HammerTap Manager is the exact same service as ChannelAdvisor Pro, just under a different name.

HammerTap

As shown in Figure 20.7, HammerTap (www. hammertap.com) offers a variety of auction management software and services, all priced separately. These tools include

- HammerTap Manager—Web-based auction posting and management
- Auction Informant—Software that sends you email alerts when your items receive bids
- BayCheck and BayCheck Pro—Software eBay user background checks
- BayMail and BayMail Pro—Software for sending emails to eBay users
- BidderBlock—Software for managing blocked bidder lists
- DeepAnalysis—Auction research tool
- FeeFinder—Software for calculating eBay, PayPal, and shipping fees

SpareDollar

SpareDollar (www.sparedollar.com) is kind of a bargain-basement auction service. As shown in Figure 20.8, all of its services are available for a flat $4.95 per month.

SpareDollar's auction tools include

- sdCounter—Traffic counters for your item listings
- sdGallery—Photo gallery of all your auction items
- sdImage—50MB of image hosting
- sdLister—Bulk listing creation with predesigned templates
- sdTracker—Post-auction tracking and emails

FIGURE 20.7

HammerTap offers both software and services.

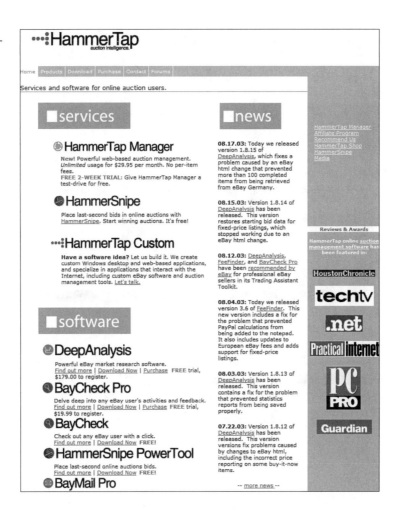

Note, however, that while SpareDollar is attractively priced, its services might prove too limited for really high-volume sellers. Give it a try to see if it fits your particular eBay business.

Vendio

Vendio (www.vendio.com), formerly known as Auctionwatch, is number-two to Ándale among auction management services. As you can see in Figure 20.9, Vendio claims 100,000 sellers use their services, which makes them a very popular site.

FIGURE 20.8

SpareDollar—
auction tools at
a bargain price.

FIGURE 20.9

Vendio claims
100,000 users.

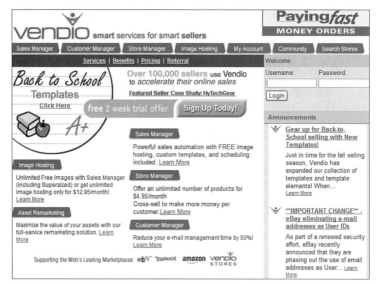

The site offers five vastly different services for auction sellers. These include

- Vendio Sales Manager—A complete package of auction management tools, including bulk listing creation, end-of-auction management and notification, and bulk feedback posting
- Vendio Image Hosting—Image hosting

- Vendio Store Manager—Your own branded fixed-price storefront

- Vendio Customer Manager—Enables you to mine your customer list for additional sales

- Vendio Asset Remarketing—Targeted at businesses wishing to unload assets in bulk

Of these services, Vendio Sales Manager is obviously the most targeted and the most popular among eBay sellers.

Vendio tries to appeal to different types of sellers by offering a mix of fixed and variable priced monthly subscriptions. For example, the Sales Manager Standard Plan carries no fixed fee, although you'll pay $0.10 per transaction and a 1% final value fee. On the other hand, the Sales Manager Variable Power Plan costs $29.95 a month, but with no listing fee and a 1.25% final value fee—and the Flat Rate Power Plan costs $39.95 a month, with a $0.10 per-transaction charge but no final value fee. Confusing? You bet—but it does let you choose the type of payment (flat versus variable versus. per-transaction) that best suits your particular business.

I like Vendio's tools almost as much as Ándale's—although the range of tools isn't quite as wide. (No research, for example.) The variable-rate pricing is actually a little more attractive to me, especially since my sales volume varies from month-to-month. And I like the fact that Vendio doesn't nickel-and-dime me to death. All in all, a service definitely worth your consideration.

Zoovy

Zoovy (www.zoovy.com) is a high-end auction management service that integrates your eBay auctions with a Web-based storefront. As you can see in Figure 20.10, Zoovy is targeted toward high-end sellers and retailers, with four different levels of service:

- Zoovy Merchant—Online auction management and basic Web storefronts

- Zoovy Hybrid—Storefronts for small online merchants

- Zoovy Developer—Storefronts and services for medium-sized online merchants

- Zoovy Enterprise—For extremely high-volume sellers and large online merchants

Zoovy Merchant is the plan for most eBay sellers, and is available with three different pricing plans. The Bronze plan costs $25 per month, plus $0.25 per transaction. The Silver plan costs $50 per month, plus $0.10 per transaction. The Gold plan costs $100 per month, plus $0.05 per transaction.

FIGURE 20.10

Zoovy offers
both auction
management
and store-
building tools.

Other Web-Based Services

The nine services just listed are the most popular of the third-party Web-based auction services. But they're not the only services; there's a lot of competition for your auction dollars. In the spirit of competition, then, I'll list a few more auction management sites that you can check out on your own time:

- Auction-X (www.auction-x.com)
- inkFrog (www.inkfrog.com)
- ManageAuctions (www.manageauctions.com)
- Trak Auctions (www.trakauction.com)

Another Option: Software Tools

Many eBay sellers prefer to manage their auctions offline, on their own time—without being tied to a single service. If you're more of a do-it-yourself kind of seller, you might want to check out some of the software programs designed to help you manage the eBay auction process. Here's a short list of programs for your consideration:

- **All My Auctions** (www.rajeware.com/auction/), $39.95. This is a basic auction management software program; it includes template-based listing creation, live auction management (including the ability to track competitors' auctions), end-of-auction email notification, and report generation.
- **Auction Information Database** (www.epigroove.com), $29.95. A.I.D. helps you monitor your eBay auctions, in database format. You can download all your auction data, send auto-generated end-of-auction emails, and print packing slips and shipping labels.

- **Auction Lizard** (www.auction-lizard.com), $29. Auction Lizard is an easy-to-use listing-creation program that uses forms and templates to generate HTML-based listings.

- **Auction Wizard 2000** (www.auctionwizard2000.com), $75/year. This full-featured software offers many of the same tools you find at the large auction management sites, including inventory management, bulk listing creation, end-of-auction emails, bulk feedback posting, and the like.

- **AuctionSage** (www.auctionsagesoftware.com), $24.95/3 months, $64.95/year. Software for posting and managing eBay auction transactions, including sending buyer emails and leaving bulk feedback.

- **AuctionTamer** (www.auctiontamer.com), $39.75/3 months, $99.95/year. AuctionTamer is an all-in-one auction management software program for both sellers and bidders. For sellers, it lets you create auction listings, schedule delayed auction listings, manage your live auctions, send post-auction emails, and print shipping labels.

- **eBay Seller's Assistant Basic** (pages.ebay.com/sellers_assistant/), $9.99/month. This is eBay's older software-based listing/management tool, still available even though it's technically been replaced by Turbo Lister and the Web-based Selling Manager. It offers HTML-based listing creation (using forms and templates), auction tracking, and basic post-auction management (including automatic email notification and feedback generation).

- **eBay Seller's Assistant Pro** (pages.ebay.com/sellers_assistant/), $15.99/month. A more fully featured program than Seller's Assistant Basic, including bulk listing creation and post-auction assistance.

- **eLister** (www.blackmagik.com/elister.html), $9.95/30 days, $29.95/6 months. eLister is an easy-to-use listing creation program, complete with HTML formatting and predesigned templates.

- **MyAuctionMate** (www.myauctionmate.com), $43. This is an auction management software program that offers listing creation, batch uploading, auction tracking and management, end-of-auction email notifications, automatic feedback posting, report generation, and more. (The company also offers its listing-creation module, MyAuctionDesigner, separately, for just $9.95.)

- **Shooting Star** (www.foodogsoftware.com), $49.95. Shooting Star is a program designed to manage the end-of-auction process. It uses what it calls a "workflow system" to move you through various post-auction operations, including email notification.

■ **Virtual Auction Ad Pro** (www.firstdesign.com/vadpro/), $14.99. This is a software program that lets you create great-looking HTML-based ad listings; it also offers templates for listing titles and descriptions, for those without strong copywriting skills.

THE ABSOLUTE MINIMUM

When you become a high-volume seller, you'll need help managing all those transactions. That help is available in the form of third-party auction tools. When choosing which service to use, keep these points in mind:

■ Some auction management sites charge a flat fee; others charge by the transaction or a percentage of the selling price.

■ These sites offer a variety of services, including research, inventory management, image hosting, gallery, bulk listing creation, end-of-auction email and checkout, bulk feedback posting, and Web-based storefronts.

■ While you can pick and choose different services from different sites, you're better off choosing a single site and using all its integrated tools.

■ Some sites bundle multiple services together into a single package; others sell their services on an a la carte basis.

■ Don't get carried away by all the different services available—every tool you use adds to your auction costs.

21

OPENING AN EBAY STORE

The next step in your creation of a successful eBay business is to set up your own online storefront. This is surprisingly easy to do, thanks to a service called eBay Stores.

Running an eBay Store (www.stores.ebay.com) is the way for a heavy seller to provide the facsimile of a retail storefront within the eBay environment. If you're thinking of making the move into real honest-to-goodness retailing, an eBay Store is a relatively painless way to start.

What Is an eBay Store?

An eBay Store, like the one shown in Figure 21.1, is a Web page where you can sell fixed-price (Buy It Now) items that are not currently up for auction on eBay, along with your current auction items. The non-auction items in your eBay Store appear only in your eBay Store—not in the eBay auction listings.

FIGURE 21.1

A typical eBay Store.

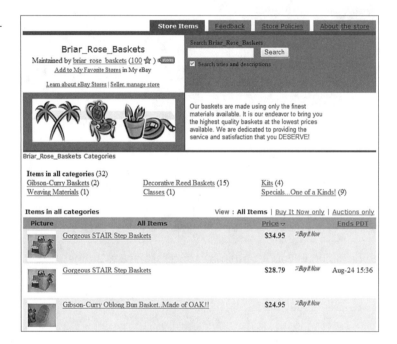

On the eBay Stores home page (www.stores.ebay.com), merchants are organized by the same categories as the eBay auction site—Antiques, Art, Books, and so on. Buyers can also search for a specific store or a store selling a certain type of item, or view an alphabetical list of all stores.

The items offered by eBay Stores merchants are a combination of items currently for auction on eBay and additional fixed-price inventory. When buyers access a particular eBay Store retailer, they have access to this entire collection of merchandise; if they tried searching on eBay proper, they wouldn't find the non-auction items the retailer might have for sale.

For a buyer, purchasing an item from an eBay Store retailer is a little like buying from any other online merchant, and a little like winning an item in an eBay auction. On the one hand, it's buying from an actual merchant at a fixed price, and the buyer can always pay by credit card. On the other hand, eBay Stores offer all the niceties found on eBay, including the ability to check the merchant's feedback rating. Checkout is handled from within the store.

Benefits of Opening Your Own eBay Store

Why would you want to open your own eBay Store? Well, it certainly isn't for casual sellers; you do have to set up your own Web page and keep the store filled with merchandise. But if you're a high-volume seller who specializes in a single category (or even a handful of categories), there are benefits to opening your own store. These include being able to sell more merchandise (through your store) than you can otherwise list in auctions; being able to display a special eBay Stores icon next to all of your auction lists; and being able to generate repeat business from future sales to current purchasers.

Opening an eBay Store is an especially good idea if you have a lot of fixed-price merchandise to sell. You can put items in your eBay Store before you offer them for auction, and thus have more merchandise for sale than you might otherwise. It's easy to direct your auction buyers to your eBay Store; if you do your job right, you can use your eBay Store to sell more merchandise to your existing customers. And, since eBay Store insertion fees are lower than auction listing fees, you'll be decreasing your costs by selling direct rather than through an auction.

Another benefit of selling merchandise in an eBay Store is that eBay will automatically advertise items from your store on the Bid Confirmation and Checkout Confirmation pages it displays to bidders in your regular auctions. These "merchandising placements" help you cross-sell additional merchandise to your auction customers.

In addition, eBay sends all eBay Store owners a monthly Seller Report. This report is divided into three major sections: Auctions, Fixed Price, and Store Inventory. Among the data reported is the following:

- Number of total listings and number of successful listings
- Number of bids
- Gross sales
- Number of unique buyers
- Percent of successful listings
- Number of bids per listing
- Average selling price per item

" Mike Sez "

If you're serious about selling merchandise outside the eBay environment, you may want to create a more full-featured e-commerce presence than available with eBay Stores. See Chapter 22, "Setting Up Your Own Web Site for Online Sales," for more information.

Featured and Anchor stores (discussed later in this chapter) also receive an eBay Marketplace Information report, with data for overall eBay performance in the categories in which they list. All eBay Store owners receive their reports via email at the end of each month.

Do You Qualify?

Just about any seller can open their own eBay Store. All you have to do is meet the following criteria:

- Be a registered eBay seller, with credit card on file
- Have a feedback rating of 20 or more, or be ID verified
- Accept credit cards for all fixed-price sales
- Maintain at least 25 item listings in your store

tip

eBay also offers a Good 'Til Cancelled option, which automatically relists unsold items every 30 days.

Given that accepting credit cards can mean using PayPal, you can see that you don't actually have to be a big traditional retailer in order to open an eBay Store. Any individual meeting the requirements can also open an eBay Store, thus making eBay Stores a great way for entrepreneurial types to get started in retailing.

The Costs of Running an eBay Store

Naturally, it costs money to open an eBay Store. (eBay isn't in this for the betterment of mankind, after all.) You pay a monthly fee to be an eBay Store merchant, and there are three subscription levels to choose from, as shown in Table 21.1.

TABLE 21.1   eBay Stores Subscription Levels

Subscription	Price	Description
Basic	$9.95/month	Store listed in every category directory where you have items listed; position based on number of items listed
Featured	$49.95/month	All features of Basic, plus store rotated through a special featured section on the eBay Stores home page; store receives priority placement in Related Stores section of search and listings pages; store featured within the top-level category pages where you have items listed; you can cross-sell products on view item pages; and you receive monthly eBay Marketplace Information reports
Anchor	$499.95/month	All features of Featured, plus premium placement in Related Stores section of search and listings pages; and your store logo will rotate through category directory pages (1 million impressions monthly)

You also have to pay eBay for each item you list and each item you sell—just as in a normal auction. The difference is you're not listing for a (relatively short) auction; you're listing for longer-term inventory.

Table 21.2 details the insertion fees that eBay charges for eBay Stores listings. Note that eBay allows listings of up to 120 days in length—although the longer listings carry an insertion fee surcharge.

TABLE 21.2   eBay Stores Insertion Fees

Listing Length	Insertion Fee (Plus Surcharge)
30 days	$0.05
60 days	$0.05 + $0.05
90 days	$0.05 + $0.10
120 days	$0.05 + $0.15

For every item you sell in your eBay Store, eBay charges a final value fee. Table 21.3 lists these selling charges.

TABLE 21.3   eBay Stores Final Value Fees

Closing Value	Fee
$0.01–$24.99	5.25%
$25.00–$999.99	5.25% on first $25 *plus* $2.75% on remaining balance
$1,000 and up	5.25% on first $25 *plus* $2.75% on the part between $25 and $1,000 *plus* 1.5% on remaining balance

eBay Stores also offers a full assortment of listing upgrades, just like the ones you can use in regular eBay auctions. These enhancements—gallery, bold, highlight, and so on—are priced according to the length of your listing. You can also offer multiples of the same item in Dutch auction format.

How to Set Up an eBay Store

Opening your own eBay store is as easy as clicking through eBay's setup pages. There's nothing overly complex involved; you'll need to create your store, customize your pages (otherwise known as your virtual storefront), and list the items you want to sell. Just follow the onscreen instructions, and you'll have your own store up and running in just a few minutes.

Here's what you need to do:

1. Go to the eBay Stores main page (www.stores.ebay.com) and click the Open Your Store Now link.

2. When the Welcome to eBay Stores page appears, click the Continue button.

3. When the Basic Store Information page appears, enter the following information:

   - Store name

   - Seller's payment information (your name and address)

   - A text description for your store's home page

   - A list of merchandise that your store specializes in

   - Item display order (select from the list: Highest Price First, Lowest Price First, Ending Soonest First, Ending Latest First)

   - Custom store categories (how you want to categorize your store's merchandise)

   - Store tier (Basic or Featured)

   - Store payment methods (which methods of payment you'll accept—PayPal, personal check, and so on)

   - Store ship-to locations (where you'll sell to—U.S. only, internationally, and so on)

   - Shipping and handling (who pays what)

   - Store sales tax

   - Store customer service and return policy

   - Additional store information

   Click the Continue button when you're done entering all this information.

4. When the Store Appearance page appears (see Figure 21.2), select a Color Scheme from the pull-down list, then select a predesigned graphic or enter the URL for your store's custom graphic (such as your logo). Click Continue when ready.

eBay now creates your store and displays the Your Store Has Been Created page. This page includes the URL for your new store; click this link to visit your store.

FIGURE 21.2

Select how your eBay Store will look.

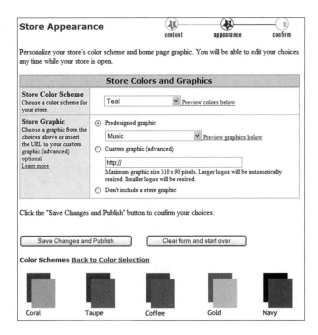

Listing Merchandise for Sale

Now that you've created your eBay store, you need to add some merchandise. Follow these steps:

1. Go to your eBay Store page and click the Seller Manage Store link.

2. When the Manage Your Store page appears, select List Items for Sale in Your Store and click the Continue button.

3. When the Sell Your Item page appears, select Sell in Your eBay Store, then click Continue.

4. Proceed through the balance of the Sell Your Item process, as you would when listing an item to sell in an auction.

That's right, eBay makes managing your eBay Store inventory almost identical to listing items in a regular eBay auction. That's one of the nice things about having an eBay Store; it's well-integrated with your other eBay activities.

Cross-Selling Merchandise

You can also specify which items in your store you want to list on your customers' Bid Confirmation and Checkout Confirmation pages. For example, if you've sold an inkjet printer, you may want to cross-sell inkjet cartridges and paper to that customer.

Follow these steps to create your merchandising links:

1. Go to your eBay Store page and click the Seller Manage Store link.

2. When the Manage Your Store page appears, select Manage Merchandising Relationships and click the Continue button.

3. When the Merchandising Manager page opens, scroll to the Select Where Your Items Appear section, highlight the items on which you'd like to display the additional merchandise, and then click the Add Item button.

4. Scroll to the Select Your Items to Show section and select up to three items you want to cross-merchandise.

5. Click the Continue button. To preview your merchandising relationships.

Repeat this procedure to cross-sell different merchandise with other auction items.

THE ABSOLUTE MINIMUM

An eBay Store is a way for you to sell more merchandise to your auction customers. Keep these points in mind:

■ An eBay Store is a Web page where you can sell fixed-price items that are not currently listed for auction on the main eBay site.

■ Just about any established seller in good standing can open an eBay store.

■ The Basic eBay Store costs $9.95 per month, plus a five-cent insertion fee and 5.25% of all sales.

■ Opening an eBay Store is as simple as filling out some forms online; just add merchandise and you're ready to roll.

IN THIS CHAPTER

- Utilizing a prepackaged storefront
- Building your own site from scratch
- Promoting your site

22

SETTING UP YOUR OWN WEB SITE FOR ONLINE SALES

In the previous chapter we looked at eBay Stores, where you can sell additional fixed-price merchandise to your auction customers. An eBay Store, however, is a rather limited online storefront. If you want to move full-force into online retailing, you'll want something more fully featured.

Fortunately, setting up your own online storefront isn't nearly as involved as you might think. There are numerous services available that provide prepackaged storefront solutions; all you have to do is point and click (and pay some money) to get your store online. Or, if you want something really fancy, you can design your own store on your own Web site, complete with your own proprietary Web domain.

However you do it, opening a dedicated Web storefront lets you sell your merchandise 24 hours a day, 365 days of the year. You don't have to wait for an auction to end to sell an item and collect your money; you're open for business anytime your customers want to buy.

So if you have dreams of turning your online auction business into the next Amazon.com, read on—and learn how to become a bona fide Internet e-tailer.

Utilizing a Prepackaged Storefront

The easiest way to create an online storefront is to let somebody else do it for you.

Several of the big auction services sites offer prepackaged Web storefronts you can use to sell both auction and non-auction merchandise. The advantage of using a prepackaged storefront is that all the hard work is done for you; you put your storefront together by filling out the appropriate forms. The disadvantage of a prepackaged storefront is that, in many cases, it's not really *your* storefront; there aren't a lot of customization options, and you have to settle for a somewhat generic look and feel. (Which means that your store is going to look like everybody else's that use the same service—not necessarily a good thing.)

Still, if you want to launch a storefront without a lot of fuss and muss—and get it up and running in record time—then a prepackaged storefront service might be for you. We'll look at some of the most popular services next.

Ándale Stores

Ándale (www.andale.com) lets you build your own storefront on its service. An Ándale Store is similar to an eBay Store, but a bit nicer looking and somewhat more functional. As you can see in Figure 22.1, an Ándale Store can be fully customized with your own personal color scheme and graphics.

Pricing to open an Ándale Store is $5.95 per month, cheaper than the $9.95 fee for an eBay Store. Of course, you also have to pay Ándale's listing and checkout fees, which are the same as for normal auction listings. However, this fee covers everything—like all of these third-party services, Ándale provides all the Web hosting and storage space you need for your store.

> **tip**
>
> When you open an Ándale Store, Ándale inserts a small Auction Gallery at the bottom of all your eBay item listings. Potential bidders can click through the items in this Gallery to shop at your Ándale Store.

FIGURE 22.1

A typical Ándale Store, from Gold Rush Games.

Auctionworks StoreFront

Auctionworks (www.auctionworks.com) offers optional Auctionworks StoreFronts as part of its package of auction management tools. Even better, Auctionworks StoreFronts are included in the service's normal monthly fees. You'll also pay Auctionworks's normal 2% fee for each item you sell.

You put together an Auctionworks StoreFront using a menu-driven setup program; it's a relatively pain-free process. Auctionworks storefronts, like the one in Figure 22.2, include shopping cart functionality and a link to your auction gallery.

FIGURE 22.2

Boca Jewelry— a typical Auctionworks StoreFront.

ChannelAdvisor

The ChannelAdvisor Merchant service (www.channeladvisor.com) helps you incorporate a full-service storefront into your eBay About Me page. Storefronts, like the one in Figure 22.3, include integrated checkout and payment services.

FIGURE 22.3

Glacier Bay
DVD—a
ChannelAdvisor
Merchant store-
front integrated
into an eBay
About Me page.

Infopia

Infopia (www.infopia.com) is one of those companies that cloak what they do in a suffocating blanket of business-to-business (B2B) buzzwords. (ChannelAdvisor is much the same way.) According to their Web site, the Infopia Marketplace Manager "delivers the technology to automate and accelerate processes that lead to customer acquisition, online marketing, and customer relationship building." In plain English, that translates into Web storefronts that link to your eBay auctions.

A full list of features includes auction listing creation, automated communication and feedback, image hosting, email marketing, tracking and reporting, inventory and order management, and a "smart" shopping cart and checkout. Figure 22.4 shows a typical Infopia-powered storefront.

Vendio

Vendio (www.vendio.com) offers Web storefronts as part of its Vendio Store Manager service. Stores, like the one in Figure 22.5, include a free gallery, mailing list management, and fully customizable look and feel. Pricing plans start at $4.95 per month, with a 1% final value fee.

Zoovy

Zoovy (www.zoovy.com) is a unique blend of Web storefront and auction management system. In essence, Zoovy Merchant lets you create an online storefront, complete with shopping cart, that links to your eBay auctions. You use the Store Builder application to build your store, and the result is a professional-looking storefront, like the one in Figure 22.6.

Pricing starts at $25 per month, with a $0.25 per-transaction fee.

FIGURE 22.4
Cartoon Passion, a typical Infopia storefront.

FIGURE 22.5
The Attic and Closet, a Vendio store.

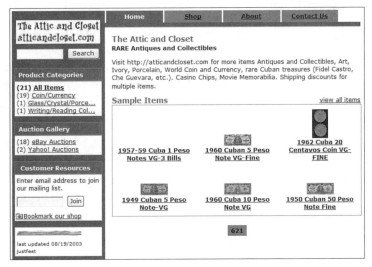

FIGURE 22.6

Abby's Place, a
Zoovy mer-
chant.

Building Your Own Site from Scratch

Prepackaged storefronts are fine, but if you want a truly full-featured Web storefront—if you want to become an honest-to-goodness *e-tailer*—then you'll need to
build your own Web site, from scratch. This is a lot of work, and will cost a lot of
money, so it's not for novice or hesitant sellers. But if you're really serious about
making a lot of money on the Internet, building your own e-commerce site is the
only way to go.

Finding a Web Host

You can't build a complex e-commerce Web site on Yahoo! GeoCities or other typical
home page communities. These sites are designed to host individual Web pages, not
complete sites; you certainly don't want your professional site to be burdened with a
URL that begins www.geocities.com/.

Instead, you need to find a professional Web hosting service, a master site that will
provide hundreds of megabytes of disk space, robust site management tools, and the
ability to use your own unique domain name. (And with your own domain name,
your site's URL will read www.*yourname*.com—just like the big sites do!)

A professional Web hosting service, at the most basic level, provides large amounts of reliable storage space for your Web site—normally for a monthly or yearly fee. Most hosting services also provide other types of services, and many offer e-commerce-specific tools.

All of these services will cost you, of course; that's part and parcel of going pro. A good Web hosting service can run as little as $10 a month—or a lot more, depending on the storage space and tools you need.

What to Look For

When you're shopping for a hosting service for your Web site, what should you look for? Here's a short list:

- Adequate storage space
- Unlimited traffic
- Affordable rates
- Reliability
- Speed
- Easy uploading and maintenance
- Domain name hosting
- Email
- Site statistics
- Technical support

Finding a Host

There are literally hundreds of site hosting services on the Web. The best way, then, to look for a Web hosting service is to use a site that performs the search for you.

There are several sites on the Internet that offer directories of Web hosting services. Most of these sites let you look for hosts by various parameters, including monthly cost, disk space provided, programming and platforms supported, and extra features offered (such as e-commerce hosting, control panels, and so on). Many also offer lists of the "best" or most popular hosting services, measured in one or another fashion.

Among the best of these host search sites are the following:

- CNET Web Hosting (www.cnet.com/internet/)
- HostIndex.com (www.hostindex.com)
- HostSearch (www.hostsearch.com)
- TopHosts.com (www.tophosts.com)
- Web Hosters (www.webhosters.com)

Top Web Site Hosts

Of all the hosting services on the Web, a handful consistently rise to the top of all the rankings. When you're looking for a hosting service, you can't go wrong by evaluating any of the sites on this list:

- Affinity (www.affinity.com)
- C I Host (www.cihost.com)
- GlobalHosting (www.globalhosting.com)
- HostCentric (www.hostcentric.com)
- Hostway (www.hostway.com)
- Interland (www.interland.com)
- Microsoft bCentral (www.bcentral.com)
- ReadyHosting.com (www.readyhosting.com)
- Website Source (www.websitesource.com)
- WebIntellects (www.webintellects.com)

All of these sites offer similar hosting services and plans, and most offer e-commerce-specific packages. You should shop around for the hosting plan that best meets your needs and budget.

Obtaining a Domain Name

A professional e-commerce Web site needs its own unique URL. The key component of the URL—the part *after* the www.—is called the *domain*. It consists of a unique domain name (before the dot) and a top-level domain (after the dot), such as .com or .net, like this: domainname.domain. You put a www. in front of this to denote your Web site. For example, eBay's domain name is ebay and its top-level domain is com; the full address becomes www.ebay.com. And to create an email address, you put a unique address and an @ sign in front of the domain information.

Reserving a domain name is just part of the process, however. Once you have a name, that name needs to be listed with the Internet's domain name system (DNS), so that users entering your URL are connected to the appropriate IP address where your site is actually hosted. Most Web site hosting services will provide DNS services if you provide a unique domain name; some will even handle the registration process for you.

If you want to receive email at your new domain you'll also need to have your hosting service (or your ISP) link your domain name to your existing email account. You can typically set up any number of specific addresses within a single domain, and have them all forwarded to the same email account.

Where to Register

All domain names are registered through a single firm, Network Solutions. You go directly to the Network Solutions Web site (www.networksolutions.com), shown in Figure 22.7, to register your Web address.

FIGURE 22.7

Register your domain name with Network Solutions.

In addition, most Web hosting services can perform domain lookup and registration for you. They'll collect the appropriate fees to register your domain (and forward those fees to Network Solutions) and arrange for the transfer of your address to their servers.

How to Register

Registering your domain is as easy as following these general steps:

1. Go to Network Solutions or any other domain registration site and search to see if the name you want is available.

2. If your name is available, reserve it by entering the appropriate contact information.

3. Arrange payment with the domain registration service, typically via credit card.

note

Network Solutions manages domain name registration on behalf of the Internet Network Information Center (InterNIC). The registration fee is $35 per year.

4. Contact your Web hosting service and arrange for your domain name to be linked to a specific IP address and added to the Internet DNS system.

5. Arrange for your Web hosting service to link your domain name to your email account.

Creating Your Web Site

Once you have a host for your storefront and a domain name registered, it's time for the really hard work—creating your site. If you're handy with HTML and have a lot of free time, you can choose to do this work yourself. Or you can bite the bullet and hire a firm that specializes in designing e-commerce Web sites and pay them to produce the kind of site you want.

Read on to learn more about what's involved.

Web Design Tools

If you opt to build your site yourself, you'll need to invest in a powerful Web site creation tool. You don't build a complex Web site using Microsoft Notepad or FrontPage Express; you need to use a fully featured program, such as one of the following:

- Adobe GoLive (www.adobe.com)
- Macromedia Dreamweaver (www.macromedia.com)
- Microsoft FrontPage (www.microsoft.com)
- NetObjects Fusion (www.netobjects.com)

These programs let you view your entire site as a single project, not just a collection of pages, as you can see with Microsoft FrontPage. You'll be able to apply universal formatting and navigation to all the pages on your site, and even generate dynamic Web pages on the fly.

This isn't the place or the time to demonstrate how to use these powerful programs. I suggest you choose the program you want, and then invest in the appropriate Que book to help you learn the basics; go to the Que bookstore (www.quepublishing.com) to find the right book for you.

Incorporating E-commerce Software

To power your new storefront, you'll need to incorporate special e-commerce software. This software will enable you to build Web pages based on your current inventory, generate customer shopping carts, funnel buyers to a checkout page, and handle all customer transactions. Here are some of the most popular:

- AbleCommerce (www.ablecommerce.com)
- BazaarBuilder (www.bazaarbuilder.com)

- bCentral Commerce Manager (www.bcentral.com)
- iNETstore (www.inetstore.com)
- Miva Merchant (www.miva.com)
- ShopZone (www.automatedshops.com)

Web Design Firms

If you're not an experienced Web page designer, you may be better off hiring someone who is to build your new storefront site. There are tons of Web design firms out there, most of them small and local. When it's time to go professional, use the following directories to find a professional Web page designer that's right for your needs:

- AAADesignList.com (www.aaadesignlist.com)
- The Firm List (www.firmlist.com)
- The List of Web Designers (webdesign.thelist.com)

note

You'll also need your new storefront to be able to handle customer payments via credit card. Learn more about enabling credit card processing in Chapter 13, "Managing Customer Payments."

Promoting Your Site

Building your Web storefront is one thing; having customers actually find it is another. If you want people to visit your new site, you just can't post a few Web pages and hope that someone stumbles across them. To generate real traffic—and real sales—you have to actively do something to *drive* users to your site.

Search Submittal Services

The easiest way to market your site is to make sure that you're included in the search results at all the major Web search sites. While you could hope that the search engines' spiders would find your site automatically, chances are they won't—or if they do, it might take them months to get to you.

A far better approach is to manually submit your site to all the search engines—which, unfortunately, is very time-consuming. For that reason, a number of search-site submittal services have sprung up, that—for a fee—will submit your site to literally hundreds of major and minor search engines and directories.

Among the most popular of these search submittal sites are

- Add Me! (www.addme.com)
- Submit Express (www.submitexpress.com)
- Submit It! (www.submitit.com)
- Submit-Pro (www.submit-pro.com)
- SubmitWizard (submitwizard.superstats.com)

Banner Exchanges

A low-cost way to tell the world about your new site is via a Web banner exchange. In a banner exchange, you agree to put banner ads on your site for other participating sites; in exchange, those sites will display banner ads for your site. It's a good deal, and very popular among smaller Web sites.

To participate in a banner exchange, you have to join a banner exchange network. Here are some of the most popular:

- bCentral Banner Network (www.bcentral.com/products/bn/)
- Home Banner Exchange (www.home-banner-exchange.com)
- NEObanners (www.neobanners.com)
- SlideInExchange.com (www.slideinexchange.com)

Web Site Marketing

Real businesses attract new customers by advertising. If you're running a real online business, you'll need to attract customers with online advertising.

How do you advertise on the Internet? There's no need to reinvent the wheel; there are a variety of companies that provide marketing and promotional services to Web retailers. These sites include

- fastclick (www.fastclick.com)
- iLOVEclicks Network (www.iloveclicks.com)
- Marcap Group (www.marcap.com)
- Promotion World (www.promotionworld.com)
- WebPromote (www.webpromote.com)

note

Linking from other sites to your eBay auctions is so important as to warrant a section in a separate chapter. Learn more in Chapter 24, "Promoting Your eBay Auctions."

Linking From Your eBay Auctions

Just because you have a separate Web storefront doesn't mean you should forget your eBay auctions. In fact, you can use your eBay auctions to advertise your storefront, and vice versa.

The problem, however, is that eBay forbids you link to other sites in your item listings. So you can't just include a link to your non-eBay storefront in your item descriptions; eBay will either block the link or cancel your auction.

If you want to promote your non-eBay storefront, then, you'll need to be creative—and devise a bit of a workaround.

The least clumsy workaround involves your eBay About Me page, which you learned about way back in Chapter 2, "Using eBay's Advanced Features." You see, eBay *does* let you include third-party links in your About Me page, which makes it the ideal place to promote your outside storefront.

Just construct your About Me page as normal, and make sure to include information about your Web storefront. Definitely include a link to the storefront. Then, in each of your individual item descriptions, add a paragraph that talks about your new Web storefront, with a line of text that says something like "Read more about my storefront on my About Me page." Then include a separate link to your About Me page in your item description (in addition to the automatic name next to your user ID), and you're in business—with a roundabout promotional link.

THE ABSOLUTE MINIMUM

When an eBay Store isn't good enough, it's time to build your own Web storefront. Keep these points in mind:

- The easiest way to create your own storefront is to use a prepackaged storefront service from Ándale, Zoovy, or other similar sites.

- To create a more fully featured storefront, you'll need to build your own Web site from scratch.

- To build a professional Web site, you'll need to find a Web hosting service, register your domain name, and either hire a Web design firm or teach yourself how to use a professional site building tool, such as Microsoft FrontPage.

- Once your site is up and running, you'll need to promote it—via search engines, online advertising, and links from your eBay auctions.

23

Integrating eBay Auctions into an Existing Business

If your eBay business gets big enough, you may be tempted to open a brick-and-mortar storefront, as well. Or, if you're already an established retailer, you may be wondering how you can supplement your existing business with sales from eBay auctions.

Either situation gives rise to the same set of challenges. In short, you need to determine just how to integrate eBay auctions into a non-online business.

It's all a matter of strategy.

Creating a Dual-Channel Sales Strategy

Where you sell your merchandise is called a *sales channel*. The Internet is one sales channel; selling in a traditional brick-and-mortar store is another sales channel. Typically, selling in more than one channel is challenging—and can even result in what is called *channel conflict*, especially if you treat each channel differently in terms of pricing or other policies.

Can you sell merchandise both online and at traditional retail? Of course; lots of businesses do it. It's all a question of what role you want each channel to play.

Selling Commodity Products

Let's take the example of a business that sells commodity products—non-unique merchandise that is available in large quantities, such as inkjet cartridges or cleaning supplies. If you sell one item, you have lots more just like it still available. In this scenario, it's relatively easy to devise your dual-channel sales strategy—you take the same SKUs and make them available in both channels. So your eBay auctions will feature the same merchandise that you have for sale at traditional retail. When you make an auction sale, you take the item out of your retail stock and manage your inventory accordingly.

Selling Unique Products

A different situation exists with a business that sells unique items—pieces of art, perhaps, or baseball cards. When you sell an item, there isn't another to take its place. In this scenario, potential problems exist when you try to sell the same item both online and in your retail store. If you have an item up for auction but then sell it to the next customer who walks in your door, you're forced to cancel the auction mid-process—even if the item has already received bids. It's an awkward situation at best, and can result in unhappy bidders (and a possible warning from eBay, if the situation repeats itself too frequently).

In this latter scenario, you have to decide in which channel you're going to sell specific merchandise. If you decide to put a particular item up for auction, you should remove it from sale at your retail location for the duration of the auction. This way you won't be forced to choose between competing customers. However, if the item doesn't sell during the specified period, you can return the item to your retail floor.

Another way to handle this situation is to offer an auction item to your retail customers on a contingency basis. That is, you offer to sell it at retail if the item doesn't sell at auction. In this scenario, you may also want to inform interested retail customers about the current auction, and encourage them to place their bids online.

Creating a Dual-Channel Pricing Strategy

Another issue you have to deal with is how to price items that sell in both online and traditional retail channels. We'll look at pricing strategies for both commodity and unique merchandise.

Pricing Commodity Products

In the case of commodity items—those items that you sell in quantity, day in and day out—you probably want to consider equivalent pricing. That is, you set the same price for both channels. In the case of your eBay auctions, that means setting either the minimum bid or the reserve price equal to the price you charge for that item in your retail store. That way your online customers won't be paying less for an item than your walk-in customers do—and you won't be accused of discriminating against your brick-and-mortar clientele.

Alternately, you set a lower minimum bid price but then set the item's Buy It Now price at your traditional retail price. This enables your online customers to *perhaps* pay a little less, if they want to wait for the entire auction process to unfold (and if they don't get outbid). But if they want the item immediately, they use the Buy It Now feature and pay the same price as your traditional retail customers.

Pricing Unique Products

Pricing is perhaps a little easier when it comes to unique products, since you don't have the issue of selling the exact same item to two different types of customers. With unique products, you only have one distinct product to sell. In this scenario, you're free to use the eBay auction process to generate as high a price as possible. Where you start the bidding is up to you. You may want to set the minimum bid lower than your retail asking price, or at the same level; that's your prerogative. In any case, you don't have to worry about potential channel conflict, as you do with commodity products.

How Other Merchants Are Using eBay to Increase Their Sales

There are many merchants, large and small, who have built businesses that incorporate both traditional and online sales. Let's look at how some of these businesses use eBay to supplement their real-world sales.

Example One: Selling More of a Good Thing

If you're selling commodity merchandise, eBay can be a great way to sell more of what you're already selling. After all, if you're selling digital cameras (for example), does it matter to you *where* you sell those cameras? If you can increase your sales by 10%, 20%, or more by running regular eBay auctions, why wouldn't you do so?

The key here is to build an eBay business that supplements your existing brick-and-mortar enterprise. You're not looking for eBay to replace your existing sales; you're looking for eBay to provide additional sales that you wouldn't have had otherwise.

You're also not looking to sell items on eBay that you don't already sell at retail. If you currently sell gift baskets, you don't want to branch out and start selling hot dog makers on eBay. No, you want to sell gift baskets—just more of them.

The nice thing about this type of operation is that you don't have to change any-thing about the purchasing part of your business—other than making larger buys, of course. You will need to set up auction listing and shipping operations, but all inventory-related operations should be able to run pretty much as-is.

The advantage of using eBay to increase sales of existing merchandise is two-fold. First, you generate higher sales. Second, you may be able to reduce your costs, by purchasing your merchandise in larger quantities. If you're now purchasing 150 items at a time instead of 100, that extra quantity may qualify you for a higher discount—all the better for your bottom line.

Example Two: Selling Slow-Moving Merchandise

Other merchants use eBay to help them move merchandise that isn't moving other-wise. If you have no takers for that last-year's model gas grill in your home town, why not offer it to the world on eBay? With millions of potential buyers logging in every day, you may be able to unload that slow-moving merchandise a lot faster online.

I know of one music retailer who uses eBay to move instruments that aren't selling at retail like he anticipated. In his case, he purchases his inventory on 90-day credit terms. If a particular item hasn't sold in 60 days or so, he puts it up for auction on eBay. Thus eBay has become his bargain center; he doesn't sell his first-line goods there, but does a good job moving less-popular items before he has to pay for them.

Other merchants use eBay to move their surplus, closeout, and returned merchan-dise. eBay is also a good place to move used goods you take in trade, or goods damaged in delivery. Just make sure you accurately represent the status of this mer-chandise in your item listings, and you'll find a whole new market for these former problem items.

Example Three: Reaching a Wider Customer Base

If you sell collectible items, the challenge you faced in the pre-Internet days was finding enough collectors in your area to make your business worthwhile. You may have had the largest comic book collection in the region, but if the region was in the middle of Montana someplace, your potential customer base was pretty small. Thanks to eBay, however, you can now sell to collectors anywhere in the world; your business is no longer constrained by geography.

eBay is a collector's paradise, and a boon for dealers everywhere. There are thousands of formerly small dealers who have gotten quite big, with the help of eBay auctions. And it doesn't matter if your base of operations is Iowa or downtown San Francisco; your customer base is just as wide, no matter where you're located. If you have the inventory, you can grow as big as you want, while still staying a "small business" in your community.

Cross-Promoting Both Channels

If you sell at both traditional retail and online, is there a way to promote both your channels and attain some sort of marketing synergy? The answer is both yes and no, depending on exactly how you want to run your business.

Some merchants prefer to keep their online and brick-and-mortar identities separate. This is a good strategy if your pricing varies significantly between the two channels, or if you sell different types of items online than you do at retail. For example, if you use eBay to move distressed merchandise at bargain prices, but your retail store moves first-line merchandise at full list price, then you may want to separate the two businesses as much as possible—even to the extent of using different names for each business. If your retail customers found out about your discount activities online, the reputation of your retail store may be tarnished. Keeping the two businesses separate enables you to sell in ways you couldn't as a single entity.

On the other hand, many online and traditional businesses successfully coexist. If you perceive no channel confusion or conflict, there's no reason not to cross-promote your two businesses. Include your eBay member name, About Me URL, and Web site address in all your real-world marketing and promotion—including your advertisements, flyers, and business cards. And include your real-world store address and phone number in all your online activities.

In reality, however, most dual-channel businesses exist in their own separate worlds. Online customers stay online, and local customers stay local. Still, there's seldom a reason *not* to cross-promote; it doesn't cost you anything. You never know—you may get an increase in brick-and-mortar sales from local customers venturing in from cyberspace.

THE ABSOLUTE MINIMUM

If you run a traditional retail business, you need to strategize how you can use eBay to increase your existing sales. Keep these points in mind:

- If you sell commodity products, it's easy to use eBay to sell more of the same—with little stress to your existing operation.

- If you sell unique products, you may run into inventory problems—especially if you try to sell the exact same items to customers in both channels.

- Be careful when setting online pricing for commodity products; channel conflict can result if your local customers find you selling the same item for less on eBay.

- Unless you use eBay to move merchandise that you don't otherwise sell at retail, there's no reason not to cross-promote your online and bricks and mortar businesses.

IN THIS CHAPTER

- Cross-promoting all your auctions
- Linking from other sites to your eBay auctions
- Advertising your auctions

24

PROMOTING YOUR EBAY AUCTIONS

If you've followed all the instructions and advice throughout this book, you should now have your eBay business up and running and generating a steady stream of sales. But no matter how much revenue you're generating, you always want more—which is what this final chapter is about. A sure-fire way to make your auctions more successful is to promote them, and there are lots of ways to do that. We'll look at some of the more efficient ways to promote your auctions, and hopefully help you increase your traffic—and your selling prices.

Cross-Promoting All Your Auctions

The most obvious place to promote your eBay auctions is on eBay itself. Once you have a potential customer interested in one thing you're selling, why not show them what else you have for sale? You'd be surprised how many customers can turn into purchasers of multiple items—and those extra sales are especially profitable.

Linking to Your Other Auctions

eBay helps you cross-sell in this fashion by including a View Seller's Other Auctions link at the top of all item listing pages, as shown in Figure 24.1. This links to a page, like the one in Figure 24.2, that lists all your current auctions.

FIGURE 24.1

Every item listing page includes a link to your other eBay auctions.

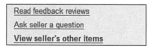

Read feedback reviews
Ask seller a question
View seller's other items

FIGURE 24.2

Your Items for Sale page, which lists all the items you currently have for sale on eBay.

Items for Sale by mojoresin (1205 ★) me

View text-only format

61 items found.

| | | All items | | Auctions | | Buy It Now | |

Show picture	Item Title	Price	Bids	Time (Ends PDT)
NEW! MY NEIGHBOR TOTORO resin model kit 📷		$35.00	1	Aug-21-03 04:49:45 PDT
1/15 scale BOBA FETT resin model kit Japan 📷		$25.00	-	Aug-23-03 09:07:17 PDT
1/15th scale STAR WARS STORMTROOPER model 📷		$25.00	-	Aug-23-03 09:07:18 PDT
120mm SET OF BLADE RUNNER MODEL KITS 📷		$50.00	-	Aug-23-03 09:07:18 PDT
AWESOME! DARKNESS(LEGEND) 120mm resin model k 📷		$25.00	-	Aug-23-03 09:07:18 PDT
COOL! FRANKENBERRY AND FRIENDS MODEL KIT 📷		$50.00	-	Aug-23-03 09:07:18 PDT

Unfortunately, this link tends to get overlooked by many buyers, so you might want to emphasize your other auctions by including another, more prominent link to this page in your item listings. You can create this link by adding the following line of HTML code to your item description:

```
<a href="http://cgi6.ebay.com/ws/ebayISAPI.dll?ViewListedItemsLinkButtons&
userid=userid">text</a>
```

Naturally, you should replace *userid* with your own eBay user ID, and *text* with the text you want for the link.

Linking to Your About Me Page

You can also create a separate link to your About Me page in your item description. You learned about About Me back in Chapter 2, "Using eBay's Advanced Features"; this page includes a list of all your current eBay auctions.

You create a link to your About Me page by adding the following HTML code to your item description:

```
<a href="http://members.ebay.com/aboutme/userid/">text</a>
```

Again, replace *userid* with your own eBay user ID, and *text* with the text you want for the link.

Linking from Other Sites to Your eBay Auctions

One of the best ways to promote your eBay auctions is to include links to your auctions on as many other Web sites as you can. For example, if you have a separate Web storefront, you should use that site to promote all the auctions you're running on eBay. You can also promote your auctions on any personal Web pages you or your family might have.

The question is, how do you promote individual auctions—particularly when those auctions have an extremely short life? If you include a link to a specific item listing page, that link will only be good for seven days (or whatever the length of the auction is). If you're okay with constantly editing and linking URLs, that's fine. For the rest of us, however, it would be nice to have a permanent URL to link to.

Linking to Your About Me Page

The good news is that you have such a permanent URL. It's called your eBay About Me page. As we just covered, your About Me page includes a list of all your current auctions, which makes it a perfect page to link to from other sites. Just add text that mentions "My eBay Auctions" or some such, and link that text to your About Me URL. The URL never changes, even though your About Me page is constantly updated with the auctions you're running.

note

Of course, another way to promote your auctions on the eBay site is to employ eBay's extra-cost listing enhancements, such as bold and highlight. Learn more about these features in Chapter 18, "Making Your Auctions More Effective."

Adding an eBay Button to Your Web Page

You can also add a Shop eBay with Me button, like the one shown in Figure 24.3, to your business or personal Web pages. When visitors click this button, they'll be taken to your Items for Sale page, which lists all your current auctions.

FIGURE 24.3

Add a Shop eBay with Me button to any Web page.

To add this button to a Web page, follow these steps:

1. Go to the Link Your Site to eBay page (see Figure 24.4), located at `pages.ebay.com/services/buyandsell/link-buttons.html`.

2. Check the box next to the My Listings on eBay button.

3. Enter the URL of the page where you want to display the button.

4. Scroll to the bottom of the page and click the I Agree button.

5. When the next page appears, copy the generated HTML code.

6. Paste the HTML code into the code for your Web page.

FIGURE 24.4

Follow the instructions on the Link Your Site to eBay page.

Link your site to eBay

If you have your own web page, you can use these buttons to link your visitors to eBay!

With these buttons, you can:

- Promote items that you are selling on eBay, or
- Provide a direct link to the eBay home page

Complete the form below to view easy instructions to install eBay buttons on your personal web site.

Select the button(s) you wish to display:

☐	Go to eb Y	Links to the eBay home page
☐	My listings on eb Y	A customized link that goes directly to a list of items you have for sale.

URL of page(s) where you plan to display buttons (required):

Example: www.ebay.com/aw/thispage.htm

www.

Advertising Your Auctions

Where else can you advertise the items you have for auction on eBay? Here are some ideas you might want to explore:

- Send emails to previous customers when you have new items for auction that they might be interested in.

- When you're sending out end-of-auction emails to your high bidders, include a link to your About Me page—or even a list of other items you have for sale, or plan to have for sale in the near future.

- Send mass emails to other eBay users. You can use HammerTap BayMail Pro (www. hammertap.com/baymailpro/) to send emails to batches of eBay users, even if you don't know their email addresses. Again, this is discussed in Chapter 15.

- Post messages on Internet message boards and Usenet newsgroups that are dedicated to the types of items you have for auction.

- Barter with other Web site owners to include links to your auctions or About Me page on their sites, in return for links to their sites on your site.

- Include your About Me URL or eBay Store URL as a signature in all your personal and business email messages

- Include your About Me or eBay Store URL on your business cards and stationery

Probably the most important type of promotion, however, is word of mouth—based on your good reputation. You want to encourage repeat bidders and drive buyers into your other auctions or online store (if you have one) for additional sales. That means treating your buyers fairly and with respect, and going the extra mile to ensure their satisfaction.

> **tip**
>
> You can facilitate this type of up-selling by using an advanced customer management tool, such as Ándale Email Manager (www.andale.com) or Vendio Customer Manager (www.vendio.com). Both of these tools are discussed in Chapter 15, "Dealing with Customers."

>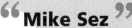
> **" Mike Sez "**
>
> I personally detest this type of unsolicited commercial email (UCE), as do many other users, and program my spam filter to block as much of this junk as possible. Still, many sellers find it a low-cost and effective means of promotion, so who's to say what's right and what's not?

THE ABSOLUTE MINIMUM

This wraps up the *Absolute Beginner's Guide to Launching an eBay Business*. I hope you've found the information and advice useful, and wish you luck on setting up and running your new eBay business. As to this chapter, you should keep the following points in mind:

- Include a prominent link to your other auctions or About Me page in every item description

- Include a link to your eBay item listings or About Me page on your Web storefront—and any personal Web pages you might have

- Send emails to previous customers when you have other items they might be interested in coming up for auction

Index

How can we make this index more useful? Email us at indexes@quepublishing.com

How can we make this index more useful? Email us at indexes@quepublishing.com

How can we make this index more useful? Email us at indexes@quepublishing.com

How can we make this index more useful? Email us at indexes@quepublishing.com

ABSOLUTE BEGINNER'S GUIDE

TO

Launching an eBay Business

Michael Miller

800 East 96th Street,
Indianapolis, Indiana 46240

Absolute Beginner's Guide to Launching an eBay Business

International Standard Book Number: 0-7897-3058-8

Library of Congress Catalog Card Number: 2003110444

Printed in the United States of America

First Printing: November 2003

06   05   04   03   4   3   2   1

Trademarks

Warning and Disclaimer

Bulk Sales

Que Publishing offers excellent discounts on this book when ordered in quantity for bulk purchases or special sales. For more information, please contact

U.S. Corporate and Government Sales
1-800-382-3419
corpsales@pearsontechgroup.com

For sales outside of the U.S., please contact

International Sales
1-317-428-3341
international@pearsontechgroup.com

Associate Publisher
Greg Wiegand

Acquisitions Editor
Angelina Ward

Development Editor
Christy Miller Kuziensky

Managing Editor
Charlotte Clapp

Project Editor
Sheila Schroeder

Production Editor
Benjamin Berg

Indexer
Kelly Castell

Proofreader
Linda Seifert

Technical Editor
Cari Skaggs

Publishing Coordinator
Sharry Lee Gregory

Interior Designer
Anne Jones

Cover Designer
Dan Armstrong

Page Layout
Bronkella Publishing
Brad Chinn